Seriously Funny

POEMS ABOUT LOVE,
DEATH, RELIGION,
ART, POLITICS, SEX,
AND EVERYTHING ELSE

EDITED BY

BARBARA HAMBY

AND

DAVID KIRBY

THE UNIVERSITY OF GEORGIA PRESS

ATHENS & LONDON

© 2010 by the University of Georgia Press
Athens, Georgia 30602
www.ugapress.org
All rights reserved
Set in Garamond MT by Graphic Composition, Inc.
Manufactured by Thomson-Shore and John P. Pow
Company

The paper in this book meets the guidelines for
permanence and durability of the Committee on
Production Guidelines for Book Longevity of the
Council on Library Resources.

Printed in the United States of America

16 15 14 13 12   P   6 5 4 3 2

Library of Congress Cataloging-in-Publication Data

Seriously funny : poems about love, death, religion,
art, politics, sex, and everything else / edited by
Barbara Hamby and David Kirby.
    xvi, 427 p. ; 24 cm.
    Includes bibliographical references and index.
    ISBN-13: 978-0-8203-3087-7 (hardcover : alk. paper)
    ISBN-10: 0-8203-3087-6 (hardcover : alk.)
    ISBN-13: 978-0-8203-3569-8 (pbk. : alk. paper)
    ISBN-10: 0-8203-3569-x (pbk. : alk. paper)
    1. American poetry—21st century. I. Hamby, Barbara,
1952– II. Kirby, David, 1944–
    PS615.S375 2010
    811'.608—dc22   2009037104

British Library Cataloging-in-Publication Data available

CONTENTS

My Old Reptile: Close Encounters of the Sexual Kind

The Heart Is a Lonely Perineum: Love, Marriage, Divorce, and Hatred

Mothers of America Let Your Kids Go to the Movies: Family Life and Strife

Let Us Be Friends a While and Understand Our Differences: Fiends and Neighbors

It Occurs to Me I Am America: Wrestling with a Huge Rococco National Identity

From My Bowels to Your Inbox: Poetry Goes to Work

We Who Love Precise Language: Poems about Writing and Literature

The Power of Weirdness: Talking Dogs, Chickens, Horses, Ducks, Bugs, and Other Entanglements Both Human and Un-

Mockery Was Still the Unforgivable Sin: Religion and Other Metaphysical Meanderings

Everything Prophesied Will Erupt: The End of the World

When the University of Georgia Press asked us to compile this anthology, immediately we began to go through the books in our libraries, searching for poems of artistic merit that contain elements of comedy. We also started to contact poets whose work succeeds "on a literary as well as the ha-ha level," in the words of the editor who commissioned the book, asking them for their poems as well as the names of other poets whose work might fit in.

As news of the project spread, people began to contact us about our "funny poem anthology," sending us light verse or promising to put us in touch with poets they knew whose work was really, really funny. Stop! we cried. We're not looking for funny poems; we're looking for *seriously* funny poems, ones that evoke poetry's timeless concerns but include a comic element as well. We have nothing against Dorothy Parker and Ogden Nash, but our interest lies only in poems of literary merit that also bring at least a smile and sometimes a belly laugh.

A lot of contemporary poetry doesn't do that. In discussing the fact that much modern poetry lacks humor, former poet laureate Billy Collins says, "It's the fault of the Romantics, who eliminated humor from poetry. Shakespeare's hilarious, Chaucer's hilarious. [Then] the Romantics killed off humor, and they also eliminated sex, things which were replaced by landscape. I thought that was a pretty bad trade-off, so I'm trying to write about humor and landscape, and occasionally sex."

More often than not, Collins's work exemplifies how humor works best, that is, in contrast with a darker mood. Just as painters use a technique called underpainting, or beginning with a base color and painting over it with an opposing shade while not entirely covering the first, so a funny Collins poem will often begin in bleakness. "The Lanyard," for example, a recollection of a geegaw the poet made at camp for his mother, is rooted in our common realization that we have failed to honor properly the person who gave us both life "and milk from her breasts":

Here are thousands of meals, she said,
and here is clothing and a good education.
And here is your lanyard, I replied,
which I made with a little help from a counselor.

Here is a breathing body and a beating heart,
strong legs, bones and teeth,
and two clear eyes to read the world, she whispered,
and here, I said, is the lanyard I made at camp.

The humor in these poems can glow with a starry sheen, but often that's
because there is a black sky behind it. As Mark Twain said, "The secret
source of humor is not joy but sorrow; there is no humor in Heaven." As
teachers of writing, we tell our students that a funny poem should appear
to have been written by a poet of deep seriousness, just as a serious poem
should seem to have been written by someone with a sense of humor.
Lorca says that all great poems have *duende*, or the shadow of death, and
especially in a funny poem, you have to hold that *duende* close.

Opposites do more than attract; they unite to create a strength that
wouldn't exist otherwise. The way we see it, seriousness and humor go
together like food and drink. Nobody would say, "The meal was okay, but
she spoiled everything by serving all these great wines" or "Can you imag-
ine? We thought we were being invited to dinner, but when we got there,
we had to eat all this food!" One of our poets, Lawrence Raab, wrote in an
e-mail message that he liked work that is both serious and funny when "its
essential seriousness emerges from its humor, rather than the humor being
a kind of overlay or a set of asides." Exactly.

In putting this book together, we learned that poets who would appear
to have the greatest claim on sorrow are often the funniest. Take Lucia
Perillo, who was diagnosed with multiple sclerosis in the 1980s. Yet her
poem "Fubar" (the title is an acronym for an expression perhaps best ren-
dered as "[fouled] up beyond all repair") is incontestably radiant. "Fubar"
appears to be addressed to a friend who is paraplegic, and Perillo starts by
wagging her finger at those who haven't earned the same right to sympa-
thy, such as the woman mourning her dead cat ("sorry, but pet death barely
puts the needle in the red zone").

Yes, the world is one big banana peel, and if we don't know that we've
got one foot on it, that's because we're not looking down: the goat (actu-

ally, it's a heifer) on Keats's immortal urn is being led to slaughter; wild-flowers nourish killer bees; the South's sylvan meadows were once bat-tlefields running with blood. "But come on," says Perillo in the poem's last lines,

> the sun is rising, I'll put a bandage on my head,
> and we'll be like those guys at the end of the movie—
> you take this crutch made from a stick.
>
> . . . .
>
> And looky, looky here at me: I'm playing the piccolo.

Incidentally, we found out later that the person Perillo addresses in "Fubar" is Paul Guest, who at age twelve was permanently paralyzed in a bike ac-cident and whose "Notes for My Body Double" we had already selected for our book.

Like these three poems, all of our selections feature a central self, some-one who is creating a reality through language rather than describing what already exists. As much as possible, we chose poems that work on the stage as well as the page. Our seriously funny poets are master rhetoricians, and we hear them even when we read silently to ourselves.

That said, each of these poems is better aloud. We drive a lot for work and pleasure, and most of the selections were made in our battered Toyota Corolla, otherwise known as the Seriously Funny Mobile Unit. During the two years in which we made our choices, we'd set out with a couple of boxes of books in the back seat, and whoever wasn't driving would read to the other. When we found that a poem made both of us think deeply but laugh as well, we earmarked it.

Seriously funny poetry has always been around. In *Beowulf*, for example, one character praises another but subtly undercuts his tribute by pointing out that the fellow is the biggest hero in *that* place on *that* day; as critics have observed, this is a little like saying "She was the most beautiful woman on *that* bar stool on *that* night." Chaucer is both serious and funny (take a look at the "Miller's Tale"), as are Shakespeare, Swift, Byron, Browning, and Dickinson.

But in order to have a book of manageable size and also identify a starting point for many of today's seriously funny poets, we decided to begin around the time of the Beats. There's no group more deadly se-rious about American culture and none that uses humor to better effect. Not everyone here is a direct descendant of Allen Ginsberg and Gregory Corso, but we imagine any of our poets would have been proud to be the opening act for those Titans of mayhem. Tonally, many of our poets are closer to the New York School, which dates from about the same time, so we're happy to include O'Hara, Koch, and Ashbery among the big daddies of seriously funny. The seriously funny approach is an equal-opportunity way of seeing the world, and this anthology presents a rich mix of race, gender, ethnicity, sexual preference, and physical ability. But most of these poets share at least some of the DNA of the hipsters on the West Coast and the surrealists on the East. We wanted the sections of *Seriously Funny* to be as self-explanatory as possible. In every case, then, we title each using a phrase from a poem in that section and then identify that section's subject matter in the subtitle. Thus "The Heart Is a Lonely Perineum: Love, Marriage, Divorce, and Hatred," for example, and "Mockery Was Still the Unforgivable Sin: Religion and Other Metaphysical Meanderings."

So love, death, religion, art, politics, sex, and everything else are at home in these seriously funny poems, and even these topics are intended as examples rather than the entire spectrum: there aren't many subjects that these poems overlook. We present both well-known poets and newcomers, as well as a range of work that includes poems capsized by their own tomfoolery, poems that glow with quiet wit, and poems in which a laugh erupts in the midst of terrible darkness. You may not find poets or poems you would expect to find. In some cases, the editors couldn't agree; in others, for one reason or another, the poems turned out to be unavailable for reprint.

As we piloted the Seriously Funny Mobile Unit across one state line or another and tossed poems back and forth, we became not only aware of how much great poetry of this type is out there but also increasingly grateful for its existence. Readers will find a true generosity in these poems, an eagerness not merely to entertain but to share ideas and emotions. The singer Ali Farka Touré said that honey is never good when it's only in one mouth, and the editors of *Seriously Funny* hope its readers find much to share with others.

SERIOUSLY FUNNY

OH LANA TURNER WE LOVE YOU GET UP

TV, Movies, Music, Cars, Cartoons—
Poetry and Popular Culture

Poem

Lana Turner has collapsed!
I was trotting along and suddenly
it started raining and snowing
and you said it was hailing
but hailing hits you on the head
hard so it was really snowing and
raining and I was in such a hurry
to meet you but the traffic
was acting exactly like the sky
and suddenly I see a headline
LANA TURNER HAS COLLAPSED!
there is no snow in Hollywood
there is no rain in California
I have been to lots of parties
and acted perfectly disgraceful
but I never actually collapsed
oh Lana Turner we love you get up

Of Time and the Line

George Burns likes to insist that he always
takes the straight lines; the cigar in his mouth
is a way of leaving space between the
lines for a laugh. He weaves lines together
by means of a picaresque narrative;
not so Henny Youngman, whose lines are strict-
ly paratactic. My father pushed a
line of ladies' dresses—not down the street
in a pushcart but upstairs in a fact'ry
office. My mother has been more concerned
with her hemline. Chairman Mao put forward
Maoist lines, but that's been abandoned (most-
ly) for the East-West line of malarkey
so popular in these parts. The prestige
of the iambic line has recently
suffered decline, since it's no longer so
clear who "I" am, much less who *you* are. When
making a line, better be double sure
what you're lining in & what you're lining
out & which side of the line you're on; the
world is made up so (Adam didn't so much
name as delineate). Every poem's got
a prosodic lining, some of which will
unzip for summer wear. The lines of an
imaginary are inscribed on the
social flesh by the knifepoint of history.
Nowadays, you can often spot a work
of poetry by whether it's in lines
or no; if it's in prose, there's a good chance
it's a poem. While there is no lesson in

the line more useful than that of the pick-
et line, the line that has caused the most ad-
versity is the bloodline. In Russia
everyone is worried about long lines;
back in the USA, it's strictly soup-
lines. "Take a chisel to write," but for an
actor a line's got to be cued. Or, as
they say in math, it takes two lines to make
an angle but only one lime to make
a Margarita.

note, passed to superman

sweet jesus superman,
if i had seen you
dressed in your blue suit
i would have known you.
maybe that choirboy clark
can stand around
listening to stories
but not you, not with
metropolis to save
and every crook in town
filthy with kryptonite.
lord, man of steel
i understand the cape,
the leggings, the whole
ball of wax.
you can trust me,
there is no planet stranger
than the one i'm from.

Farm Implements and Rutabagas in a Landscape

The first of the undecoded messages read: "Popeye sits in thunder,
Unthought of. From that shoebox of an apartment,
From livid curtain's hue, a tangram emerges: a country."
Meanwhile the Sea Hag was relaxing on a green couch: "How pleasant
To spend one's vacation en *la casa de Popeye*," she scratched
Her cleft chin's solitary hair. She remembered spinach

And was going to ask Wimpy if he had bought any spinach.
"M'love," he intercepted, "the plains are decked out in thunder
Today, and it shall be as you wish." He scratched
The part of his head under his hat. The apartment
Seemed to grow smaller. "But what if no pleasant
Inspiration plunge us now to the stars? *For this is my country*."

Suddenly they remembered how it was cheaper in the country.
Wimpy was thoughtfully cutting open a number 2 can of spinach
When the door opened and Swee'pea crept in. "How pleasant!"
But Swee'pea looked morose. A note was pinned to his bib. "Thunder
And tears are unavailing," it read. "Henceforth shall Popeye's apartment
Be but remembered space, toxic or salubrious, whole or scratched."

Olive came hurtling through the window; its geraniums scratched
Her long thigh. "I have news!" she gasped. "Popeye, forced as you know
    to flee the country
One musty gusty evening, by the schemes of his wizened, duplicate
    father, jealous of the apartment
And all that it contains, myself and spinach
In particular, heaves bolts of loving thunder
At his own astonished becoming, rupturing the pleasant

Arpeggio of our years. No more shall pleasant
Rays of the sun refresh your sense of growing old, nor the scratched
Tree-trunks and mossy foliage, only immaculate darkness and thunder."
She grabbed Swee'pea. "I'm taking the brat to the country."
"But you can't do that—he hasn't even finished his spinach,"
Urged the Sea Hag, looking fearfully around at the apartment.

But Olive was already out of earshot. Now the apartment
Succumbed to a strange new hush. "Actually it's quite pleasant
Here," thought the Sea Hag. "If this is all we need fear from spinach
Then I don't mind so much. Perhaps we could invite Alice the Goon
    over"—she scratched
One dug pensively—"but Wimpy is such a country
Bumpkin, always burping like that." Minute at first, the thunder

Soon filled the apartment. It was domestic thunder,
The color of spinach. Popeye chuckled and scratched
His balls: it sure was pleasant to spend a day in the country.

The Motorcyclists

My cuticles are a mess. Oh honey, by the way,
did you like my new negligee? It's a replica
of one Kim Novak wore in some movie or other.
I wish I had a foot-long chili dog right now.
Do you like fireworks, I mean not just on the 4th of July,
but fireworks any time? There are people
like that, you know. They're like people who like
orchestra music, listen to it any time of day.
Lopsided people, that's what my father calls them.
Me, I'm easy to please. I like ping-pong and bobcats,
shatterproof drinking glasses, the smell of kerosene,
the crunch of carrots. I like caterpillars and
whirlpools, too. What I hate most is being the first
one at the scene of a bad accident.

Do I smell like garlic? Are we still in Kansas?
I once had a chiropractor make a pass at me,
did I ever tell you that? He said that your spine
is happiest when you're snuggling. Sounds kind
of sweet now when I tell you, but he was a creep.
Do you know that I have never understood what they meant
by "grassy knoll." It sounds so idyllic, a place to go
to dream your life away, not kill somebody. They
should have called it something like "the grudging notch."
But I guess that's life. What is it they always say?
"It's always the sweetest ones that break your heart."
You getting hungry yet, hon? I am. When I was seven
I sat in our field and ate an entire eggplant
right off the vine. Dad loves to tell that story,

but I still can't eat eggplant. He says I'll be the first
woman President, it'd be a waste since I talk so much.
Which do you think the fixtures are in the bathroom
at the White House, gold or brass? It'd be okay with me
if they were just brass. Honey, can we stop soon?
I really hate to say it but I need a lady's room.

Country-Western Singer

I used to feel like a new man
After the day's first brew.
But then the new man I became
Would need a tall one too.

As would the new man he became,
And the new one after him
And so on and so forth till the new men made
The dizzy room go dim.

And each one said, I'll be your muse,
I'll trade you song for beer:
He said, I'll be your salt lick, honey,
If you will be my deer.

He said, I'll be your happy hour,
And you, boy, you'll be mine
And mine won't end at six or seven
Or even at closing time.

Yes, son, I'll be your spirit guide;
I'll lead you to Absolut,
To Dewar's, Bushmills and Jameson
Then down to Old Tangle Foot.

And there I'll drain the pretense from you
That propped you up so high;
I'll teach you how salvation's just
Salivation without the I.

To hear his sweet talk was to think
You'd gone from rags to riches,
Till going from drink to drink became
Like going from hags to bitches,

Like going from bed to barroom stool,
From stool to bathroom stall,
From stall to sink, from sink to stool,
From stool to hospital.

The monitors beep like pinball machines,
And coldly the IV drips;
And a nurse runs a moistened washcloth over
My parched and bleeding lips.

And the blood I taste, the blood I swallow
Is as far away from wine
As 5:10 is for the one who dies
At 5:09.

I'd Rather Look for Keys

with you all night than be on time to see
The Red Hot Chili Peppers

even though I've been dying
to see them

since *Blood Sugar Sex Magic* came out
when I was twelve

because I know you have too and so I'm guaranteed
a frantic search

and how often do most people get
frantic?

A sofa cushion flies past my
head,

and "Apache Rose Peacock"
and "Give it Away"

or whatever it is they play now
loud as hell

and even the fact that we promised each other
we'd mosh

wouldn't make me miss this for all the funk-rock
in the world,

and it's no contest whether I'd rather
look at Flea

thumping his bass in all his tattooed glory
or at you

in butterfly-embroidered jeans with a hole in the hip
and a bra

trying desperately to decide what color T-shirt to wear
while you look for keys

because—though you'll look better in any of them
than anyone else—

you remember colors most and it wouldn't do for this
evening to come back

in taupe or maroon when it should have been bright
emergency red.

Understanding Al Green

When I was twelve, a wiser sixteen-
year-old told me: *If you really want
to get that, homeboy, you best be bringing
Al Green's Greatest Hits. And if you ain't
in the mix by song five, either she's
dyking it or you need to re-evaluate your
sexual orientation. Know what I'm saying?*

With those words, I was off—borrowed Al
Green in the clutch in search of that *thing.*
Socks pulled up to my neck. Jeri curl. Real
tight Hoyas jersey was nothing but regulation
and I knew I was smooth and I knew
I was going to be in the mix by song five.
The whole walk from the ball court,

the wise man's words echoed like somebody's
mama banging on the door: *the panties
just be slippin' off when the women hear
Al's voice. Slippin'.* Slippin' because Al
hits notes mellow, like the silk that silk
wears. His voice is all hardworking night time
things. Not fake breasts, but you

and your woman, squeezed onto the couch,
taking a nap while the aquarium stutters
beside you. Nodding off on drizzly days
when you should be at work. The first smoke
after a glass of fine wine you know

you can't afford. Nobody, not woman
or man, knows how to handle Al Green.

That Girl from Ipanema would have
dug Al. Her panties, flip-flopping right
there by the sea. That sexy passing
the Pharcyde by would have stopped to say
What up? if they were Al. But they weren't.
And neither were you, last night when
that woman at the club shut you down:

I got a man . . . blah, blah, blah. Hate to tell you,
player, but she's at Al's place right now asking
for an autograph and maybe a little sumpin-
sumpin. What is sumpin-sumpin? I don't know.
But Al knows. And I'm sure you've heard that old
jive about Al getting scalding grits thrown on him.
You have to recognize those lies because

he would have started singing and those grits
would have been in the mix, too. For real.
I never believed the pimp-to-preacher story
anyway. The point is, Al's voice is like G-strings
and afro wigs and trying to be quiet when
the parents are home. The point is Al Green
hums better than most people dream.

My Life at the Movies

Village of the Damned was the movie I'd chosen
for my first date with Emily, my first
date ever, as well as my last with Emily.
It was a good movie—children with supernatural powers
turn against their parents and take over the village.
But I kept remembering how embarrassed I'd felt
telling Emily on the phone that we'd be going
to a horror movie. Science fiction, I thought
immediately. God, that sounds so much better.

Then there was *The Wreck of the Mary Deare*
with Barbara, who showed up late, so we missed
the credits and the opening scene, and never
went out again. Later *Hour of the Wolf* with Wendy
and Max von Sydow as a demented artist
who must stay awake all night to fend off his demons.

These were not, I can see now, the very best choices.
Certainly they failed to create a comfortable
romantic mood. At least with *Blow-Up*, Nancy and I
had the mystery of the end to talk about.
What does it mean when the photographer
walks away and vanishes, like the body
he'd discovered in the park? That was the Sixties,
a good time to discuss illusion and reality,
an easy time to favor illusion. When we got stoned

and watched *A Night at the Opera* it was amazing
to see how much was going on. Groucho,
we agreed, was a genius, like James Joyce,

in fact very much like James Joyce.
Our teachers were resistant, failing to grasp
the necessary connections. Was Stephen Dedalus
like all four Marx Brothers, or only Groucho?
It was so difficult to explain. We cited
Baudelaire, mentioned the limitations
of rational thought, and were given extensions.

Movies, of course, were much better
than rational thought. Plus they had music.
How could I drive off down the highway without
the right song in my mind? How could I
break up with Nancy without seeing it played out
on the screen: a crane shot, lifting me up
and back and away in one long sweet and floating glide.
Then a slow dissolve. Or the final frame
frozen into significance. Of course

it didn't happen that way, and now
I don't remember the truth. Instead
I think of the last scene of *La Dolce Vita*—
Mastroianni on the beach, so handsome
and anguished. A young girl at the water's edge
calls to him, but he can't hear what she's saying.
Then he smiles and shrugs
as only he could shrug, as if to say he knew

that whatever lost part of his life
she represented, it was too far away from him now.
Knowing that, he could only smile
and shrug, which meant: What can I do?
We can't take the world
too seriously, no matter how lovely
you are in your white dress this morning.

What I Learned from the Incredible Hulk

When it comes to clothes, make
an allowance for the unexpected.
Be sure the spare in the trunk
of your station wagon with wood paneling

isn't in need of repair. A simple jean jacket
says *Hey, if you aren't trying to smuggle
rare Incan coins through this peaceful
little town and kidnap the local orphan,*

I can be one heck of a mellow kinda guy.
But no matter how angry a man gets, a smile
and a soft stroke on his bicep can work
wonders. I learned that male chests

also have nipples, warm and established—
green doesn't always mean envy.
It's the meadows full of clover
and chicory the Hulk seeks for rest, a return

to normal. And sometimes, a woman
gets to go with him, her tiny hands
correcting his rumpled hair, the cuts
in his hand. Green is the space between

water and sun, cover for a quiet man,
each rib shuttling drops of liquid light.

Jackass: The Viewer

Why do I remember *Jackass: The Movie* when so much
has gushed from the cracked crankcase of my mind?
My brain has dumped the words King Lear howled

on the heath, but saved some Fool promising some car-
rental guy, "I'll take good care of this baby," then driving
straight to Demolition Derby. I've fuzzed the year

of William's Conquest, but see clearly the car, crumpled
like a paper-wad, the same Fool claiming, "It was like this
when I got it." I can't recall women I've slept with,

or forget Sir Wastebasket-Head, his bike careening
through a Mini Mart, push-broom lance scattering canned
goods as he falls. I can't define *Bauhaus*, but recall

the industrial-strength moron who paper-cut his own tongue,
begged to be shot with a bean-bag gun, then screamed,
wriggled, writhed on the floor, and later showed off

a black and purple bruise big as a fist. Paying the phone
bill slips my mind, but not "Bungee Jump Wedgie."
Brains save what they think they need to survive—

not Nobel Prize economics, but "Ass Kicked by a [Karate
Champion] Girl." I barely smile watching that French
genius-mime, but nearly fill my pantaloons watching a guy

crack a newspaper in a hardware store, then deflower
the display commode. I can't contain the sense
of *teleology*, but can't let go of sqwonking air-horns

as pro putters flail. I can't quote one line of Hart Crane,
or grasp why celebrated critics celebrate certain poets
of today, but I remember the dwarf (Wee Man)

who high-kicked his own head, then strolled down
a jammed street under a red traffic cone as heedless
rivers of Japanese flowed by. I can't recall my wife's

birthday, but can't forget the limo-shape in the X-ray
of that imbecile who shoved a toy car where the sun
don't want to shine. I draw a blank on *tenth birthday*,

though I know my parents spent a mint on mine; yet
I remember "Alligator Tightrope's" dope-with-a-dead-
chicken-in-his-shorts, and Señor Power-Suit washing-

machined down two city blocks by "Tidal Wave."
Why is High Culture so hard to grasp today?
Why is History so easily displaced? Is my life a waste

because I can't recite the periodic table, or Boyle's Law,
or the first bars of Beethoven's Ninth, or my password
to the *Times* on-line archives, or how many cups

in a gallon, or my city councilman (if I have one),
or my state senator or national representative, or how
to take square roots, or who won the Battle of Bull Run,

or what side of trees moss grows on, or the difference
between Lope de Vega and Cabeza de Vaca, or exactly
why my ex filed on me, but I remember the white guy

in Tokyo who snorted hot wasabi until he threw up.
His fellow diners seemed incredulous at first, then laughed
so hard that one bent down and threw up too.

Jeep Cherokee

You've never known
a single Indian
who wasn't painted
onto a football helmet
or branded in chrome
on a tailgate, but there you go,
off mashing the landscape
like some edge-city explorer,
flinging yourself toward
new worlds beyond the driveway,
Lewis and Clark
with a seat belt.
Go ahead, you trampling trooper,
you goose-stepping little
Godzilla, you shining beast
of raging fashion,
riding the big teeth
of your tires as if you
would ever follow a dirt road
anywhere but to a car wash.
This is America,
and you're free to drive
anything you can buy
but I will tell you:
Hitler would love this car—
a machine in which even the middle class
can master the world,
purchase their way through peril
safely as senators.
This is a car for

a uniformed strongman,
a one-car motorcade
through a thatched village
of strangers.
This is the car that will
replace Prozac.
This is the car that Barbie buys
with mad money
after the date with Angry White Ken.
This is the car that makes it safe
to be hateful in public.
Go ahead. Climb in. Look
at yourself, way up there
on the bridge of this
thick-windowed ship of enterprise.
Everybody knows
the only way today is to
buy your way through,
be bigger, be better,
be a bully, be a barger,
be sure you're safe from the poor,
bustle your way through
each day's bombardment
with the muscle of royalty.
You've got the power
to bring back the monarchy
four fat tires at a time.
Go anywhere. You're entitled.
You have squasher's rights.
Onward! Accelerate,
you brawny bruising winner,
you self-saluting junta on wheels,
you reclaimer of gold-bricked streets.
Democracy is for people
stuck in small cars
and God has never ruled

through traffic laws.
Get used to the feeling
of having your way.
Each broad cut of the steering wheel
is your turn at conquest.
The power-assisted triumph
of the me
in heavy traffic.
You are rolling proof
that voting is stupid,
that the whole damn machine is fixed
before it leaves the factory,
that fairness is a showroom,
that togetherness is for bus riders,
that TV has the right idea:
there is just you in a small room
on the safe side of glass,
with desire spread out before you
like a ballroom without walls,
and you will not be denied,
you've got the moves and the view,
you don't need government, unions,
bank regulation, mercy,
the soft hands of strangers.
You've got 4-wheel drive
and a phone, you've got
the friendship of a reinforced chassis,
you've got empathy for dictators
without knowing it,
you've got freedom from rear-view mirrors,
you've got wide-bodied citizenship,
you've gained Custer's Revenge:
caissons packed with children and soccer balls
coasting across the plowed prairie,

history remodeled with one great
blaring of jingles and horns:

Hail Citizen King!
Hail the unswerving settler!
Hail the rule of logo!
Hail Jeep Cherokee!

Two Trains

Then there was that song called "Two Trains Running,"
a Mississippi blues they play on late night radio,
that program after midnight called *FM in the AM*,
—well, I always thought it was about *trains*.

Then somebody told me it was about what a man and woman do
under the covers of their bed, moving back and forth
like slow pistons in a shiny black locomotive,
the rods and valves trying to stay coordinated

long enough that they will "get to the station"
at the same time. And one of the trains
goes out of sight into the mountain tunnel,
but when they break back into the light

the other train has somehow pulled ahead,
the two trains running like that, side by side,
first one and then the other; with the fierce white
bursts of smoke puffing from their stacks,
into a sky so sharp and blue you want to die.

So then for a long time I thought the song was about sex.

But then Mack told me that all train songs
are really about Jesus, about how the second train
is shadowing the first, so He walks in your footsteps
and He watches you from behind, He is running with you,

He is your brakeman and your engineer,
your coolant and your coal,

and He will catch you when you fall,
and when you stall He will push you through
the darkest mountain valley, up the steepest hill,

and the rough *chuff chuff* of His fingers on the washboard
and the harmonica *woo woo* is the long soul cry by which He
pulls you through the bloody tunnel of the world.
So then I thought the two trains song was a gospel song.

Then I quit my job in Santa Fe and Sharon
drove her spike heel through the center of my heart

and I got twelve years older and Dean moved away,
and now I think the song might be about goodbyes—

because we are not even in the same time zone,
or moving at the same speed, or perhaps even
headed towards the same destination—
forgodsakes, we are not even trains!

What grief it is to love some people like your own
blood and then to see them simply disappear;
to feel time bearing us away
                    one boxcar at a time.

And sometimes sitting in my chair
I can feel the absence stretching out in all directions—
like the deaf, defoliated silence
just after a train has thundered past the platform,

just before the mindless birds begin to chirp again
—and the wildflowers that grow along the tracks
wobble wildly on their little stems,
              then gradually grow still and stand

motherless and vertical in the middle of everything.

Billy Joel Gets Philosophical on Bravo

That thing Billy said about how we enter someone's heart when we die?

It's not *A Brief History of Time* or anything, but what if Billy's right?

What if the heart really *is* a doorway with a silver lock and dying, that's
    the key?

Let's say you die and live in a little apartment in someone's heart.

Let's say you've got a red velvet chair, an old floor lamp,
    and a library filled with all the books you didn't get to read alive.

Let's say there's a cute little deli down the road
    and a radio that plays all your favorite songs from the sixties and
      seventies
    and also, on Sunday afternoons, the folk songs, the Knees Deep in
      Big Muddy.

There'd also be tea bags and after dinner mints.

There'd be a mammoth pile of handwritten letters from
    everyone who ever hurt you,
    sealed at the point of envelope entry with the person's initials in wax,
    and the prose—the prose would be outstanding—

it would include that loneliness of horses line
    from James Wright's *if I could step out of my body* poem
    and descriptions of everything Hieronymous Bosch
    ever thought he shouldn't, but couldn't help but think.

The weird thing would be when someone *else* died
    and entered this heart that was your apartment and library and deli.

What if he or she didn't like your radio?

What if he or she turned off your floor lamp and sat in the dark
    despondent about the lack of drugs in this, the Piano Man hereafter?

I'm finding it difficult to live with people. Even the people I love.

As for strangers: you may as well know that's asking a bit too much—
    that's like knocking on my door and wanting me to believe in angels.

When the housekeeping women in their delicate, prairie-girl clothing
    show up with their bibles and small-print documents on the splendor
      of heaven,
    I say I'm sorry, but I'm quite the homosexual.

My sister, on the other hand, once hid in her closet.

What was it like in there? Was there a single light bulb
    hanging from a white socket in the ceiling?

Did she stare at all the coats or rummage through the pockets
    of the rejected toddler trousers
    while the women knocked and hollered *yoo-hoo*
    in their high-wire voices?

Is that what being dead is? Hiding in the dark with out-of-
    style outerwear?

What kind of person would stay up all night
    thinking about the philosophy of Billy Joel?

Do you know?

Would you please just *tell me* before the angels materialize
    in their onionskin caps and black taxicabs?

Vince Neil Meets Josh in a Chinese Restaurant in Malibu (after Ezra Pound)

Back when my voicebox
was a cabinet-full of golden vibrators, and my hair
fell white across the middle of my back
like a child's wedding dress,
I made love to at least a dozen girls
dressed up to look like me: the hotel bed a sky
filled with the spastic flock
of our South-Flying mic scarves,
the back of my head and the front
appearing simultaneously
in hotel mirrors, and the twin crusts of our make-up
sliding off into satin seas
like bits of California coast. I heard my own lyrics
coming out of the greasy tent
of their beautiful wigs, my lyrics driven back
towards me, poled into me, demanding of me
the willing completion of vague circus acts
I'd scribbled down, once, on the back of a golf card
or a piece of toilet paper. Sometimes I myself
wonder what I was thinking then, but those words
went on to live forever, didn't they, radioed out
into the giant Midwestern backseat
and blasted into kneecaps and tailbones
by that endless tongue of berber carpeting
blanketing the American suburbs, boys and girls
strung like paper lanterns from here to Syracuse
along my microphone cord. Who rocks you now
rocks you always, I told them all,
and all of them somehow wearing

a homemade version of the same leather pants
I'd chosen to wear on stage that night;
all of them hoping to enter me—to enter anyone—
the way they thought I entered them,
and the way I entered them was wishing
I was somewhere else, or wishing I was
the someone else who'd come along
to enter me, which was the same thing.
I am no fag, my new friend.
Love in battle conditions requires a broad
taxonomy, queerness has its ever-more-visible degrees.
Josh, I know you know what I'm talking about,
you have the build of a stevedore. Which reminds me—more shrimp
fried rice?—as a child in Nanjing,
I sculled the junks for my bread and I slept
in a hovel along the Chiang Jiang River.
In a cage there, I bred mice who built their nests
from the frayed rope I'd taken from the decks, and one Spring,
when the babies did not emerge, I lifted
up the rock that hid them, and I found
they'd grown together, fused with each other
and the tendrils of the nest. I held them up, eleven blind tomatoes
wriggling on a blackened vine. My friends and I
performed many surgeries. And now you come to me
in this Chinese restaurant in Malibu,
asking if you can help me. Please tell *Circus Magazine* I love them
forever, and please pass Pamela this message:
If you get back to Malibu by springtime, drop by the boathouse,
and I'll rock your ass as far as Cho-Fu-Sa.

Foley

It *is* Harrison Ford who just saved the world,
but when he walks down a dirt road toward the ultralarge sun
what sounds like his boots are really bricks being drudged
through a boxful of coffee beans. And the mare you've seen
clopping along those 19th-century pebbles—
she's a coconut struck by a ball peen hammer.
And the three girls riding in the hansom,
where the jouncing rustles their silk-and-bone:
that's a toothbrush moving across birchbark.
Even the moment when one kickboxer's perfect body
makes contact with the other kickboxer's perfect body
has nothing to do with kickboxing, or bodies,
but the concrete colliding with the abstract of perfection,
which molts into a leather belt spanking a side of beef.
This is the problem with movies:
go to enough of them and pretty soon the world
starts sounding wrongly synced against itself: e.g.,
last night when I heard a noise below my bedroom window
that sounded like the yowl a cat would make
if its tongue were being yanked backwards out its ass.
Pain, I thought. *Help*, I thought,
so at 2:00 A.M. I went outside with a flashlight
and found a she-cat corkscrewed to a tom,
both of them humped and quivering where the beam flattened
against the grass whose damp was already wicking
through my slippers. *Aaah . . . love*, I thought,
or some distantly-cousined feline analogue of love,
or the feline analogue of the way love came out of the radio
in certain sixties pop songs that had the singer keening
antonyms: how can something so right feel so wrong,

so good hurt so bad . . . you know what I'm talking about.
And don't you think it's peculiar:
in the first half of the sixties they made the black girl-groups
sing with white accents and in the second half of the sixties
they made the white girl-groups sing with black accents,
which proves that what you hear is always
some strange alchemy of what somebody thinks you'll pay for
and what you expect. Love in particular
it seems to me we've never properly nailed down
so we'll know it when we hear it coming, the way
screaming "Fire!" *means* something to the world.
I remember this guy who made noises against my neck
that sounded like when after much tugging on a jar lid
you stick a can opener under its lip—that little *tsuck*.
At first I thought this must be
one of love's least common dialects, though later
when I found the blue spots all over I realized
it was malicious mischief, it was vandalism, it was damage.
Everybody has a story about the chorus of these
love's faulty hermeneutics: the muffler in retreat
mistaken for the motor coming, the declaration
of loathing construed as the minor reproach;
how "Babe, can I borrow five hundred bucks?"
gets dubbed over "Goodbye, chump"—of course,
of course, and you slap your head but it sounds funny,
not enough sizzle, not enough snap. If only
Berlitz had cracked the translations or we had conventions
like the international code of semaphores,
if only some equivalent of the Captain Nemo decoder ring
had been muscled across the border. As it has
for my friend who does phone sex
because it's a job that lets her keep at her typewriter all day,
tapping out poems. Somehow she can work
both sides of her brain simultaneously, the poem
being what's really going on and the sex being what sounds
like what's going on; the only time she stops typing
is when she pinches her cheek away from her gums,
which is supposed to sound like oral sex

though she says it's less that it really *sounds* like oral sex
than that these men have established a pact, a convention
that permits them to *believe* it sounds like oral sex.
When they know
it's a woman pinching her cheek and not a blow job,
it's a telephone call and not a blow job,
it's a light beam whistling down a fiber, for god's sake,
and not a blow job. Most days I'm amazed
we're not all schizophrenics, hearing voices
that have been edited out of what calls to us
from across the fourth wall. I've heard
that in *To Have and Have Not* Lauren Bacall's singing
comes from the throat of a man; also that Bart Simpson is really
a middle-aged woman; and last week not once but twice
I heard different women wailing
in public parking lots, the full throttle
of unrestrained grief, and both times I looked straight at them
and pretended nothing unusual was going on,
as though what I was hearing were only the sound of air
shrieking through the spoiler on someone's Camaro.
That's also part of the pact my friend's talking about,
not to offer condolence, not to take note.
You don't tell the men they're sorry creatures,
you don't ask the women what went wrong.
If you're being mugged or raped or even killed,
you have to scream "Fire!" instead of "Help!"
to get someone to help you. Though soon, if not already,
all the helpers will have caught on
and then you'll have to start screaming something else,
like that you've spotted Bacall or Harrison Ford on the street,
Bart Simpson even—no wait a minute, he's not real,
though I remember a time when even the president talked about him
as if he were human. It's not the sleaziness
of phone sex I bristle at, but rather the way it assists
the world in becoming imprecise
about what is real and what is not, what is a blow job
and what is only my friend jimmying her finger
in her mouth or making a sucky noise

against the back of her hand. Which is oddly exactly
how the professor of the ornithology class I took my junior year
taught us to lure birds in, because birds
would think these were the sounds of other birds.
And in that other life of mine,
when bird-watching was part of what I did for a living,
I remember packing high into the mountains
before the snow melted, when the trail couldn't be followed,
so mine would be the only soul for miles.
One reason I went up there was because at sundown
when the wind climbed the backs of the mountains
along with the spreading violet light,
you could hear the distinct murmuring that the Indians said
were the collective voices of the dead. And I'd lie there,
just my sleeping bag and pad set down on snow,
and I'd look hard at the sky, as though
the wind were something I could see if I looked hard enough,
listening equally hard to convince myself
about the voices of the dead, though always
I was tugged back from true belief
by that one side of my brain that insisted: *Wind.*
And also I remember
how once at the trailhead a man popped out of his motor home
and pointed a camcorder at me, asking
where I was going, what I was doing—though of course,
alone, I wasn't going to say.
But even as I turned away, I heard
the whirr of the movie being made
and the man making up his own narration: *see this little girl,*
she says she's going to climb a mountain,
and briefly I thought about pulling a Trotsky on him
with my ice axe. But as the New Agers say I
"let it go," and I left,
and he didn't follow me, and nothing bad ever happened,
though from time to time I think about strangers watching that movie
in the man's living room, his voice overdubbing
(see this little girl, she says she's going to climb a mountain)
the sound of me, of my boots walking.

I WAS ALONE WHEN IT HIT ME

The Self

To My Twenties

How lucky that I ran into you
When everything was possible
For my legs and arms, and with hope in my heart
And so happy to see any woman—
O woman! O my twentieth year!
Basking in you, you
Oasis from both growing and decay
Fantastic unheard of nine- or ten-year oasis
A palm tree, hey! And then another
And another—and water!
I'm still very impressed by you. Whither,
Midst falling decades, have you gone? Oh in what lucky fellow,
Unsure of himself, upset, and unemployable
For the moment in any case, do you live now?
From my window I drop a nickel
By mistake. With
You I race down to get it
But I find there on
The street instead, a good friend,
X—— N——, who says to me
Kenneth do you have a minute?
And I say yes! I am in my twenties!
I have plenty of time! In you I marry,
In you I first go to France; I make my best friends
In you, and a few enemies. I
Write a lot and am living all the time
And thinking about living. I loved to frequent you
After my teens and before my thirties.
You three together in a bar
I always preferred you because you were midmost

Most lustrous apparently strongest
Although now that I look back on you
What part have you played?
You never, ever, were stingy.
What you gave me you gave whole
But as for telling
Me how best to use it
You weren't a genius at that.
Twenties, my soul
Is yours for the asking
You know that, if you ever come back.

To Jewishness, Paris, Ambition, Trees, My Heart, and Destiny

Now that you all have gathered here to talk with me,
Let's bring everything out into the open.
It's almost too exciting to have all of you here—
One of you physically and another spiritually inside me,
Another worn into me by my upbringing, another a quality
I picked up someplace west of here, and two of you at least fixed things
    outside me,
Paris and trees. Who would like to ask the first question?
Silence. Noble, eternal-seeming silence. Well, destiny, what do you think?
Did you bring Jewishness here or did it bring you, or what?
You two are simply smiling and stay close together. Well, trees and Paris
You have been together before. What do you make of being here
With Jewishness, my heart, ambition, and destiny? It's a frightening, even
    awe-inspiring thing,
Don't you think so? Ambition you've been moving my heart
For a long time—will you take some time off now?
Should we go to lunch? Just sit here? Or, perhaps, sing
A song about all of you. "Including you?" one of you speaks for the
    first time
And it is you, my heart, a great chatterbox all the same! And now you,
    Jewishness, chime in
With a Hebrew melody you'd like us to enjoy and you Paris and trees
    step out
Of the shadows of each other and say "Look
At these beautiful purple and white blossoms!" Destiny you wink at me
    and shrug
A shoulder toward ambition who (you) now begin to sing
"Yes, yes it will include all of us, and it is about time!"
Jewishness and ambition go off to a tree-greened-out corner

And start their confab. Destiny walks with Paris and me

To a house where an old friend is living. You, heart, in the padded dark
    as usual,

Seem nonetheless to be making a very good effort. "Oh, this stirs me,"
    you say, excitedly—

"To be with Jewishness and trees and destiny at the same time makes me
    leap up!"

And you do. Ambition you return but don't take hold.

Destiny, you have taken my heart to Paris, you have hidden it among
    these trees.

Heart, the rest of this story is yours. Let it go forward in any way it needs
    to go.

MARILYN CHIN

How I Got That Name
an essay on assimilation

I am Marilyn Mei Ling Chin.
Oh, how I love the resoluteness
of that first person singular
followed by that stalwart indicative
of "be," without the uncertain i-n-g
of "becoming." Of course,
the name had been changed
somewhere between Angel Island and the sea,
when my father the person
in the late 1950s
obsessed with a bombshell blond
transliterated "Mei Ling" to "Marilyn."
And nobody dared question
his initial impulse—for we all know
lust drove men to greatness,
not goodness, not decency.
And there I was, a wayward pink baby,
named after some tragic white woman
swollen with gin and Nembutal.
My mother couldn't pronounce the "r."
She dubbed me "Numba one female offshoot"
for brevity: henceforth, she will live and die
in sublime ignorance, flanked
by loving children and the "kitchen deity."
While my father dithers,
a tomcat in Hong Kong trash—
a gambler, a petty thug,
who bought a chain of chopsuey joints
in Piss River, Oregon,

with bootlegged Gucci cash.
Nobody dared question his integrity given
his nice, devout daughters
and his bright, industrious sons
as if filial piety were the standard
by which all earthly men are measured.

•   •   •

Oh, how trustworthy our daughters,
how thrifty our sons!
How we've managed to fool the experts
in education, statistics and demography—
We're not very creative but not adverse to rote-learning.
Indeed, they can use us.
But the "Model Minority" is a tease.
We know you are watching now,
so we refuse to give you any!
Oh, bamboo shoots, bamboo shoots!
The further west we go, we'll hit east;
the deeper down we dig, we'll find China.
History has turned its stomach
on a black polluted beach—
where life doesn't hinge
on that red, red wheelbarrow,
but whether or not our new lover
in the final episode of "Santa Barbara"
will lean over a scented candle
and call us a "bitch."
Oh God, where have we gone wrong?
We have no inner resources!

•   •   •

Then, one redolent spring morning
the Great Patriarch Chin
peered down from his kiosk in heaven
and saw that his descendants were ugly.
One had a squarish head and a nose without a bridge.
Another's profile—long and knobbed as a gourd.

44

A third, the sad, brutish one
may never, never marry.
And I, his least favorite—
"not quite boiled, not quite cooked,"
a plump pomfret simmering in my juices—
too listless to fight for my people's destiny.
"To kill without resistance is not slaughter"
says the proverb. So, I wait for imminent death.
The fact that this death is also metaphorical
is testament to my lethargy.

* * *

So here lies Marilyn Mei Ling Chin,
married once, twice to so-and-so, a Lee and a Wong,
granddaughter of Jack "the patriarch"
and the brooding Suilin Fong,
daughter of the virtuous Yuet Kuen Wong
and G.G. Chin the infamous,
sister of a dozen, cousin of a million,
survived by everybody and forgotten by all.
She was neither black nor white,
neither cherished nor vanquished,
just another squatter in her own bamboo grove
minding her poetry—
when one day heaven was unmerciful,
and a chasm opened where she stood.
Like the jowls of a mighty white whale,
or the jaws of a metaphysical Godzilla,
it swallowed her whole.
She did not flinch nor writhe,
nor fret about the afterlife,
but stayed! Solid as wood, happily
a little gnawed, tattered, mesmerized
by all that was lavished upon her
and all that was taken away!

Ode to Pork

I wouldn't be here
without you. Without you
I'd be umpteen
pounds lighter & a lot
less alive. You stuck
round my ribs even
when I treated you like a dog
dirty, I dare not eat.
I know you're the blues
because loving you
may kill me—but still you
rock me down slow
as hamhocks on the stove.
Anyway you come
fried, cued, burnt
to within one inch
of your life I love. Babe,
I revere your every
nickname—bacon, chitlin
cracklin, sin.
Some call you murder,
shame's stepsister—
then dress you up
& declare you white
& healthy, but you always
come back, sauced, to me.
Adam himself gave up
a rib to see yours
piled pink beside him.

Your heaven is the only one
worth wanting—
you keep me all night
cursing your four-
letter name, the next
begging for you again.

Vim

Some people just seem to exist, as opposed to *live*,
in a foggy drift. I am so glad that's not me!

I am certainly so glad I have such thumping
zest for life. The way I dig into life
like a bowl of hot Texas chili with sour cream
and shredded sharp cheddar—I'm so glad

I have such a pulsing intuitive grasp
of how short and precious life is
and how we are impassioned clay
and each incredible *diem* is there to be *carped*

so therefore I skim speedingly over the waters of life
alert to every flick of fin
and super-ready to jab my osprey talons into
the flesh of whatever sensation swims my way
not fretting for a second about any other plump fish in the sea

and so for example when I see young couples
groobling moistly at each other's burger-fed gamoofs
I certainly don't waste my time with any type of envy,
I'm just like Yeah you kids go for it!—
Meanwhile I am going to listen to *Let It Bleed* LOUD
and totally rock out with all my teeth bared!

Man, it's so great not to be the type who falls asleep watching baseball
and wakes up with Cherry Garcia on my shirt.
I figure I am at least as alive as Little Richard was in 1958
and it's such a kick!

Does it get tiring?

                      Well sure, occasionally,
but who cares? I *embrace* the fatigue,
I KISS it till it flips and becomes defiantly voracious vim

and when I read that line in Wallace Stevens
"being part is an exertion that declines"
I'm like What in heck is that old guy talking about?

BILL ZAVATSKY

Bald

In the mirror it's plain to see:
soon I'll be bald, like the two faceless men
staring at each other in the word SOON.
Left profile crowding mirror, I can still pretend
it isn't happening—enough tangled skeins
of hair hide the gleam. But from the right,
where the wave lifts, I don't have to push my face
close to see it winking at me—
the mysterious island of my skull,
the dinky coastline of my baby head
swimming back to me at last.
Through the sparse shore weeds
that dot the beach (I mean my
miserable hairs), it glints. Soon
I'll crawl ashore where all uncles live—
the ones who never grew any hair,
their clown cannibal heads hilarious
in photographs, glaring like chromosomes
from dresser picture frames the way
they always did when I and my cousins
stopped short in a game of tag to stare at them,
trapped under glass in their dumb grown-up world,
a phrenology of how I'd never be. Then
two years ago I saw my head in a three-way mirror
buying a coat: three pink slivers of skin like slices
of pizza radiated from my part. The overhead lighting
shriveled my scalp, scorching my silk purse
to a sow's ass. Soon the morning hairs in the sink
reached out their arms and wailed to me.
Soon the moonlight with its chilly hands

seized my cranium, taking measurements.
Everybody kept quiet. I was the last to know.
Yes, I'm drifting closer. Closer
to the desert island where I'll live out my days
training to be ever more the skeleton
that's taking over my body pore by pore.
Hair by hair its fingerbone scissors snip me
away, I who in the sixties fell in love
with my own hair! Who swooned among
battalions of Narcissuses over the ripples
our long tresses made in that mirror
of our generation, the President's face!
I who have always known
that Death is a haircut!
Walking the streets I pause to study my scalp
where it hangs in a butcher shop window,
reflected beside the other meat.
Under my breath I sing the song I'm learning
that goes, "Bald is anonymous . . . bald is goodbye."
I will not grow the hair above my ear
until it's ten feet long, then drape it suavely
over the empty parking lot atop my head
where the forest used to loom, then plaster it down
with goo. No, I don't want a toupee
to fall in my soup, or a hair transplant
driven into my brain with giant needles!
I shoo away the mysterious weave
spun from the dead hair of unfortunate ones,
rich only in what grows from their heads.
I reject the compensatory beard—I refuse
to live my life upside-down!
I prepare myself to receive the litanies
chanted by the kids as I enter the classroom:
"Chrome dome, marble head, baldy bean, skin head,
Bowling ball brain, reflector head, bubble top. . . ."
I urge them on in the making of metaphor!
I am content to merge with the reflection
of every bald barber who ever adjusted my head.

I am enchanted, so late, to be becoming
someone else—the face in the mirror which,
by the time I claim it, won't even look like me!
I am thrilled to realize that the scythe
of the grim reaper is nothing more
than a cheap plastic comb
you can buy in any drugstore,
and even its teeth fall out

BETH ANN FENNELLY

I Need to Be More French. Or Japanese.

Then I wouldn't prefer the California wine,
its big sugar, big fruit rolling down my tongue,
a cornucopia spilled across a tacky tablecloth.
I'd prefer the French, its smoke and rot.
Said Cézanne: *Le monde—c'est terrible!*
Which means, *The world—it bites the big weenie.*
People sound smarter in French.
The Japanese prefer the crescent moon to the full,
prefer the rose before it blooms.
Oh, I have been to the temples of Kyoto,
I have stood on the Pont Neuf, and my eyes,
they drank it in, but my taste buds
shuffled along in the beer line at Wrigley Field.
It was the day they gave out foam fingers.
I hereby pledge to wear more gray, less yellow
of the beaks of baby mockingbirds,
that huge yellow yawping open on wobbly necks,
trusting something yummy will be dropped inside,
soon. I hereby pledge to be reserved.
When the French designer learned
I didn't like her mock-ups for my book cover,
she sniffed, *They're not for everyone. They're*
subtle. What area code is 662 anyway? I said,
Mississippi, sweetheart. Bet you couldn't find it
with a map. OK: I didn't really. But so what
if I'm subtle as May in Mississippi, my nose
in the wine-bowl of this magnolia bloom, so what
if I'm mellow as the punch-drunk bee.
If I were Japanese I'd write a tone poem
about magnolias in March, each bud long as a pencil,

sheathed in celadon suede, jutting from a cluster
of glossy leaves. I'd end the poem before anything
bloomed, end with rain swelling the buds
and the sheaths bursting, then falling to the grass
like a fairy's cast-off slippers, like candy wrappers,
like spent firecrackers. Yes, my poem
would end there, spent firecrackers.
If I were French, I'd capture post-peak, in July,
the petals floppy, creased brown with age,
the stamens naked, stripped of yellow filaments.
The bees lazy now, bungling the ballet, thinking
for the first time about October. If I were French,
I'd prefer this, end with the red-tipped filaments
scattered on the scorched brown grass,
and my poem would incite the sophisticated,
the French and the Japanese readers—
because the filaments look like matchsticks,
and it's matchsticks, we all know, that start the fire.

Very Hot Day

I know what's going to happen
to those two plastic produce bags of crushed ice
I perched atop the garden wall:
one's floppy, droopy, flabby,
its overhanging pooch of ice-melt
already about to pull the whole bag down
into the dirt, bursting it, turning it
into a fistful of filthy gummy polyethelene;
the other's centered, poised—even
its ice-melt seems to know where to settle
so the bag stays upright and stable:
if it were a person, he'd radiate
smiling confidence and good health,
a team player wanting only to be useful,
to stand as an example of how to adjust
conflicting parts of himself for the general good.
His effortless balance and bright red twisty-tie
might seem flashy and arrogant
were he not so persistently mindful
that he shares the other bag's fate.
How could he not, since they're almost touching?
He'd have to be completely oblivious
not to witness the moment his twin
plops into the dirt.
He'd have to know he's heading there, too,
no matter how solid he feels at present—
that even now he's really broken and helpless

and destined for the recycle bin
where like an omniscient god I throw
useless used bags for crushed ice
the butcher gives me to keep my raw meat
safe while I drive home on a very hot day.

Shame: An Aria

You think you've grown up in various ways
and then the elevator door opens and you're standing inside
reaming out your nose—something about the dry air
in the mountains—and find yourself facing two spruce elderly couples
dressed like improbable wildfires in their primary color
definitely on vacation sports outfits, a wormy curl of one of the body's
shameful and congealed lubricants gleaming on your fingertip
under the fluorescent lights, and there really isn't too much to say
as you descend the remaining two flights with them in silence,
all five of you staring straight ahead in this commodious
aluminum group coffin toward the ground floor. You are,
of course, trying to think of something witty to say. Your hand
is, of course, in your pocket discreetly transferring the offending article
into its accumulation of lint. One man clears his throat
and you admit to yourself that there are kinds of people—if not
people in particular—you hate, that these are they,
and that your mind is nevertheless, is nevertheless working
like a demented cicada drying its wings after rain to find some way
to save yourself in your craven, small child's large ego's idea
of their eyes. You even crank it up a notch, getting more high-minded
and lugubrious in the seconds it takes for the almost silent
gears and oiled hydraulic or pneumatic plungers and cables
of the machine to set you down. "Nosepicking," you imagine explaining
to the upturned, reverential faces, "is in no way the ground floor
of being. The body's fluids and solids, its various despised disjecta,
toenail parings left absently on the bedside table that your lover
the next night notices there, shit streaks in underwear or little, faint
odorous pee-blossoms of the palest polleny color, the stiffened
small droplets in the sheets of the body's shuddering late-night loneliness
and self-love, russets of menstrual blood, toejam, ear wax,

phlegm, the little dead militias of white corpuscles
we call pus, what are they after all but the twins of the juices
of mortal glory: sap, wine, breast milk, sperm and blood. The most
      intimate hygienes,
those deepest tribal rules that teach a child
trying to struggle up out of the fear of loss and love
from anger, hatred, fear, they get taught to us, don't they,
as boundaries, terrible thresholds, what can be said (or thought, or done)
inside the house but not out, what can be said (or thought, or done)
only by oneself, which must therefore best not be done at all.
so that the core of the self, we learn early, is where shame lives
and where we also learn doubleness, and a certain practical cunning
and what a theater is, and the ability to lie—"
the elevator has opened and closed, the silver-haired columbines
of the mountain are murmuring over breakfast menus in a room full of
      bright plastics
somewhere, and you, grown up in various ways, are at the typewriter,
thinking of all the slimes and jellies of decay, thinking
that the zombie passages, ghoul corridors, radiant death's head
entries to that realm of terror claim us in the sick middle-of-the-night
sessions of self-hatred and remorse, in the day's most hidden,
watchful self, the man not farting in line at the bank,
no trace of discomfort on his mild, neighbor-loving face, the woman
calculating the distance to the next person she can borrow a
      tampon from
when she smiles attentively into this new man's explanation
of his theory of deforestation, claims us also, by seepage, in our lies,
small malices, razor knicks on the skin of others of our meannesses,
deprivations, rage, and what to do but face that way
and praise the kingdom of the dead, praise the power which we have
      all kinds
of phrases to elide, that none of us can worm our way out of—
"which all must kneel to in the end," "that no man can evade,"
praise it by calling it time, say it is master of the seasons,
mistress of the moment of the hunting hawk's sudden sheen of
      grape-brown
gleaming in the morning sun, the characteristic slow gesture,

two fingers across the cheekbone deliberately, of the lover dreamily
oiling her skin, in this moment, no other, before she turns to you
the face she wants you to see and the rest
that she hopes, when she can't keep it hidden, you can somehow love
and, which, if you could love yourself, you would.

Praying Drunk

Our Father who art in heaven, I am drunk.
Again. Red wine. For which I offer thanks.
I ought to start with praise, but praise
comes hard to me. I stutter. Did I tell you
about the woman whom I taught, in bed,
this prayer? It starts with praise; the simple form
keeps things in order. I hear from her sometimes.
Do you? And after love, when I was hungry,
I said, *Make me something to eat.* She yelled,
Poof! You're a casserole!—and laughed so hard
she fell out of the bed. Take care of her.

Next, confession—the dreary part. At night
deer drift from the dark woods and eat my garden.
They're like enormous rats on stilts except,
of course, they're beautiful. But why? What *makes*
them beautiful? I haven't shot one yet.
I might. When I was twelve, I'd ride my bike
out to the dump and shoot the rats. It's hard
to kill your rats, our Father. You have to use
a hollow point and hit them solidly.
A leg is not enough. The rat won't pause.
Yeep! Yeep! it screams, and scrabbles, three-legged, back
into the trash, and I would feel a little bad
to kill something that wants to live
more savagely than I do, even if
it's just a rat. My garden's vanishing.
Perhaps I'll merely plant more beans, though that
might mean more beautiful and hungry deer.
Who knows? I'm sorry for the times I've driven

home past a black, enormous, twilight ridge.
Crested with mist, it looked like a giant wave
about to break and sweep across the valley,
and in my loneliness and fear I've thought,
O let it come and wash the whole world clean.
Forgive me. This is my favorite sin: despair—
whose love I celebrate with wine and prayer.

Our Father, thank you for all the birds and trees,
that nature stuff. I'm grateful for good health,
food, air, some laughs, and all the other things
I'm grateful that I've never had to do
without. I have confused myself. I'm glad
there's not a rattrap large enough for deer.
While at the zoo last week, I sat and wept
when I saw one elephant insert his trunk
into another's ass, pull out a lump,
and whip it back and forth impatiently
to free the goodies hidden in the lump.
I could have let it mean most anything,
but I was stunned again at just how little
we ask for in our lives. *Don't look! Don't look!*
Two young nuns tried to herd their giggling
schoolkids away. *Line up*, they called. *Let's go
and watch the monkeys in the monkey house.*
I laughed, and got a dirty look. Dear Lord,
we lurch from metaphor to metaphor,
which is—let it be so—a form of praying.

I'm usually asleep by now—the time
for supplication. Requests. As if I'd stayed
up late and called the radio and asked
they play a sentimental song. Embarrassed.
I want a lot of money and a woman.
And, also, I want vanishing cream. You know—
a character like Popeye rubs it on
and disappears. Although you see right through him,
he's there. He chuckles, stumbles into things,

and smoke that's clearly visible escapes
from his invisible pipe. It makes me think,
sometimes, of you. What makes me think of me
is the poor jerk who wanders out on air
and then looks down. Below his feet, he sees
eternity, and suddenly his shoes
no longer work on nothingness, and down
he goes. As I fall past, remember me.

JYNNE DILLING MARTIN

How You See Depends on Where You Go

If I were a hot dog, no way would I want to hang around
all week in the boiling water of a metal hot dog cart.

The dark would make me claustrophobic, the smell
must be pungent, and though we'd all pretend to be friends,

each time the sky split open and the aluminum tongs
came down everyone would hustle hoping to be chosen

and then be so pissed afterwards about life's randomness
and inequality, since the dog selected would totally suck.

With nothing else to go on, we'd idiotically think
hot dogs were the only food and our cart the only cart

and our vendor the one who invented the light and dark.
We'd carve a fresco of our cart's history on the metal

using a rusted knife that had fallen into our water.
We'd be such a joke to the ketchup and the mustard!

No, I'd rather be an eight-pack dog in the refrigeration aisle
of a grocery store, and not just anywhere in that pack,

but one of the four on bottom with a transparent plastic view
of the suburban shoppers. Then I could scan all the people

and feel quietly superior to the ugly and unhappy ones,
knowing my snug life at least is better than that.

Grapefruit

I'm eating breakfast even if it means standing
in front of the sink and tearing at the grapefruit,
even if I'm leaning over to keep the juices
away from my chest and stomach and even if a spider
is hanging from my ear and a wild flea
is crawling down my leg. My window is wavy
and dirty. There is a wavy tree outside
with pitiful leaves in front of the rusty fence
and there is a patch of useless rhubarb, the leaves
bent over, the stalks too large and bitter for eating,
and there is some lettuce and spinach too old for picking
beside the rhubarb. This is the way the saints
ate, only they dug for thistles, the feel
of thorns in the throat it was a blessing, my pity
it knows no bounds. There is a thin tomato plant
inside a rolled-up piece of wire, the worms
are already there, the birds are bored. In time
I'll stand beside the rolled-up fence with tears
of gratitude in my eyes. I'll hold a puny
pinched tomato in my open hand,
I'll hold it to my lips. Blessed art Thou,
King of tomatoes, King of grapefruit. The thistle
must have juices, there must be a trick. I hate
to say it but I'm thinking if there is a saint
in our time what will he be, and what will he eat?
I hated rhubarb, all that stringy sweetness—
a fake applesauce—I hated spinach,
always with egg and vinegar, I hated
oranges when they were quartered, that was the signal
for castor oil—aside from the peeled navel

I love the Florida cut in two. I bend
my head forward, my chin is in the air,
I hold my right hand off to the side, the pinkie
is waving; I am back again at the sink;
oh loneliness, I stand at the sink, my garden
is dry and blooming, I love my lettuce, I love
my cornflowers, the sun is doing it all,
the sun and a little dirt and a little water.
I lie on the ground out there, there is one yard
between the house and the tree; I am more calm there
looking back at this window, looking up
a little at the sky, a blue passageway
with smears of white—and gray—a bird crossing
from berm to berm, from ditch to ditch, another one,
a wild highway, a wild skyway, a flock
of little ones to make me feel gay, they fly
down the thruway, I move my eyes back and forth
to see them appear and disappear, I stretch
my neck, a kind of exercise. Ah sky,
my breakfast is over, my lunch is over, the wind
has stopped, it is the hour of deepest thought.
Now I brood, I grimace, how quickly the day goes,
how full it is of sunshine, and wind, how many
smells there are, how gorgeous is the distant
sound of dogs, and engines—Blessed art Thou
Lord of the falling leaf, Lord of the rhubarb,
Lord of the roving cat, Lord of the cloud.
Blessed art Thou oh grapefruit King of the universe,
Blessed art Thou my sink, oh Blessed art Thou
Thou milkweed Queen of the sky, burster of seeds,
Who bringeth forth juice from the earth.

RAY A. YOUNG BEAR

A Season of Provocations and Other Ethnic Dreams

1.
It began near the site
of a smoldering but vacant
mobile home. East Quail
Road. There, blared the scanner,
relatives conveyed a teenager
was upset for being deprived
of a "real Three Stooges
videotape." Thus was the day
ignited. Next, through the jet's
window, I waved to my wife,
Selene Buffalo Husband,
as the bus-like craft turned
over a runway of corn stalk
stumps. And then we ascended,
westward. Unbuckled, I sat in
the back and stretched my arms
across the tops of a soft bench.
Standing beside me, an ethnic
pilot was uneasy. He deflected
my questions with stares toward
earth of concern. Like an amateur
verbal boxer I recited: "Best to leave
a rock that refuses to talk alone;
best just to listen to the water
rippling around it."

2.
Once, after an all-night drive
to Taos, New Mexico, I became

disoriented. At some plaza square,
perhaps close to the designated
meeting place with the poetry
reading contact, I approached
a group of ethnics on a balcony
and, thinking they were other
invited poets, asked: "Are you
here to meet Peter Cottontail?"
Unflinchingly, while wiping salad
bits from their mouths, they pointed
to each other. "No, but we have Bugs
Bunny here—and, oh, here's Daffy!"
Travel-faced in their expensive sun-
glasses I was convex at the ethnologic
query about who I was. Si, I said, an
Indio, from a nearby immiscible history.
Years later, I recall this exchange
and wonder if Woody Woodpecker
really has a daughter and what
her name might be. Is it Splinter?
you knothead. Methinks it's a clue
from Oklahoma via the Lazy-Boy
quest sessions in the disappearances
of Laura and Ashley.

3.
English for Black Eagle Childs,
Pat "Dirty" Red Hat once noted,
is saturated with linguistic pitfalls.
For example, he once asked
a coy waitress at an old German-
style restaurant on Interstate 80,
"Do you serve alcoholics?"
"Yes, we do," he was told
that Sunday morning. At a Sears
auto garage the manager peace-
signed when Pat asked about
"Hallucinogenic" rather than

halogen headlights. And at
the Youth Services Facility
co-workers oft-reflected when
he "applied a Heineken" on
a muskmelon pulp-choking
girl. That singular misapplication
had more notice than the turbulent
adolescence saved. But no one quipped
at the line given when he mis-addressed
himself: "I am completely reverse
of what I am." Because that term
could fit anyone, ethnic—
or otherwise.

Pronouncing My Name

When someone leans in and says, "Koohurch?
Curcheese? Curgoo?" I just nod. Believe me,
it's easier.

When someone wipes his brow and asks,
"What the hell kind of name is that, anyway?"
I say it's probably German. Like Goethe.

To whom I was related. Closely. I also let it be
known that my great grandparents, being modest
immigrants, had dropped the noble *Von*.
Actually I was an aristocrat.

Sure, Ronald Von Koertge the Twerp.

"*Coeur*," said Robert one day. "Maybe it's French."
Could it be Ronald Heart, like in sweetheart?
How wonderful! What did the Germans invent,
anyway, but anal retentiveness.

But the French—they drink wine all the time
and think nudity is okay. Now I can stop
worrying that I would look good in a long,
leather coat. I have a great new hometown,
France! Where, by the way, my great, great,
great, great grandfather invented the sweetest
kiss of them all.

Constant Defender

My little finger's stuck in a
Coca-Cola bottle and I've got three
red checkers lodged in my watchpocket.
In a rush to meet my angel, now
I don't even know who my angel was.
I can see seven crimson jeeps lined up
outside Pigboy's Barbecue Shack—
must be a napkin salesmen's convention.
I don't care what cargo as long as
their hats are back on by eleven.
The thing I'm trying to avoid
is talking to my mule about glue futures.
What's a fellow going to do? I must
have a ceiling fan. I can't postpone
twirling blades. And my one stuffed chair
was owned by a hunchback from a hundred years
before I came along. I need some new
knickknacks to suggest an air of cleanliness
to this sluggish pit of extinct sweet potatoes.
Ah, trickery, you sassy lark, withered black pearl,
unfetter me from these latches, make me
the Director at every meatball's burial,
lacerate this too, too static air
I've been eating my way through.
I lunch on eels and larks in lemonade, Lord,
I'm so happy I woke up in my right mind today.
And those kleptomaniacs, Smitty and Bob,
stole peanuts from a hunchback, snuff from an angel.
My knees click, I won't budge, like a wind-up toy

unwound, my guitar held tightly between my thighs.
Last night a clam fell from the stars:
a festive, if slippery occasion, a vibrating blob
entered our midst—I say "ours" out of some need—
I was alone when it hit me.

STEPHEN DOBYNS

How to Like It

These are the first days of fall. The wind
at evening smells of roads still to be traveled,
while the sound of leaves blowing across the lawns
is like an unsettled feeling in the blood,
the desire to get in a car and just keep driving.
A man and a dog descend their front steps.
The dog says, Let's go downtown and get crazy drunk.
Let's tip over all the trash cans we can find.
This is how dogs deal with the prospect of change.
But in his sense of the season, the man is struck
by the oppressiveness of his past, how his memories
which were shifting and fluid have grown more solid
until it seems he can see remembered faces
caught up among the dark places in the trees.
The dog says, Let's pick up some girls and just
rip off their clothes. Let's dig holes everywhere.
Above his house, the man notices wisps of cloud
crossing the face of the moon. Like in a movie,
he says to himself, a movie about a person
leaving on a journey. He looks down the street
to the hills outside of town and finds the cut
where the road heads north. He thinks of driving
on that road and the dusty smell of the car
heater, which hasn't been used since last winter.
The dog says, Let's go down to the diner and sniff
people's legs. Let's stuff ourselves on burgers.
In the man's mind, the road is empty and dark.
Pine trees press down to the edge of the shoulder,
where the eyes of animals, fixed in his headlights,
shine like small cautions against the night.

Sometimes a passing truck makes his whole car shake.
The dog says, Let's go to sleep. Let's lie down
by the fire and put our tails over our noses.
But the man wants to drive all night, crossing
one state line after another, and never stop
until the sun creeps into his rearview mirror.
Then he'll pull over and rest awhile before
starting again, and at dusk he'll crest a hill
and there, filling a valley, will be the lights
of a city entirely new to him.
But the dog says, Let's just go back inside.
Let's not do anything tonight. So they
walk back up the sidewalk to the front steps.
How is it possible to want so many things
and still want nothing? The man wants to sleep
and wants to hit his head again and again
against a wall. Why is it all so difficult?
But the dog says, Let's go make a sandwich.
Let's make the tallest sandwich anyone's ever seen.
And that's what they do and that's where the man's
wife finds him, staring into the refrigerator
as if into the place where the answers are kept—
the ones telling why you get up in the morning
and how it is possible to sleep at night,
answers to what comes next and how to like it.

MY OLD REPTILE

Close Encounters of the Sexual Kind

Dream Song 4

Filling her compact & delicious body
with chicken páprika, she glanced at me
twice.
Fainting with interest, I hungered back
and only the fact of her husband & four other people
kept me from springing on her

or falling at her little feet and crying
'You are the hottest one for years of night
Henry's dazed eyes
have enjoyed, Brilliance.' I advanced upon
(despairing) my spumoni.—Sir Bones: is stuffed,
de world, wif feeding girls.

—Black hair, complexion Latin, jewelled eyes
downcast ... The slob beside her   feasts ... What wonders is
she sitting on, over there?
The restaurant buzzes. She might as well be on Mars.
Where did it all go wrong? There ought to be a law against Henry.
—Mr. Bones: there is.

The Devils

You were a "victim of semiromantic anarchism
In its most irrational form."
I was "ill at ease in an ambiguous world

Deserted by Providence." We drank wine
And made love in the afternoon. The neighbors'
TVs were tuned to soap operas.

The unhappy couples spoke little.
There were interminable pauses.
Soft organ music. Someone coughing.

"It's like Strindberg's *Dream Play*," you said.
"What is?" I asked and got no reply.
I was watching a spider on the ceiling.

It was the kind St. Veronica ate in her martyrdom.
"That woman subsisted on spiders only,"
I told the janitor when he came to fix the faucet.

He wore dirty overalls and a derby hat.
Once he had been an inmate of a notorious state institution.
"I'm no longer Jesus," he informed us happily.

He believed only in devils now.
"This building is full of them," he confided.
One could see their horns and tails

If one caught them in their baths.
"He's got Dark Ages on his brain," you said.
"Who does?" I asked and got no reply.

The spider had the beginnings of a web
Over our heads. The world was quiet.
Except when one of us took a sip of wine.

The Sausage Parade

When the Roman Empire, like an overcooked
kielbasa, began to shrivel up, Christians made them

illegal. Peperone, Calabrese, Sanguinaccio:
from speakeasy kitchens, butter, lard and onion

hissed. Holsteiner, Genoa, Cervelats:
20 centuries later, the High-Production

Pickle Injector ensures a steady supply.
Presskopf, Figatelli, Jagdwurst:

could it be their names? That each must form
to its casing? Whose nose hasn't longed

for the scent of fennel and pork?
Who can say sausage isn't onomatopoeic?

"Cook them slowly," Dishes of the World
insists. "To keep from bursting, prick."

Robert was my first: red pepper, pimento
pinch. Chorizo de Lomo. Taught me

sizzle, avoidance of smokehouse shrink. Never
would I settle for less. Byron Speer—oatmeal, vinegar,

thyme—loved to go shirtless March to November.
Skin silken gravy, oven-baked. Chuck, a Drisheen—

running ox, tansy-tinged; two parts blood
to one part cream. Helmut, all-hands-in-the-pot

simmering shallots, 6'2", 220; sweetness
soaked (lawyer by day, Braunschweiger

by night); Dylan a Rotwurst, keeping sausage—
sage, chestnut purée, lemon, Muscadet—

would have kept and kept. . . .

The man I love doesn't love my bread-crumb-soaked,
sputtering-pork-and-chipolata past—

salsiccie, budini, zamponi.
But the past is long as Italy's boot.

It is made of leeks, red wine,
crushed garlic, whole peppercorns.

There is plenty of room at the table.

Chit-Chat with the Junior League Women

A Junior League woman in blue
Showed me enough panty
To keep my back straight,
To keep my wine glass lifting
Every three minutes,
Time enough for the sun to wrench
More sweat from the workers
Shouldering cement and lumber,
The scaffolding of hard labor
That keeps this hill view up.
Do you have children? She asked.
Oh, yes, I chimed. Sip, sip.
Her legs spread just enough to stir
The lint from my eyelashes,
Just enough to think of a porpoise
Smacking me with sea-scented kisses.
The Junior League woman in yellow
Turned to the writer next to me,
Bearded fellow with two remaindered books,
His words smoldering for any goddamn reader.
This gave me time. Sip, sip,
Then a hard, undeceitful swallow
Of really good Napa Valley wine.
My mind, stung with drink,
Felt tight, like it had panty hose
Over its cranium. I thought
About the sun between sips,
How I once told my older brother,
Pale vampire of psychedelic music,
That I was working on a tan.

That summer my mom thought I had worms—
I was thin as a flattened straw,
Nearly invisible, a mere vapor
As I biked up and down the block.
I rolled out an orange towel in the back yard
And sun sucked more weight
From my body. After two hours,
My skin hollered. . . . I let the reminiscence
Pass and reached for the bottle,
Delicately because I was in a house
With a hill view held up by cement and lumber
And other people's work.
A Junior League woman in red
Sat with her charming hands
On her lap, studying us two writers,
Now with the panty hose of drunkenness
Pulled over our heads and down to our eyes.
What do you do exactly, Mr. Soto?
And I looked at her blinding
Underwear and—sip, sip—said, Everything.

Sex with a Famous Poet

I had sex with a famous poet last night
and when I rolled over and found myself beside him I shuddered
because I was married to someone else,
because I wasn't supposed to have been drinking,
because I was in a fancy hotel room
I didn't recognize. I would have told you
right off this was a dream, but recently
a friend told me, *write about a dream,*
lose a reader and I didn't want to lose you
right away. I wanted you to hear
that I didn't even like the poet in the dream, that he has
four kids, the youngest one my age, and I find him
rather unattractive, that I only met him once,
that is, in real life, and that was in a large group
in which I barely spoke up. He disgusted me
with his disparaging remarks about women.
He even used the word "Jap,"
which I took as a direct insult to my husband who's Asian.
When we were first dating, I told him,
"You were talking in your sleep last night
and I listened, just to make sure you didn't
call out anyone else's name." My future husband said
that he couldn't be held responsible for his subconscious,
which worried me, which made me think his dreams
were full of blonde vixens in rabbit-fur bikinis,
but he said no, he dreamt mostly about boulders
and the ocean and volcanoes, dangerous weather
he witnessed but could do nothing to stop.
And I said, "I dream only of you,"
which was romantic and silly and untrue.

But I never thought I'd dream of another man—
my husband and I hadn't even had a fight,
my head tucked sweetly in his armpit, my arm
around his belly, which lifted up and down
all night, gently like water in a lake.
If I passed that famous poet on the street,
he would walk by, famous in his sunglasses
and blazer with the suede patches at the elbows,
without so much as a glance in my direction.
I know you're probably curious about who the poet is,
so I should tell you the clues I've left aren't
accurate, that I've disguised his identity,
that you shouldn't guess *I bet it's him* . . .
because you'll never guess correctly
and even if you do, I won't tell you that you have.
I wouldn't want to embarrass a stranger
who is, after all, probably a nice person,
who was probably just having a bad day when I met him,
who is probably growing a little tired of his fame—
which my husband and I perceive as enormous,
but how much fame can an American poet
really have, let's say, compared to a rock star
or film director of equal talent? Not that much,
and the famous poet knows it, knows that he's not
truly given his due. Knows that many
of these young poets tugging on his sleeve
are only pretending to have read all his books.
But he smiles anyway, tries to be helpful.
I mean, this poet has to have some redeeming qualities, right?
For instance, he writes a mean iambic.
Otherwise, what was I doing in his arms?

DAVID BOTTOMS

Crawling Out at Parties

My old reptile loves the Scotch,
the way it drugs the cells that keep him caged
in the ancient swamps of the brain.
He likes crawling out at parties
among tight-skirted girls. He takes
the gold glitter of earrings
for small yellow birds wading in shallow water,
the swish of nyloned legs for muskrats in the reeds.

But he moves awkwardly in the hardwood forests
of early American furniture, stumbles on grassy
throw rugs, and the yellow birds
flutter toward the foggy horizons of the room.
Out of date, he just can't swing
so slides back always to his antique home,
the stagnant, sobering water.

Breasts

If I were French, I'd write
about breasts, structuralist treatments
of breasts, deconstructionist breasts,
Gertrude Stein's breasts in Père-Lachaise
under stately marble. Film noir breasts
no larger than olives, Edith Piaf's breasts
shadowed under a song, mad breasts raving
in the bird market on Sunday.
Tanguy breast softening the landscape,
the politics of nipples (we're all equal).
A friend remembers nursing,
his twin in a menacing blur. But wait,
we're in America, where breasts
were pointy until 1968. I once invented
a Busby Berkeley musical with naked women
underwater sitting at a counter
where David Bowie soda-jerked them
ice-cream glaciers. It sounds so sexual
but had a Platonic air-brushed air.
Beckett calls them dugs, which makes me think
of potatoes, but who calls breasts potatoes?
Bolshoi dancers strap down their breasts
while practicing at the barre.
You guess they're thinking of sailing
but probably it's bread, dinner,
and the *Igor Zlatik Show* (their
Phil Donahue). There's a photo of me
getting dressed where I'm surprised
by Paul and try to hide my breasts, and another
this year, posed on a pier, with my breasts

reflected in silver sunglasses. I blame
it on summer when flowers overcome gardens
and breasts point at the stars. Cats
have eight of them, and Colette tells
of a cat nursing its young while
being nursed by its mother. Imagine the scene
rendered human. And then there's the Russian
story about the woman . . . but wait,
they've turned the lights down, and Humphrey
Bogart is staring at Lauren Bacall's breasts
as if they might start speaking.

So Thick?

Freud, presented with a copy of Wilhelm Reich's The Function of the Orgasm,
is said to have remarked "So thick?"

As thieves, as clotted cream, molasses poured in March,
or dullards duly quizzed, as thin's mate in
the marriage vow, or black fly hoverings
upon Katahdin, ketchup in the kitchen's
bottleneck, or traffic's slow red ooze
on I-5 every dusk, as musk
in the mind of an elephant,
or malice in the minds of men,
this treatise on the uses
of the human love-cramp

isn't surely anywhere as thick.
But what's the use of use, at this

imponderable juncture? Just
how practical are practices? Is poetry
poetic? And to what high end
the spondee's spasm? If the seizure leaves us
sobered up, we're lucky. Lucky

(after the humpback's beached) to have a bath
of modest aftermath, a tristesse to
redress the tryst! We're lucky to escape
the clutch of Sophocles' "furious master" (feeling's fist),
for the rest of the evening. A breather from breathing!
If the world for a merciful while be spared our craving,
or if spilling brine by brimfuls can

(for only the blink of an animal eye)
undo a few of our meaning's demeanings,
our siring's desirings, and give us one
pure moment's peace, I'd say the fucking
function's clear. One fewer war for now!

(Meanwhile, in the wombs
engorged with worm,
the drumroll starts
its endlessness again.
They'll come from some
deep months away,
the humped-up little beating forms of men . . .)

Roughhousing

Tonight I let loose the weasel of my body
across the plantation of your body,
bird eater, mouse eater scampering across
your pale meadows on sandpaper feet.
Tonight I let my snake lips slide over you.
Tonight my domesticated paws have removed
their gloves and as pink as baby rats
they scurry nimble-footed into your dark parts.
You heave yourself—what is this earthquake?
You cry out—in what jungle does that bird fly?
You grunt—let's make these pink things hurry.
Let's take a whip and make them trot faster.
These lips already torn and bleeding—
let's plunder them. These teeth banging together—
prison bars against prison bars. Who really
is ever set free? Belly and breasts—
my snout roots in your dirt like a pig
rooting for scraps. Arm bones, hip bones—
I'll suck their marrow, then carve a whistle.
Woman, what would you be like seen from the sky?
My little plane sputters and coughs. I scramble
onto the wing. The wind whips across the fuselage.
Who needs a parachute? Wheat fields, a river,
your pastures rush toward me to embrace me.

While You Were Away . . .

I thought about sex. I turned 40, drank beer
on the back porch by myself. Called an ex.
Last night, the woman across the alley, the one
with that green porch light, suddenly appeared
in a white-and-black Dalmatian-spotted bathrobe,
bare legs, and slippers and shuffled down wet bricks.
She may have seen me, but she also saw
our other neighbor's Datsun gone, that guy
she dated once or twice, out all night,
and so she quickly shuffled right back home.
From the front side of the house, across the street,
a guy kept yelling "April! April! April!"
He pounded on the door. "C'mon, April!"
I am also sick of the month of March.
The season sucks us out of our houses, pulls
us onto porches and down damp alleys. We keep
testing our breaths against the cool night air.

This afternoon I made corn chowder, baked bread,
roasted asparagus for the Bollingers,
the mother deep in chemotherapy
for the second time. Their ten-year-old daughter
plays sweeper on the fifth-grade soccer team.
I wonder if the couple still has sex,
and if they do each time feels like the last.

Tonight the neighborhood is quiet.
No dogs bark. Everyone must have been
sucked back inside, maybe licking their wounds.
Our neighbor's light still burns a fungus green.

The roots begin to stir in the cold March rain.
I feel like I've been 40 all my life.
My daughter is at her mother's, and tonight,
you are so much further away than sleep.
I finish another High Life, go upstairs
and crawl beneath the covers, shiver, naked.
The dog's been on the bed, smelly but warm—
the only warmth tonight, so I'll take it.

Disrespect at the Mall

As I strolled through the mall one Saturday
in the unforgivable month of May
at the age of fifty-five
feeling really quite alive
I became aware that every attractive young woman there
(and there were hundreds) was wearing a sign
in cool dark blue letters across her chest that said
NOT FOR MARK
—and finally I was exasperated enough to approach
one who may have been twenty-six and looked intelligent
and I said "Why are you wearing this sign?"
and she said "Excuse me?"
and I said "This sign—it's so unfriendly—can't you take it off?"
and she said "What are you *talking* about?"
and so I did a kind of twinkling Sean Connery eyebrow thing
and I said "Sweetie, I'm only fifty-five"
and then she said, in this murderous mix of politeness and mirth
"Oh really? Whatever!" and she turned and walked away
with that extremely coordinated music of rump and thighs
so frequently described by midlife guys
and mingled with the shopping throng.
Then home I drove with droopy dong
to heal my soul in deathless song.

And I do feel calmer now, but still I resent
the way time turns me into some horny old gent
ostensibly, when in my heart I'm so appreciative, and vital,
and my appreciation deserves requital—

oh God, this is just how my old daddy felt
till he was eighty-five at least:
young beauty should not be untouchably svelte
if its magnetic tyranny has not ceased!
Ashley, Brenda, Cindy, Doreen,
you're just oblivious, not really mean,
yet you do my old heart vivisect.
Time and fate, not you, are guilty of disrespect.
(Notice though, girls, how deftly I rhyme;
younger guys can't do that, can they? Can they?
Not yet they can't. But give them time.)

THOMAS LUX

Sex in History

Only the Pope partook, the cardinals, priests, monks,
and nuns, it seems,
when you read the revisions. How the peasantry
reproduced itself despite
the bans is a mystery: no sex
on Thursday, the day of Christ's arrest,
Friday to honor His death,
Saturday in honor of His Mom,
Sunday, He has risen,
Monday to honor all who have not risen . . .
It seems, given festivals and fasts
around Easter, Pentecost, Xmas,
that there were two or three days a year for sex if:
You did not enjoy it (1) and (2)
It was conceptual, heterosexual, man and wife, man
on top. Chronic
food shortages were made more bearable
by penitential fasting (bread
and water) for infractions: 7 days
for wet dreams, 20 days
for masturbation, 2 years
for interfemoral connection (penis
between thighs of passive partner). . . .
And despite inbreeding
as an offshoot of snobbery, the nobility
did not believe the priests either,
which is why today there are so many sterile, dumb,
educated, and vacantly lovely humans
sitting in outdoor cafes
along the famous shopping boulevards.

Sex was sex: flesh
to flesh, eons of it, say one thing,
do another—fast, furtive,
fearful, and God
was always watching,
with His big wide eyes,
watching what He had made.

TIM SEIBLES

Bonobo

Bonobo apes employ sex — all kinds — as their primary mode of social interaction.
Violence is virtually unheard of among them.

Call Drea and Carlo   Jaretta, Josefina and George.
Ring Zhao, then Yusef   Dvora, Savannah and Dee.

Let's not be so useless today. Let's find a field
and, Andre, bring some birds—a thousand sparrows

to pepper the sky, a ruckus of toucans for color.
And Renée, don't forget the sunlight and no more

than 75 degrees with the friendly breeze that sings to us.
José, we stand in a place where no one can run naked,

but the police go public with their billy clubs and guns.
Red automobiles might be waxed and shown off,

but the genitals are locked up, gaberdined, touched
in secret and dubbed "privates." Let's not mingle

with the *forgive-me-my-sinners* or their grim
and constipated God. Jeanette, make sure the field

is a quilt of monkey-grass and periwinkle.
Send the numbskulls to the city for a shopping day.

Then, let's get with the kisses—
who with who, who cares? Who cares!

As long as the lips are excellent
pastries and the tongues, circumspect

and merciless. It should take half a day
to spill the vulva's quick honey   longer

to key the relentless clarinet of the cock—half a day
or the sun will consider the good light wasted on us.

And why not be deliberately lazy with the buttery rays
like a broth ladled over us? Why not a languid

and mellifluous career grooving hallelujah with our hips,
as if this flammable symmetry were a ship always

turning between two ports: *wanting* and *having.*
Don't let Masala and Sissy double-up

on Susanna. Watch out for JT and Bernard.
Tell them to hold their horny horses—

tell them   *the orgasm, like a favorite*
auntie   always saves a place at her table,

the dinner ready whenever we arrive.
But nobody can stop them. Who can ever stop

any of us   and why: as if we haven't already lost
too much time working—and too many lives.

So let there be lots of licking, every mouth
on loan to the loud song of our loneliness,

and fucking, of course—crisp, proud, posh,
preemptive, unimpeachable, forever and ever—

from these front yards to Zimbabwe and the Taj Mahal,
fucking in the loosest, most elaborate sense

of the word. Forget the word. Let thighs be questions
and other thighs be answers. When we're true like this

even the sky rolls onto its back, even the most reluctant
shade slides over us: Eros in the air—bold fish

stroll from the lake, a lone bonobo brings a symphony
of oboes   spilling all the unsaid things.

Let's take this one chance and be terribly
kind to each other. I'm sick of wafting around

like a fart in the attic. Leave the money
to the morticians and their cadavers.

Let's make the most noise with our hearts.

The Secret Life of Barbie and Mr. Potato Head

It began the year Jane received her first Barbie, and Dick was given
Mr. Potato Head for Christmas. Jane loved Barbie. She especially loved
undressing Barbie. So did Mr. Potato Head. Soon Barbie and Mr. Potato
Head were slipping off alone to dark corners. The first time it happened
Jane's mother was fixing a salad for supper: cottage cheese nestled on
a crisp bed of lettuce with canned pears on top. Barbie was nervously
popping her head off and on. *Jane,* her mother called, *would you please set
the table?* That's when Jane told her mother that Barbie was engaged to
marry Mr. Potato Head.

Of course even Jane knew Mr. Potato Head wasn't the perfect match
for Barbie. She was afraid her Barbie might be jealous of all the other
Barbies in her neighborhood who had acquired handsome Kens for
their husbands. But she soon realized her mother was right. Her mother
always said looks aren't everything. Besides, Mr. Potato Head could make
Barbie laugh. And he could do a lot more things with his detachable nose
and pipe and ears when her mother wasn't looking. He, unlike Ken, was
the kind of man who could change himself for a woman like Barbie.
No problem, Mr. Potato Head would say whenever Barbie requested yet
another body part.

Bad Girl

She's the one sleeping all day, in a room
at the back of your brain. She wakes up
at the sound of a cork twisted free
of a bottle, a stabbed olive

plopped into gin. She's prettier than you
and right now you bore the shit out of her,
sitting there sipping when she wants
to stand on the rim of the glass, naked,

dive straight to the bottom and lie there
looking up, amazed at how the world
wavers and then comes clear. You're not
going to let her. You've locked her in

with her perfume and cheap novels,
her deep need for trouble. She's the one
calling to you through the keyhole,
then sneaking away to squirm out

a window and tear her silk dress.
You can't guess where she's going,
or who you'll wake up with
when you finally wake up,

your head throbbing like a heart.
She's the one you're scared of,

the one who dares you to go ahead
and completely disappear. It's not

you the boys are noticing, not you
turning toward them and throwing off light.
You're crouched in a corner, coming undone.
She's in love with you now. She's the one.

STEPHEN DOBYNS

He Told Her He Loved Her

Party all day, party all night—a man
wakes up on the floor of a friend's kitchen.
It's still dark. He can hear people snoring.
He reaches out and touches long silky hair.
He thinks it's his friend's daughter. Actually,
it's a collie dog. He can't see a thing
without his glasses. He embraces the dog.
Why is the daughter wearing a fur coat?
He gropes around for the dog's breasts
but can't find them. The dog licks his face.
So that's how it's going to be, is it?
The man licks the collie dog back. He tries
to take off his pants but gets his underwear
caught in the zipper, so they only smooch.
He tells the collie dog about his wife,
how they only make love once a month.
He tells the collie dog about his two sons,
how they have robbed him blind and ruined
the record player. The dog licks his face.
The man tells the collie dog that he loves her.
He decides in the morning he and the daughter
will run away and immigrate to New Zealand.
They will raise sheep and children. Each evening
as the sun sets they will embrace on their
front porch with a deep sense of accomplishment.
He will stop drinking and playing cards.
The man falls asleep with the image of
the little log house clearly before his eyes.
When he wakes in the morning, he finds
the collie dog curled up beside him. You bitch,

he cries, and kicks her out of the kitchen.
He staggers off to find the daughter's bedroom.
Time to leave for New Zealand, my precious.
The daughter screams. The father comes running,
grabs his friend, and throws him out of the house.
Later the father has lunch with a priest.
He describes how this fat old clerk had tried
to rape his daughter. Was it drugs, whiskey,
or general depravity? They both wonder at
the world's impending collapse. The waitress
brings them coffee. The father can't take
his eyes off her. She has breasts the size
of his head. He wants to take off his shoes
and run back and forth across her naked body.
Let us leave him with his preoccupation.
Like an airborne camera, the eye of the poem
lifts and lifts until the two men are only
two dark shapes seated at the round table
of an outdoor café. The season is autumn.
The street is full of cars. It is cloudy.
This is the world where Socrates was born;
where Jesse James was shot in the back
when he reached up to straighten a picture;
where a fat old clerk prowls the streets,
staring in the face of each dog he meets,
seeking out the face of his one true love.

Girls, Look Out for Todd Bernstein

Because after sitting out for a spell
he's back with a degree in accounting and a high
paying position in one of the leading
pharmaceutical corporations in the country
and aspirations of owning that exotic yellow
sports car, license plate EVIL.
And like Dennis Meng at Sycamore Chevrolet
stakes his reputation on his fully reconditioned
used cars, I stake my reputation
on telling you Todd Bernstein means business
this time, girls. No more of this being passed over
for abusive arm wrestling stars. He's got
a velour shirt now. No more of your excuses—
if he wants you, you're there. None of this
I'm shaving my pubes Friday night nonsense—
come on, you think Todd Bernstein's
going to fall for that? He knows you're not
studying, not busy working on some local
political campaign, not having the guy
who played Cockroach on *The Cosby Show* over
for dinner, not writing any great American
novel. He's seen your stuff and it's nothing more
than mediocre lyric poetry with titles
like "The Falling" and "Crucible" and "Waking to Death"
that force impossible metaphors, despairing
about love and womanhood and how bad
your life is even though you grew up happily
in suburban America, or at least as happily
as anyone can grow up in suburban America,
which normally, you know, consists of

the appearance of happiness while your dad is doing
three secretaries on the side and your mom
pretends not to know and brags to the entire
town about how you're an actress about to star
in a sitcom about the misadventures of a cable TV
repairperson who, while out on a routine
installation one day, accidentally
electrically blasts herself into the living room
of a family of barbarian warlords on a planet
near Alpha Centauri who force her into slavery
before sending her on a pillage mission
to a planet of Cloxnors who capture her and place
her in a torture institution where she meets
a vulnerable Meeb whom she convinces, because of
her cable TV repairperson skills, to let her
become nanny to its impressionable Meeblets just
before it's about to rip off her limbs
with its ferocious abnons and devour her.
The results, according to your mom, are hilarious,
but come on, you and I both know the story
is just so *predictable*. And Todd knows
your writing doesn't pull off any metaphors
for the happiness taken from you by some dude
who played bass and called himself a musician
when all he could really do was play a couple
of chords and sing about true love and alligators
and how the alligator represents true love
which somehow explains the legend where the guy
cut open an alligator one time in Florida
and found a golfer. There's just no fooling
Todd. Sure, he'll act like he's interested, that's
Todd Bernstein, and he'll make claims
that he too has written or been artistic
at some point in his life, but Todd Bernstein
knows all you girls really want is a piece
of good old Todd Bernstein. No longer
will any strange auras enter the bedroom
during sex and keep him from maintaining

an erection, no longer will any women
walk out on him repulsed. If anybody's walking out
after sex, it'll be Todd Bernstein, I can assure you.
He won't be humiliating himself by falling down
a flight of stairs in front of a group of Japanese
tourists anymore, but rather coaxing entire
masses of women into his bedroom. Because
that's Todd Bernstein. He's on the move.
And he wants you to know, girls, that he's well aware
you certainly can't learn Korean sitting around here
which is why he's out there right now, preparing
for the slew of women just beyond his sexual
horizon, spray-painting GIRLS, LOOK OUT
FOR TODD BERNSTEIN on the side
of a Village Pantry.

THE HEART IS A LONELY PERINEUM

Love, Marriage, Divorce, and Hatred

Marriage

Should I get married? Should I be good?
Astound the girl next door with my velvet suit and faustus hood?
Don't take her to movies but to cemeteries
tell all about werewolf bathtubs and forked clarinets
then desire her and kiss her and all the preliminaries
and she going just so far and I understanding why
not getting angry saying You must feel! It's beautiful to feel!
Instead take her in my arms lean against an old crooked tombstone
and woo her the entire night the constellations in the sky—

When she introduces me to her parents
back straightened, hair finally combed, strangled by a tie,
should I sit with my knees together on their 3rd degree sofa
and not ask Where's the bathroom?
How else to feel other than I am,
often thinking Flash Gordon soap—
O how terrible it must be for a young man
seated before a family and the family thinking
We never saw him before! He wants our Mary Lou!
After tea and homemade cookies they ask What do you do for a living?

Should I tell them? Would they like me then?
Say All right get married, we're losing a daughter
but we're gaining a son—
And should I then ask Where's the bathroom?

O God, and the wedding! All her family and her friends
and only a handful of mine all scroungy and bearded
just wait to get at the drinks and food—
And the priest! he looking at me as if I masturbated

asking me Do you take this woman for your lawful wedded wife?
And I trembling what to say say Pie Glue!
I kiss the bride all those corny men slapping me on the back
She's all yours, boy! Ha-ha-ha!
And in their eyes you could see some obscene honeymoon going on—

Then all that absurd rice and clanky cans and shoes
Niagara Falls! Hordes of us! Husbands! Wives! Flowers! Chocolates!

All streaming into cozy hotels
All going to do the same thing tonight
The indifferent clerk he knowing what was going to happen
The lobby zombies they knowing what
The whistling elevator man he knowing
Everybody knowing! I'd almost be inclined not to do anything!
Stay up all night! Stare that hotel clerk in the eye!
Screaming: I deny honeymoon! I deny honeymoon!
running rampant into those almost climactic suites
yelling Radio belly! Cat shovel!
O I'd live in Niagara forever! in a dark cave beneath the Falls
I'd sit there the Mad Honeymooner
devising ways to break marriages, a scourge of bigamy
a saint of divorce—

But I should get married I should be good
How nice it'd be to come home to her
and sit by the fireplace and she in the kitchen
aproned young and lovely wanting my baby
and so happy about me she burns the roast beef
and comes crying to me and I get up from my big papa chair
saying Christmas teeth! Radiant brains! Apple deaf!
God what a husband I'd make! Yes, I should get married!
So much to do! Like sneaking into Mr Jones' house late at night
and cover his golf clubs with 1920 Norwegian books
Like hanging a picture of Rimbaud on the lawnmower
like pasting Tannu Tuva postage stamps all over the picket fence
like when Mrs Kindhead comes to collect for the Community Chest

grab her and tell her There are unfavorable omens in the sky!
And when the mayor comes to get my vote tell him
When are you going to stop people killing whales!
And when the milkman comes leave him a note in the bottle
Penguin dust, bring me penguin dust, I want penguin dust—

Yes if I should get married and it's Connecticut and snow
and she gives birth to a child and I am sleepless, worn,
up for nights, head bowed against a quiet window, the past behind me,

finding myself in the most common of situations a trembling man
knowledged with responsibility not twig-smear nor Roman coin soup—

O what would that be like!
Surely I'd give it for a nipple a rubber Tacitus
For a rattle a bag of broken Bach records
Tack Della Francesca all over its crib
Sew the Greek alphabet on its bib
And build for its playpen a roofless Parthenon

No, I doubt I'd be that kind of father
Not rural not snow no quiet window
but hot smelly tight New York City
seven flights up, roaches and rats in the walls
a fat Reichian wife screeching over potatoes Get a job!
And five nose running brats in love with Batman
And the neighbors all toothless and dry haired
like those hag masses of the 18th century
all wanting to come in and watch TV
The landlord wants his rent
Grocery store Blue Cross Gas & Electric Knights of Columbus
impossible to lie back and dream Telephone snow, ghost parking—
No! I should not get married! I should never get married!
But—imagine if I were married to a beautiful sophisticated woman
tall and pale wearing an elegant black dress and long black gloves
holding a cigarette holder in one hand and a highball in the other
and we lived high up in a penthouse with a huge window

from which we could see all of New York and even farther on
   clearer days
No, can't imagine myself married to that pleasant prison dream—

O but what about love? I forget love
not that I am incapable of love
It's just that I see love as odd as wearing shoes—
I never wanted to marry a girl who was like my mother
And Ingrid Bergman was always impossible
And there's maybe a girl now but she's already married
And I don't like men and—
but there's got to be somebody!
Because what if I'm 60 years old and not married,
all alone in a furnished room with pee stains on my underwear
and everybody else is married! All the universe married but me!

Ah, yet well I know that were a woman possible as I am possible
then marriage would be possible—
Like SHE in her lonely alien gaud waiting her Egyptian lover
so I wait—bereft of 2,000 years and the bath of life.

DENISE DUHAMEL

Yes

According to *Culture Shock:*
A Guide to Customs and Etiquette
of Filipinos, when my husband says yes,
he could also mean one of the following:
a.) *I don't know.*
b.) *If you say so.*
c.) *If it will please you.*
d.) *I hope I have said yes unenthusiastically enough*
for you to realize I mean no.
You can imagine the confusion
surrounding our movie dates, the laundry,
who will take out the garbage
and when. I remind him
I'm an American, that all his yeses sound alike to me.
I tell him here in America we have shrinks
who can help him to be less of a people-pleaser.
We have two-year-olds who love to scream "No!"
when they don't get their way. I tell him,
in America we have a popular book,
When I Say No I Feel Guilty.
"Should I get you a copy?" I ask.
He says yes, but I think he means
"If it will please you," i.e., "I won't read it."
"I'm trying," I tell him, "but you have to try too."
"Yes," he says, then makes *tampo,*
a sulking that the book *Culture Shock* describes as
"subliminal hostility . . . withdrawal of customary cheerfulness
in the presence of the one who has displeased" him.
The book says it's up to me to make things all right,
"to restore goodwill, not by talking the problem out,

but by showing concern about the wounded person's
well-being." Forget it, I think, even though I know
if I'm not nice, *tampo* can quickly escalate into *nagdadabog*—
foot stomping, grumbling, the slamming
of doors. Instead of talking to my husband, I storm off
to talk to my porcelain Kwan Yin,
the Chinese goddess of mercy
that I bought on Canal Street years before
my husband and I started dating.
"The real Kwan Yin is in Manila,"
he tells me. "She's called Nuestra Señora de Guia.
Her Asian features prove Christianity
was in the Philippines before the Spanish arrived."
My husband's telling me this
tells me he's sorry. Kwan Yin seems to wink,
congratulating me—my short prayer worked.
"Will you love me forever?" I ask,
then study his lips, wondering if I'll be able to decipher
what he means by his yes.

The Theory of the Leisure Classes

In theory the sky was gray all that winter in London: no central heating, a
  constant drizzle, your feet were constantly cold.
In practice it was the same old overheated New York City apartment —
  but once you went outside, how near the sky, how blue.

In theory a man watching as a woman dresses, slowly, slowly, for the
  benefit of his gaze, is a man to be envied.
In practice he needs a shave.

In theory a man choosing among three women—his past wife, his future
  wife, and his current mistress—chooses the mistress.
In practice he is choosing among the daughters of King Lear.

In theory the revolver in the desk drawer was not meant to be used—it
  was a prop in a play, to be brandished once or twice by the hero in a fit
  of temperament.
In practice the newlyweds soon discovered the limits of their tolerance
  for each other's quirks.

In theory it was a trip to the places on the postage stamps in the
  collection I had as a boy: Magyar Poste, Ceskoslovensko, Jugoslavia,
  Deutsches Reich, Österreich.
In practice it was the experience of examining a 1957 Duke Snider
  baseball card fifteen years later, and noticing how young Snider looked.
  He hit forty home runs that season, the Dodgers' last in Brooklyn.

In theory she was the right woman at the wrong airport. It was the first
  time he had seen her without her makeup.
In practice, she wears flats and never comes into Manhattan without
  having stockings on. Watching her walk back and forth back and

forth in front of him, the auburn-haired man in the dark shirt and tie calculates the exact relation of danger to desire.

In theory the passengers are irate. "You are inept," an owlish-looking gentleman hooted at a red-faced customer service agent. Two cops turn up and the unattended shoe box in the TWA ticket area becomes the object of lively discussion. Then the announcement is made. Everyone has to clear the area—it's a real live bomb scare, folks.
In practice you take a cab into the city and notice for the first time the little shopfront at Lexington Avenue and 94th Street: Chao's Laundry. Remove the apostrophe and you arrive at your chosen destination. The adrenaline automatically starts to flow.

In theory the voice of authority is never heard—the word unspoken is what commands us.
In practice I was having lunch with an executive in the publishing industry. He said that success in management meant "having not only the responsibility but also the authority." Later I heard the same phrase from the general manager of the San Francisco Giants and from a guy I know in middle management in Rochester. I figured it must be true.

In theory a man does his best work under the pressure of deadlines and production schedules.
In practice a man does his best work on a beach in Bermuda, on an exceptionally clear October day, followed by rum swizzles at sundown and a little night reading.

In theory the woman was absent.
In practice every inch of the canvas implicated her in the man's idle fantasies of leisure and success.

Seriousness

Driving the Garden State Parkway to New York, I pointed out two crows to a woman who believed crows always travel in threes. And later just one crow eating the carcass of a squirrel. "The others are nearby," she said, "hidden in trees." She was sure. Now and then she'd say "See!" and a clear dark trinity of crows would be standing on the grass. I told her she was wrong to under- or overestimate crows, and wondered out loud if three crows together made any evolutionary sense. I was almost getting serious now. Near Forked River we saw five. "There's three," she said, "and two others with a friend in a tree." I looked to see if she was smiling. She wasn't. Or she was. "Men like you," she said, "need it written down, notarized, and signed."

My Wife's Therapist

My wife's therapist is explaining how counterproductive anger is.
There's a difference between asserting oneself and aggression, she says.
Flying into tirades can cause others to withdraw,
And then we can't negotiate
With them anymore.
She illustrates her point.
I have to get into a new office, right away, she says.
Yeah, I agree, this place is a mess.
Fixing her hair with both hands, she continues:
At the meeting to sign the new lease, the other party
Makes impossible demands
And suddenly walks out, slams the door, leaves.
I want to blow up, Angelo, but I don't.
Do I know what her response should be? She asks suddenly.
I shake my head.
She doesn't scream fuck you or kick ass, I bet.
I examine my feelings, Angelo, and then I cry. She leans toward me:
The realtor will set up another meeting later in the week and I'll get to
    try again.
My wife is breathing deeply so I know she is being moved.
Do I understand how this example is useful?
Sure. Definitely. It's clear to me.
How do I feel about it? What changes
Can I make in myself to show what I've learned?
I stand up, smack my head, and grasp
Everything she's been leading me to.
I'm transformed by her analysis.
I grasp her hands in my hands:
Ann, would you like me to go over there and fuck with them for you?
I could yell and curse. I could make them treat you good.

I could scare the piss out of them.

No, she says, crossing and uncrossing her legs. Let's begin again.

Anger is hurtful. Anger is bad.

Understand?

I nod my head.

Midnight

Speak to me, aching heart: what
ridiculous errand are you inventing for yourself
weeping in the dark garage
with your sack of garbage: it is not your job
to take out the garbage, it is your job
to empty the dishwasher. You are showing off again,
exactly as you did in childhood—where
is your sporting side, your famous
ironic detachment? A little moonlight hits
the broken window, a little summer moonlight, tender
murmurs from the earth with its ready sweetnesses—
is this the way you communicate
with your husband, not answering
when he calls, or is this the way the heart
behaves when it grieves: it wants to be
alone with the garbage? If I were you,
I'd think ahead. After fifteen years,
his voice could be getting tired; some night
if you don't answer, someone else will answer.

Purple Bathing Suit

I like watching you garden
with your back to me in your purple bathing suit:
your back is my favorite part of you,
the part furthest away from your mouth.

You might give some thought to that mouth.
Also to the way you weed, breaking
the grass off at ground level
when you should pull it up by the roots.

How many times do I have to tell you
how the grass spreads, your little
pile notwithstanding, in a dark mass which
by smoothing over the surface you have finally
fully obscured? Watching you

stare into space in the tidy
rows of the vegetable garden, ostensibly
working hard while actually
doing the worst job possible, I think

you are a small irritating purple thing
and I would like to see you walk off the face of the earth
because you are all that's wrong with my life
and I need you and I claim you.

What I Want

For my marriage, 1996–2000

I want a good night's sleep.
I want to get up without feeling
That to waken is to plunge through a trap door.

I want to ride my motorcycle
In late spring through the Elysian Fields
Of the Rocky Mountains

And lie once more with Cecelia
In the summer of 1985
On a blanket in the backyard of her house

In Denver and watch the clouds expand.
And it would be great to see my mother
Alive again, at the stove, frying up a pan of noodles

Into that peculiar carbonized disk that has never been replicated.
I would like for my ex-wife to get leprosy,
Her beauty falling away in little chunks

To the disgust of everyone in the chic café
Where she exercises her gift
For doing absolutely nothing.

I want world peace.
I want to come home one evening
And find that Julia, the new assistant professor

In the history department,
Has let herself into my apartment
For the express purpose of lecturing me

On the history of lingerie.
I don't ask for much: a good merlot.
An afternoon thunderstorm cooling off

The city as I sit listening to Ella
Sing "Spring is Here," so the air goes lyrical
And perhaps a stray bolt of lightning

Strikes my ex-wife as she steps from her car,
Setting her on fire, to the unqualified delight
Of the friends she has come to visit,

Who are thoroughly sick of her self-aggrandizing stories.
I want to spark a bowl of Maui Wowie
And spend the entire afternoon in my dorm room

With Corrine Spellman, trying to remember
What we were talking about, wondering
Whether, in fact, we had had sex yet.

I'd like to sit at the little outdoor restaurant
By the lake in Forest Park, talking with my aunt
In the humid summer twilight, as the hot

St. Louis day expires upon the water
And the moth-eaten Chinese lanterns
Glow like faded Kodachrome.

We would argue about the great tenor voices
Of the century, or causes for the dearth
Of poetry about the Gulf War,

Or why my father drank himself into an elegy
We never stop revising,
While couples on their paddleboats come in

From the darkening lake, as they've done
Since the beginning of time, and children
Call each other across the shadowy fields.

Yes, that would be nice.
I want a good woman
With a sweet bosom

And a wicked sense of humor.
I want to wake up in London on a spring morning
And read in the paper that my ex-wife

Has received a lethal injection, courtesy of the state
Of Ohio, as part of a citywide program aimed
At improving the civic pride of Cleveland,

But something went terribly wrong
And she's been left in a persistent
Vegetative state,

Which everyone agrees
Is nonetheless an improvement.
And it would be wonderful

To sit down with Maria
At our favorite restaurant in Madrid
With some good red wine

And listen to her Spanish
Caress the evening.
I want to read that a new manuscript

Of poetry by James Wright
Has been discovered in someone's attic,
And someone I haven't yet met,

In some future I have yet to despoil,
Has bought it for my birthday.
And after the kids are asleep

We sit out in the backyard,
A little drunk, and read it
Aloud to each other,

Something we often do
In summer, before climbing upstairs to the bedroom
In the big old house we love so much.

Mr. X

All my Ex's
live in Texas, so the country song says and no excuses,
it's mostly true for me too that the spade-shaped extra
big state with its cotton lints and Ruby Reds holds the crux
of my semi-truck-I've-never-had-any-kind-of-luck-deluxe-
super-high-jinx-born-to-be-unhappy-if-it-ain't-broken-don't-fix-

it loves, for example, there was the snakebit mudlogger who fixed
himself forever diving off that hexed bridge, and that foxy ex-
patriot who imported exotic parrots, he'd pump me up with his deluxe
stuff, the salesman who felt so guilty for the wide-eyed excuses
he told his wife that at the Big Six Motel just outside Las Cruces
he spent the afternoon hunched over Exodus, bemoaning the sin
    of extra-

marital sex, and the harmonica player, his mouth organ could extract
an oily bended blues, on sticky nights we'd hit the 12th hole pond with
    a fix
of Dos Equis and a hit of Ecstasy and I'd wrap my legs around his
    lanky crux,
as moonlight cut through the water like a giant X-ray, his Hohner ax
glistened in and out. And then there was the feckless shrink. No excuse
for his fixation, the tax man, the cute butcher from the Deluxe,

the Kilim dealer, the defrocked priest. So what if my mother was deluxe
luscious, my father with a Baptist streak, I can't blame them, I was born
    just extra
affectionate. Don't ask about the abortions, and who can ever
    make excuses

for the time I spent holed up with the Port-O-Can tycoon my friend fixed me up with, or the Mexican sculptor who made cathedral-sized onyx Xs, twisted crucifixes. Art, he quoted Marx, was history at its crux.

Then there was the Ph.D. who took me to Peru and showed me Crux (the Southern Cross), Centaurus, Musca, Vela, Lupus, and another deluxe equatorial constellation that I forgot. For fun I ascribed each sparkly X a name and date, so now I have a star chart to exalt each of my extraordinary, heavenly bodies. But that night I dreamed the stars were fixed on stacks of pages: pica asterisks to indicate omission, footnotes, excuses,

explanations. I stood there, Ms. D. Giovanni, with a million excuses. Now in exile I journey on the Styx with Mr. X in our boat the *Crux Criticorum*. I wear an aqua slicker, he a sharkskin suit. He's non-fiction, never incognito. We've got our sextant and spy manual open on
    our deluxe
waterbed. I can just make out the tattoo above his boxers in this extra dark, there's the curve of his back. Now we'll break the code and go
    beyond X.

Dim Lady

My honeybunch's peepers are nothing like neon. Today's special at Red Lobster is redder than her kisser. If Liquid Paper is white, her racks are institutional beige. If her mop were Slinkys, dishwater Slinkys would grow on her noggin. I have seen tablecloths in Shakey's Pizza Parlors, red and white, but no such picnic colors do I see in her mug. And in some minty-fresh mouthwashes there is more sweetness than in the garlic breeze my main squeeze wheezes. I love to hear her rap, yet I'm aware that Muzak has a hipper beat. I don't know any Marilyn Monroes. My ball and chain is plain from head to toe. And yet, by gosh, my scrumptious Twinkie has as much sex appeal for me as any lanky model or platinum movie idol who's hyped beyond belief.

My Beloved

In the fine print of her face
Her eyes are two loopholes.
No, let me start again.
Her eyes are flies in milk,
Her eyes are baby Draculas.

To hell with her eyes.
Let me tell you about her mouth.
Her mouth's the red cottage
Where the wolf ate grandma.

Ah, forget about her mouth,
Let me talk of her breasts.
I get a peek at them now and then
And even that's more than enough
To make me lose my head,
So I better tell you about her legs.

When she crosses them on the sofa
It's like the jailer unwrapping a parcel
And in that parcel is a Christmas cake
And in that cake a sweet little file
That gasps her name as it files my chains.

Song

Her nose is like a satellite,
her face a map of France,
her eyebrows like the Pyrenees
crossed by an ambulance.

Her shoulders are like mussel shells,
her breasts nouvelle cuisine,
but underneath her dress she moves
her ass like a stretch limousine.

Her heart is like a cordless phone,
her mouth a microwave,
her voice is like a coat of paint
or a sign by Burma Shave.

Her feet are like the income tax,
her legs a fire escape,
her eyes are like a videogame,
her breath like videotape.

True love is like a physics test
or a novel by Nabokov.
My love is like ward politics
or drinks by Molotov.

You Were Wearing

You were wearing your Edgar Allan Poe printed cotton blouse.
In each divided up square of the blouse was a picture of Edgar
　　Allan Poe.
Your hair was blonde and you were cute. You asked me, "Do most boys
　　think that most girls are bad?"
I smelled the mould of your seaside resort hotel bedroom on your hair
　　held in place by a John Greenleaf Whittier clip.
"No," I said, "it's girls who think that boys are bad." Then we read
　　Snowbound together
And ran around in an attic, so that a little of the blue enamel was scraped
　　off my George Washington, Father of His Country, shoes.

Mother was walking in the living room, her Strauss Waltzes comb in
　　her hair.
We waited for a time and then joined her, only to be served tea in cups
　　painted with pictures of Herman Melville.
As well as with illustrations from his book *Moby Dick* and from his
　　novella *Benito Cereno*.
Father came in wearing his Dick Tracy necktie: "How about a
　　drink, everyone?"
I said, "Let's go outside a while." Then we went onto the porch and sat
　　on the Abraham Lincoln swing.
You sat on the eyes, mouth, and beard part, and I sat on the knees.
In the yard across the street we saw a snowman holding a garbage can lid
　　smashed into a likeness of the mad English king, George the Third.

And Day Brought Back My Night

It was so simple: you came back to me
and I was happy. Nothing seemed to matter
but that. That you had gone away from me
and lived for days with him—it didn't matter.
That I had been left to care for our old dog
and house alone—couldn't have mattered less!
On all this, you and I and our happy dog
agreed. We slept. The world was worriless.

I woke in the morning, brimming with old joys
till the fact-checker showed up, late, for work
and started in: *Item: it's years, not days.*
Item: you had no dog. Item: she isn't back,
in fact, she just remarried. And oh yes, item: you
left her, remember? I did? I did. (I do.)

DANIEL BORZUTSKY

The Heart Is a Lonely Perineum

And if it is true that all I can do is float
through these tunnels of dust and pain in which
capital swims in the arms of mercilessness,
then I will put you in the coffin I wear
around my waist and bind you with a rose to the
small triangular bone at the end of my
spinal column where the you that is not you shall
meet the you that might be you and together we
will form a family who will flourish inside this
golden abyss whose entryway is guarded by
a gaggle of slithering creditors with
pee-pees for guns and Chinese porcelain for
eyeballs. For who is to say that the air we breathe
is anything more than a secret code both
capricious in structure and marketable in
the substance of its sad and tender humility.
I was teaching the Laotians about the
existential implications of the
conditional voice when a man came on the
loudspeaker and said we were all a bunch of
Mexican widows with secret Jewish husbands
in our titties. A woman in a velvet dress
jumped out of the rosemary bush and showed us
how to hide those we have murdered in our bodies. I
did not know the blind were invisible to
themselves until I chopped up an old harpy, shoved
her into my underpants, and chuckled as she
struggled to put herself back together. Then we
hopped into my Hybrid Honda Civic and sped
across the border to the all-you-can-eat

rotisserie chicken shack whose drive-thru window
clerk is the Virgin Mary on whose lips you must
tap three times before telling her there is a
handful of dust on her posterior vulva
junction, at which point she will become all the
women you should have kissed but didn't. This will come
true, even if you don't believe it.

For You, Sweetheart, I'll Sell Plutonium Reactors

For you, sweetheart, I'll ride back down
into black smoke early Sunday morning
cutting fog, grab the moneysack
of gold teeth. Diamond mines
soil creep groan ancient cities, archaeological
diggings, & yellow bulldozers turn around all night
in blood-lit villages. Inhabitants here once gathered seashells
that glimmered like pearls. When the smoke clears, you'll see
an erected throne like a mountain to scale,
institutions built with bones, guns hidden in walls
that swing open like big-mouthed B-52s.
Your face in the mirror is my face. You tapdance
on tabletops for me, while corporate bosses
arm wrestle in back rooms for your essential downfall.
I entice homosexuals into my basement butcher shop.
I put my hands around another sharecropper's throat
for that mink coat you want from Saks Fifth,
short-change another beggarwoman,
steal another hit song from Sleepy
John Estes, salt another gold mine in Cripple Creek,
drive another motorcycle up a circular ice wall,
face another public gunslinger like a bad chest wound,
just to slide hands under black silk.
Like the Ancient Mariner steering a skeleton ship
against the moon, I'm their hired gunman
if the price is right, take a contract on myself.
They'll name mountains & rivers in my honor.

I'm a drawbridge over manholes for you, sweetheart.
I'm paid two hundred grand
to pick up a red telephone anytime & call up God.
I'm making tobacco pouches out of the breasts of Indian maidens
so we can stand in a valley & watch the grass grow.

Why I Hate Martin Frobisher

Because he says I look like Deborah Kerr
Because he leaves wet towels on the bedspread
Because all mothers, waitresses, and bank ladies love him on the spot
Because he wears T-shirts with girls on them
Because he never gets parking tickets
Because he never breaks the Sorrento wineglasses
Because when he's mad we duke it out, and when I'm mad I need to
    calm down
Because he looks at me when I reach for the Land O'Lakes unsalted
    when Breakstone's on sale for a dollar fifty a pound
Because he watches sports on TV
Because he works and I just read books
Because when I'm screaming like an ocean liner, he can answer the phone
    and say, "Sure, no problem"
Because my mother thinks he's the spotty pup and I'm Cruella de Vil
Because he plays with his food, cuts curlicues into my 4-hour
    crème brûlée
Because he's always wrong and I'm the first to say sorry
Because he tries to placate me

Because he buys generic fabric softener instead of Downy
Because he does not want to go to the Red Party and gives me a 15-Watt
    excuse and we do not go to the Red Party
Because when he's stupid I'm too tired to point it out and when I'm
    stupid he's all there
Because he strains to hear *All Things Considered* when I'm biting his ankles
Because when I'm weepy and refuse to get out of the car it's time for the
    shrink, but when he puts his fist through my grandmother's beveled
    mirror he's just getting things out

Because he's glued to *The MacNeil/Lehrer Report* while I preview my
   upcoming suicide
Because he never trips me up

Because he made me his grandmother
Because he notices water spots on the glassware but hasn't an inkling
   about the man I've been sleeping with for over a year
Because he's so unlayered he doesn't know when I'm being mean
Because he no longer puts notes in my pockets for me to find later at the
   office by the Mr. Coffee machine
Because he no longer reads me to sleep from *One Thousand and One
   Arabian Nights*

Because in front of the judge he looks like Clark Gable and I look like
   the stepmother
Because he's got a heart the size of a chipped acorn, the brains
   of a squirrel, he's a jerk,
   a little girl's blouse,
   a felon, but straight-seamed,
   a cream-faced, two-penny
   scoundrel and a kitten kicker,
   a real badass and
   I want him back, oh yeah.

MOTHERS OF AMERICA LET YOUR KIDS GO TO THE MOVIES

Family Life and Strife

Ave Maria

Mothers of America
          let your kids go to the movies!
get them out of the house so they won't know what you're up to
it's true that fresh air is good for the body
             but what about the soul
that grows in darkness, embossed by silvery images
and when you grow old as grow old you must
             they won't hate you
they won't criticize you they won't know
        they'll be in some glamorous country
they first saw on a Saturday afternoon or playing hookey

they may even be grateful to you
        for their first sexual experience
which only cost you a quarter
        and didn't upset the peaceful home
they will know where candy bars come from
        and gratuitous bags of popcorn
as gratuitous as leaving the movie before it's over
with a pleasant stranger whose apartment is in the
        Heaven on Earth Bldg
near the Williamsburg Bridge
        oh mothers you will have made the little tykes
so happy because if nobody does pick them up in the movies
they won't know the difference
        and if somebody does it'll be sheer gravy
and they'll have been truly entertained either way
instead of hanging around the yard
        or up in their room
          hating you

prematurely since you won't have done anything horribly

                                                       mean yet

except keeping them from life's darker joys

                                   it's unforgivable the latter

so don't blame me if you won't take this advice

                                      and the family breaks up

and your children grow old and blind in front of a TV set

                                          seeing

movies you wouldn't let them see when they were young

The Lanyard

The other day as I was ricocheting slowly
off the pale blue walls of this room,
bouncing from typewriter to piano,
from bookshelf to an envelope lying on the floor,
I found myself in the L section of the dictionary
where my eyes fell upon the word *lanyard*.

No cookie nibbled by a French novelist
could send one more suddenly into the past—
a past where I sat at a workbench at a camp
by a deep Adirondack lake
learning how to braid thin plastic strips
into a lanyard, a gift for my mother.

I had never seen anyone use a lanyard
or wear one, if that's what you did with them,
but that did not keep me from crossing
strand over strand again and again
until I had made a boxy
red and white lanyard for my mother.

She gave me life and milk from her breasts,
and I gave her a lanyard.
She nursed me in many a sick room,
lifted teaspoons of medicine to my lips,
set cold face-cloths on my forehead,
and then led me out into the airy light

and taught me to walk and swim,
and I, in turn, presented her with a lanyard.

Here are thousands of meals, she said,
and here is clothing and a good education.
And here is your lanyard, I replied,
which I made with a little help from a counselor.

Here is a breathing body and a beating heart,
strong legs, bones and teeth,
and two clear eyes to read the world, she whispered,
and here, I said, is the lanyard I made at camp.
And here, I wish to say to her now,
is a smaller gift—not the archaic truth

that you can never repay your mother,
but the rueful admission that when she took
the two-tone lanyard from my hands,
I was as sure as a boy could be
that this useless, worthless thing I wove
out of boredom would be enough to make us even.

Phone Call

Maybe I overdid it
when I called my father an enemy of humanity.
That might have been a little strongly put,
a slight exaggeration, ˙

an immoderate description of the person
who at the moment, two thousand miles away,
holding the telephone receiver six inches from his ear,
must have regretted paying for my therapy.

What I meant was that my father
was an enemy of *my* humanity
and what I meant behind that
was that my father was split
into two people, one of them

living deep inside of me
like a bad king or an incurable disease—
blighting my crops,
striking down my herds,
poisoning my wells—the other
standing in another time zone,
in a kitchen in Wyoming
with bad knees and white hair spouting from his ears.

I don't want to scream forever,
I don't want to live without proportion
Like some kind of infection from the past,

so I have to remember the second father,
the one whose TV dinner is getting cold
while he holds the phone in his left hand
and stares blankly out the window

where just now the sun is going down
and the last fingertips of sunlight
are withdrawing from the hills
they once touched like a child.

CAMPBELL McGRATH

Delphos, Ohio

is where we turned around, surrendered to fate, gave in to defeat and abandoned our journey at a town with three stoplights, one good mechanic and a name of possibly oracular significance.

Which is how we came to consider calling the baby Delphos.

Which is why we never made it to Pennsylvania, never arrived to help J.B. plant trees on the naked mountaintop he calls a farm, never hiked down the brush-choked trail for groceries in the gnomic hamlet of Mann's Choice, never hefted those truckloads of bundled bodies nor buried their delicate rootling toes in the ice and mud of rocky meadows.

Blue spruce, black walnut, white pine, silver maple.

And that name! Mann's Choice. Finger of individual will poked in the face of inexorable destiny.

Which is how we came to consider calling the baby Hamlet, Spruce or Pennsylvania.

But we didn't make it there. Never even got to Lima or Bucyrus, let alone Martin's Ferry, let alone West Virginia, let alone the Alleghenies tumbled across the state line like the worn-out molars of a broken-down plow horse munching grass in a hayfield along the slate-grey Juniata.

Because the engine balked.

Because the shakes kicked in and grew like cornstalks hard as we tried to ignore them, as if we could push that battered blue Volvo across the wintry heart of the Midwest through sheer determination.

Which is foolish.

And the man in Delphos told us so.

Fuel injector, he says. Can't find even a sparkplug for foreign cars in these parts. Nearest dealer would be Toledo or Columbus, or down the road in Fort Wayne.

Which is Indiana. Which is going backwards.

Which is why they drive Fords in Ohio.

Which is how we came to consider calling the baby Edsel, Henry, Pinto or Sparks.

Which is why we spent the last short hour of evening lurching and vibrating back through those prosperous beanfields just waiting for spring to burst the green-shingled barns of Van Wert County.

Which is how we came to consider calling the baby Verna, Daisy, Persephone or Soy.

By this time we're back on the freeway, bypassing beautiful downtown Fort Wayne in favor of the rain forest at Exit 11, such is the cognomen of this illuminated Babel, this litany, this sculptural aviary for neon birds, these towering aluminum and tungsten weeds,

bright names raised up like burning irons to brand their sign upon the heavens.

Exxon, Burger King, Budgetel, Super 8.

Which is how we came to consider calling the baby Bob Evans.

Which is how we came to consider calling the baby Big Boy, Wendy, Long John Silver or Starvin' Marvin.

Which is how we came to salve our wounds by choosing a slightly better than average motel, and bringing in the Colonel to watch *Barnaby Jones* while Elizabeth passes out quick as you like

leaving me alone with my thoughts and reruns

in the oversized bed of an antiseptic room on an anonymous strip of indistinguishable modules among the unzoned outskirts of a small Midwestern city named for the Indian killer Mad Anthony Wayne.

Which is why I'm awake at 4 a.m. as the first trucks sheet their thunder down toward the interstate.

Which is when I feel my unborn child kick and roll within the belly of its sleeping mother, three heartbeats in two bodies, two bodies in one blanket, one perfect and inviolable will like a flower preparing to burst into bloom,

and its aurora lights the edge of the window like nothing I've ever seen.

Rice and Beans

"Dad?" Yes. "You are a wimp." That's very nice, thank you. Eat your grilled cheese. "I say you are a *little* wimp. I learn that at school. From a *big* kid." Of course. "Tyrannosaurus Rex, King of the Dinosaurs!" Sam is not yet three. When he roars I stick a spoonful of rice and beans into his mouth. "Dad, did Rex eat ricey-beans?" I think so. "No! He was a *meat* eater." That's right. "They *think* he was a meat eater." Who? "*Scientists*. Dad?" Yes. "Does beans have bones?" No. "Do cheese have bones?" No. "Why do they change the name of *bronto*saurus to *apato*saurus?" I honestly don't know. "*Scientists* know. They know, Dad." Yes. Probably. Drink some water, please. "Dad, water does not have bones." True. "Water does not have hands." Right. "Usually, dogs have no hands. But Scooby Doo have hands. Why, Dad?" He's not a real dog. "Did he *die out?*" He's just a cartoon dog. "Do Scooby Doo eat ricey-beans—*cartoon* ricey-beans?" No. Yes. Probably. I think so. Eat your sandwich. "Dad, I no call you little wimp before. *Rex* call you little wimp." That's not a nice thing to call someone, is it? "Rex is not nice. Rex *mean!*" Sam roars and I stick a crust of sandwich in his mouth. "Dad, can I have a cookie? Vanilla cookie? *Please.*" You haven't finished your grilled cheese, have you? "That's just the bones, Dad. *Toast* bones."

Our Other Sister

The cruelest thing I did to my younger sister
wasn't shooting a homemade blowdart into her knee,
where it dangled for a breathless second

before dropping off, but telling her we had
another, older sister who'd gone away.
What my motives were I can't recall: a whim,

or was it some need of mine to toy with loss,
to probe the ache of imaginary wounds?
But that first sentence was like a strand of DNA

that replicated itself in coiling lies
when my sister began asking her desperate questions.
I called our older sister Isabel

and gave her hazel eyes and long blonde hair.
I had her run away to California
where she took drugs and made hippie jewelry.

Before I knew it, she'd moved to Santa Fe
and opened a shop. She sent a postcard
every year or so, but she'd stopped calling.

I can still see my younger sister staring at me,
her eyes widening with desolation
then filling with tears. I can still remember

how thrilled and horrified I was
that something I'd just made up
had that kind of power, and I can still feel

the blowdart of remorse stabbing me in the heart
as I rushed to tell her none of it was true.
But it was too late. Our other sister

had already taken shape, and we could not
call her back from her life far away
or tell her how badly we missed her.

Boss of the Food

Before time, everytime my sista like be the boss
of the food. We stay shopping in Mizuno Superette
and my madda pull the Oreos off the shelf
and my sista already saying, Mommy,
can be the boss of the Oreos?

The worse was when she was the boss
of the sunflower seeds.
She give me and my other sistas
one seed at a time.
We no could eat the meat.
Us had to put um in one pile on one Kleenex.
Then, when we wen' take all the meat
out of the shells and our lips stay all cho cho,
she give us the seeds one at a time
cause my sista, she the boss
of the sunflower seeds.

One time she was the boss
of the Raisinettes.
Us was riding in the back
of my granpa's Bronco down Kaunakakai Wharf.
There she was, passing us one Raisinette at a time.
My mouth was all watery
'cause I like eat um all one time, eh?
So I wen' tell her, Gimme that bag.
And I wen' grab um.
She said, I'ng tell Mommy.
And I said, Go you fuckin' bird killa;
tell Mommy.

She wen' let go the bag.
And I wen' start eating the Raisinettes all one time.
But when I wen' look at her,
I felt kinda bad cause I wen' call her bird killa.
She was boss of the parakeet too, eh,
and she suppose to cover the cage every night.
But one time, she wen' forget.
When us wen' wake up, the bugga was on its back,
legs in the air all stiff.
The bugga was cold.
And I guess the thing that made me feel bad
was I neva think calling her bird killa
would make her feel so bad
that she let go the bag Raisinettes.

But I neva give her back the bag.
I figga what the fuck.
I ain't going suffer eating one Raisinette at a time.
Then beg her for one mo
and I mean one mo
fuckin' candy.

Prayer

God bless the chick in Alaska
who took in my sister's ex,
an abusive alcoholic hunk.
Bless all borderline brainless ex-cheerleaders
with long blonde hair, boobs,
and waists no bigger around than a coke bottle
who've broken up somebody else's home.
Forgive my thrill
should they put on seventy-five pounds,
develop stretch marks, spider veins,
and suffer through endless days of deep depression.

Bless those who remarry on the rebound.
Bless me and all my sisters,
the ball and chain baggage
we've carried into our second marriages.
Bless my broken brother and his live-in.
Grant him SSI. Consider
how the deeper the wounds in my family,
the funnier we've become.
Bless those who've learned to laugh at what's longed for.
Keep us from becoming hilarious.
Bless our children.
Bless all our ex's,
and bless the fat chick in Alaska.

The Wrestler's Heart

I had no choice but to shave my hair
And wrestle—thirty guys humping one another
On a mat. I didn't like high school.
There were no classes in archeology,
And the girls were too much like flowers
To bother with them. My brother, I think,
Was a hippie, and my sister, I know,
Was the runner-up queen of the Latin American Club.
When I saw her in the cafeteria, waved
And said things like, Debbie, is it your turn
To do the dishes tonight? she would smile and
Make real scary eyes. When I saw my brother
In his long hair and sissy bell-bottom pants,
He would look through me at a little snotty
Piece of gum on the ground. Neither of them
Liked me. So I sided with the wrestling coach,
The same person who taught you how to drive.
But first there was wrestling, young dudes
In a steam room, and coach with his silver whistle,
His clipboard, his pencil behind his clubbed ear.
I was not good. Everyone was better
Than me. Everyone was larger
In the showers, their cocks like heavy wrenches,
Their hair like the scribbling of a mad child.
I would lather as best I could to hide
What I didn't have, then walk home
In the dark. When we wrestled
Madera High, I was pinned in twelve seconds.
My Mom threw me a half stick of gum
From the bleachers. She shouted, It's Juicy Fruit!

And I just looked at her. I looked at
The three spectators, all crunching corn nuts,
Their faces like punched-in paper bags.
We lost that night. The next day in Biology
I chewed my half stick of Juicy Fruit
And thought about what can go wrong
In twelve seconds. The guy who pinned
Me was named Bloodworth, a meaningful name.
That night I asked Mom what our name meant in Spanish.
She stirred crackling *papas* and said it meant Mexican.
I asked her what was the worst thing that happened
To her in the shortest period
Of time. She looked at my stepfather's chair
And told me to take out the garbage.
That year I gained weight, lost weight,
And lost more matches, nearly all by pins.
I wore my arm in a sling when
I got blood poisoning from a dirty fingernail.
I liked that. I liked being hurt. I even went so far
As limping, which I thought would attract girls.

One day at lunch the counselor called me to his office.
I killed my sandwich in three bites. In his
Office of unwashed coffee mugs,
He asked what I wanted from life.
I told him I wanted to be an archeologist,
And if not that, then an oceanographer.
I told him that I had these feelings
I was Chinese, that I had lived before
And was going to live again. He told me
To get a drink of water and that by fifth period
I should reconsider what I was saying.
I studied some, dated once, ate the same sandwich
Until it was spring in most of the trees
That circled the campus, and wrestling was over.
Then school was over. That summer I mowed lawns,
Picked grapes, and rode my bike
Up and down my block because it was good

For heart and legs. The next year I took Driver's Ed.
Coach was the teacher. He said, Don't be scared
But you're going to see some punks
Getting killed. If you're going to cry,
Do it later. He turned on the projector,
A funnel of silver light that showed motes of dust,
Then six seconds of car wreck from different angles.
The narrator with a wrestler's haircut came on.
His face was thick like a canned ham
Sliding onto a platter. He held up a black tennis shoe.
He said, The boy who wore this sneaker is dead.
Two girls cried. Three boys laughed.
Coach smiled and slapped the clipboard
Against his leg, kind of hard.
With one year of wrestling behind me,
I barely peeked but thought,
Six seconds for the kid with the sneakers,
Twelve seconds for Bloodworth to throw me on my back.
Tough luck in half the time.

We Take Our Children to Ireland

What will they remember best? The barbed wire
still looped around the Belfast airport,
the building-high Ulster murals—
but those were fleeting, car window sights,
more likely the turf fires lit each night,
the cups of tea their father brought
and the buttered soda farls, the sea wall
where they leaped shrieking into the Irish Sea
and emerged, purpling, to applause;
perhaps the green castle at Carrickfergus,
but more likely the candy store
with its alien crisps—vinegar? They ask,
prawn cocktail? Worcestershire leek?
More certainly still the sleekly syllabled
odd new words, gleet and shite,
and grand responses to everyday events:
How was your breakfast? Brilliant.
How's your crust? Gorgeous.
Everything after that was gorgeous,
brilliant. How's your gleeted shite?
And the polite indictment from parents
everywhere, the nicely dressed matrons
pushing prams, brushing away their older kids
with a Fuck off, will ye? Which stopped
our children cold. Is the water cold,
they asked Damian, before they dared it.
No, he said, it's not cold, it's
fooking cold, ye idjits.
And the mundane hyperbole of rebuke—
you little puke, I'll tear your arm off

and beat you with it, I'll row you out to sea
and drop you, I'll bury you in sand
and top you off with rocks—
to which the toddler would contentedly nod
and continue to drill his shovel
into the sill. All this will play on
long past the fisherman's cottage and farmer's
slurry, the tall hedgerows lining the narrow
drive up the coast, the most beautiful
of Irish landscapes indelibly fixed
in the smeared face of two-year-old Jack—
Would you look at that, his father said
to Ben and Zach, shite everywhere, brilliant.
Gorgeous, they replied. And meant it.

El Zapato

Not the wooden spoon,
primordial source
of sweetness and pain,
flying at me from across the kitchen—
I barely bothered to duck.
Not my father reaching for his belt,
I would be long gone before
it could slap across the table-top
in a sample *nalgada*,
but my mother's shoe, El Zapato:
black leather, high-topped
with the long tongue laced
all the way up, thick square high heel.
Shoe from a hundred years ago,
puritanical shoe, witch's shoe,
shoe of the Dutch Cleanser lady,
peasant shoe, gypsy shoe, shoe
for clogging around a hat flung down
on the grave of your enemy.
Not the pain, brief humiliating clunk
of leather striking flesh,
but her aim, the way I knew that
if I ran out the kitchen door
down the back stairs, over the fence,
around the corner, if I glanced
over my shoulder while my arms and legs
were flailing away, El Zapato
would still be there, its primitive
but infallible radar homed in on my back.
Even now, years later, El Zapato

sails toward me turning slowly
like charred meat on a spit.
It lands on the bed with a thump,
and clamps on to my foot. I kick
the blankets, as if my foot were stuck
in the mouth of a dog,
an old dog, without teeth.

Don't Know What Love Is

My mother can't recall the exact
infamous year but Mama does know
that she and her friends were teenagers
when they sneaked out to an official joint
in the middle of the woods to listen
to Dinah Washington sing their favorite
love song. They wanted to dance together
so close they'd be standing behind
each other but Mama says, *Dinah showed*
up late and acted ugly and on top of
that she didn't want to sing the song.
This is supposed to be the story of Mama's
blues and how she threw good money
after bad but this is South Georgia
and Dinah's standing in high heels on a Jim
Crow stage two feet off the ground.
She's sniffing the perfume of homemade
cigarettes, chitlin plates, hair grease one
grade above Vaseline, and the premature
funk wafting up from the rowdy kids
with no home training. Can't even pee
straight much less recognize a silver lamé
dress. All they know to do is demand
one song because they risked a certain
butt whipping to be in this joint, in these woods.
Dinah won't sing it, though.
She just won't sing the song.
I'm an evil gal, she hollers out instead.
Don't you bother with me!

Upon Seeing an Ultrasound Photo of an Unborn Child

Tadpole, it's not time yet to nag you
about college (though I have some thoughts
on that), baseball (ditto), or abstract
principles. Enjoy your delicious,
soupy womb-warmth, do some rolls and saults
(it'll be too crowded soon), delight in your early
dreams—which no one will attempt to analyze.
For now: may your toes blossom, your fingers
lengthen, your sexual organs grow (too soon
to tell which yet) sensitive, your teeth
form their buds in their forming jawbone, your already
booming heart expand (literally
now, metaphorically later); O your spine,
eyebrows, nape, knees, fibulae,
lungs, lips . . . But your soul,
dear child: I don't see it here, when
does that come in, whence? Perhaps God,
and your mother, and even I—we'll all contribute
and you'll learn yourself to coax it
from wherever: your soul, which holds your bones
together and lets you live
on earth.—Fingerling, sidecar, nubbin,
I'm waiting, it's me, Dad,
I'm out here. You already know
where Mom is. I'll see you more directly
upon arrival. You'll recognize
me—I'll be the tall-seeming, delighted
blond guy, and I'll have
your nose.

THOMAS LUX

Autobiographical

The minute I get out of jail I want
some answers: when our mother
murdered our father
did she find out first, did he tell her—the pistol's tip
parting his temple's fine hairs—did he
tell her where our sister (the youngest, Alice)
hid the money Grandma (mother's side)
stole from her Golden Age Group?
It was a lot of money but *enough to die for?*
was what Mom said she asked him,
giving him a choice. *I'll see you in Hell,*
she said Dad said
and then she said (this is in the trial transcript): *Not*
any time soon, needle dick!
We know Alice hid the money—she was arrested

a week later in Tacoma for armed robbery,
which she would not have done
if she had it. Alice was (she died
of a heroin overdose six hours after making bail)
syphilitic, stupid, and rude
but not greedy. So she hid the money,
or Grandma did,
but since her stroke can't say a word,
doesn't seem to know anybody.
Doing a dime at Dannemora
for an unrelated sex crime, my brother
might know something but won't answer
my letters, refuses to see me,
though he was the one who called me

at divinity school
after Mom was arrested. He could hardly
get the story out from laughing
so much: Dad had missed
his third in a row the day before with his parole officer,
the cops were sent
to pick him up (*Bad timing*, said Mom) and found him
before he was cold.
He was going back to jail anyway, Mom said,
said the cops,
which they could and did use against her
to the tune of double digits, which means,
what with the lupus, she's guaranteed
to die inside. Ask her?
She won't talk to me.
She won't give me the time of day.

Muck-Clump

My wife was being too *busy* around the kitchen one morning
I think to give herself the sense of being on top of things
and when I poured a bowl of Shredded Wheat Spoonfuls for Devon
my wife bustled over and said "Oh Devon likes to have more cereal
   than that"
so she poured more Spoonfuls on top of the considerable number I
   had poured.
This griped me because now it was as if I hadn't given Devon
   her breakfast
because it might as well have been my wife who did it all
which would imply that I wasn't really making a contribution,
as if I were just a log of driftwood on the sand of time
while everyone else built the boats and caught the fish
and made the whole human drama fare forward against the void.

So I watched Devon pour a lot of milk on her Shredded Spoonfuls
and I figured she would hardly eat half of them
and when she went out to the schoolbus there would be
this awful soggy mass of decomposing cereal left behind
which would resemble the way I sometimes see myself
so I figured then I could show the bowl to my wife
and I'd say "Do you think Devon got enough cereal?"
and the moment of sarcasm would be exquisite.
While Devon ate Spoonfuls I tied her shoes—I did accomplish that—
and I imagined how I would say it with measured irony
that would sting slightly but also come across as witty—
"Do you think Devon got enough cereal?"—I would say it
and then vigorously dump the sodden milky muck-clump into the trash.
It would be a moment in which I would be quite noticeably

on top of things . . . Then the bus came
and Devon hoisted her backpack and hurried outside, calling Goodbye,

and I saw with astonishment that her cereal bowl was empty.
How was I going to deal with this? It wouldn't be fair
to be angry at Devon for her unreasonable appetite; but
I could possibly complain about my wife's failure to provide
a more balanced breakfast for our daughter—but I sensed
that this challenge would backfire because my wife is the one
who really does think about nutrition and besides there were, actually,
some strawberries on Devon's placemat.
So I decided to rise above the entire episode, to be large-minded,
to wash a few dishes nonchalantly and read the newspaper
and make an insightful remark about something in the news.
Awareness of a larger world, after all, is
a central part of being mature, which is
something I want to believe I am—
when you see some old chunk of driftwood on the beach
you might say "That looks so calm, so peaceful"
or you might say "That is so dry and dead"
but you don't say "That is really mature."

Praise for the Ford LTD

When I walk out of the store with my cigar and BEE LUCKY
scratch-off card, I think I see our old LTD idling in its nest
of smoke, the car my father bought from one-armed Bernie Trotter
for three hundred bucks, the one with the muffler that swung like
an elephant trunk and failed to leave a trail of sparks only because
of the coat hanger my father rigged to hold it up. I want to ask
the man behind the wheel if maybe this isn't the exact LTD
that my sister turned from umber soot to golden tan with a water hose
and dish soap, the same seats that I rubbed down with baby oil,
though the seats before me are covered in what looks like
the cured hide of an exceptionally large Dalmation, which I
hate to see, because if this is the same two-tone, two-door, vinyl top
LTD, then it is the one in which my father backed over our dog
who that day wore a green dog sweater and got placed with her sweater
in the trunk and made an awful thudding rolling forward
then back when the car started and stopped until my father
pulled over at a dumpster and unloaded her, and was embarrassed
for us to see him crying. Not the story I'd tell a stranger
without buying him a beer first. And this guy would likely
get pissed off if he knew that his car had been wrecked,
that my father stomped out of the house one night and returned
in three days with the front bumper missing and the back
boasting a sticker that read "Tyson's Beer Garden." That car
with its teeth knocked out. My father slept in the back seat
for a week after that, empty cans of potted meat and cracker
wrappers junking up the dash. Still, I want to say to this man
"Excuse me sir, we had this car when I was a kid," but I don't
because he might take it wrong, like I was saying "damn
that car sure is old," and it had been more than twenty years
since my parents decided to stay together and drove

along the canopied roads outside of town until they had
to scream at each other. My mother traded that car
for one day's use of a moving truck, and I didn't miss
my father much at first, but I missed that car, and bolted
baskets to my ten-speed, which it must have seemed
I didn't quite know how to ride, wobbling home with the weight
of canned beans, Tab, toilet paper, and milk. "Nice ride,"
I say to the man before he pulls off. "I'll sell it to you,"
he says, and revs the engine, lets off the gas, and the car
goes dead. But I don't care, for in this moment, I do
want to buy it, if for no other reason than to ride once again
with the radio stuck on A.M. *W God is Lord in Mississippi!*
To say amen to the viscous stench of scorched oil, to the slack
brakes and the stuck horn and the shot rod. Amen to the people
looking down at us from the windows of the city bus
while the upholstery above our heads flapped like a flag
in a hurricane of spilt beer, Little Debbies, and the combustible
fumes of hot tamales. "How much?" I say to the man, but he's
not paying attention because the car won't crank. He gets out
and lets loose with "Son of a Bitch! Son of a Bitch!" and I
think of telling the man that the car's only flooded, that if
he waits a minute it'll start, but he's too wound up,
"It's yours!" he says. "Try it again," I say, and he does,
and it starts, and he backs out of the parking lot, and I stand there
waving like I just got the better end of that deal, which is how
Bernie Trotter must have felt with his cigar hanging out
of his mouth and him waving us off with his one good arm
after my father had kicked the tires and honked the horn,
and my mother sat in the middle close to him, and even my sister
seemed happy when she punched me in the leg and called me
a dumbass, and we both laughed our guts sore with our hair
blowing and our hands held out, cupping the new wind.

LET US BE FRIENDS A WHILE AND UNDERSTAND OUR DIFFERENCES

Fiends and Neighbors

FRANK O'HARA

Personal Poem

Now when I walk around at lunchtime
I have only two charms in my pocket
an old Roman coin Mike Kanemitsu gave me
and a bolt-head that broke off a packing case
when I was in Madrid the others never
brought me too much luck they did
help keep me in New York against coercion
but now I'm happy for a time and interested

I walk through the luminous humidity
passing the house of Seagram with its wet
and its loungers and the construction to
the left that closed the sidewalk if
I ever get to be a construction worker
I'd like to have a silver hat please
and get to Moriarty's where I wait for
LeRoi and hear who wants to be a mover and
shaker the last five years my batting average
is .016 that's that, and LeRoi comes in
and tells me Miles Davis was clubbed 12
times last night outside BIRDLAND by a cop
a lady asks us for a nickel for a terrible
disease but we don't give her one we
don't like terrible diseases, then

we go eat some fish and some ale it's
cool but crowded we don't like Lionel Trilling
we decide, we like Don Allen we don't like
Henry James so much we like Herman Melville
we don't want to be in the poet's walk in

San Francisco even we just want to be rich
and walk on girders in our silver hats
I wonder if one person out of the 8,000,000 is
thinking of me as I shake hands with LeRoi
and buy a strap for my wristwatch and go
back to work happy at the thought possibly so

You Can Change Your Life through Psychic Power

I was evidently just staring into space.
I had gone downtown for something and couldn't
remember what it was. I know it had seemed
important at the time. A man I knew slightly,
but whose name escaped me, if I ever knew it at
all, said to me, "Hey, Luther, what have you
been up to lately?" I was startled but tried
not to show it. "Oh, busy as usual. Too much
work, not enough time. How about yourself?" I
said. "Oh, Crystal and I did manage to go camp-
ing for a week recently. It rained most of the
time, but still we had a great time. Crystal
always asks about you," he said. "She does?"
I said. "Sure. She thinks you're a great guy.
You should come over for dinner some time. She'll
cook you a great meal. Take care, pal, I gotta
run," he said. "Yeah, take care, good to see
you," I said. I watched him disappear down the
street. Quite a stride, definitely a man on a
mission. I like that, well, sort of. Brad and
Crystal Austin—I met them at Renata's party
several years ago. They talked about their
sublime villa in Tuscany all night until I was
nearly comatose. Flashlight batteries and
toothpaste, these were all I needed for the
good life.

To Whoever Set My Truck on Fire

But let us be friends awhile and understand our differences
are small and that they float like dust in sunny rooms
and let us settle into the good work of being strangers
simply who have something to say in the middle of the night
for you have said something that interests me—something of flames,

footsteps and the hard heavy charge of an engine gunning away
into the June cool of four in the morning here in West Virginia
where last night I woke to the sound of a door slamming,
five or six fading footsteps, and through the window saw
my impossible truck bright orange like a maverick sun and

ran—I did—panicked in my underwear bobbling the dumb
extinguisher too complex it seemed for putting out fires
and so grabbed a skillet and jumped about like one
needing to piss while the faucet like honey issued its slow
sweet water and you I noticed then were watching

from your idling car far enough away I could not make
your plate number but you could see me—half naked
figuring out the puzzle of a fire thirty seconds from
a dream never to be remembered while the local chaos
of a growing fire crackled through the books and boots

burning in my truck, you bastard, you watched as I sprayed
finally the flames with a gardenhose under the moon
and yes I cut what was surely a ridiculous figure there
and worsened it later that morning after the bored police
drove home lazily and I stalked the road in front of my house

with an ax in my hand and walked into the road after
every car to memorize the plates of who might have done this:
LB 7329, NT 7663, and you may have passed by—
I don't know—you may have passed by as I committed
the innocent numbers of neighbors to memory and maybe

you were miles away and I, like the woodsman of fairy tales,
threatened all with my bright ax shining with the evil
joy of vengeance and mad hunger to bring harm—heavy
harm—to the coward who did this and if I find you,
my friend, I promise you I will lay the sharp blade deep

into your body until the humid grabbing hands of what must be
death have mercy and take you away from the constant
murderous swinging my mind makes my words make
swinging down on your body and may your children
weep a thousand tears at your small and bewildered grave.

The Crybaby at the Library

There was a crybaby at the library.
Tears were pouring heavily down his face.
He had omitted to do his math
and thought of the anger of his teacher
as the tears fell on his knitted
mittens between fingers and thumb.

It is raining all over inside the library.
Parts of the brick walls are curling up
and plaster is falling on the heads and beards of students.
It is very dangerous for the books.
The rain comes down from every beam
and the professors do not know whether they should wrap
their articles in themselves or themselves in their articles.
The beautiful new botany professor who is only twenty-six
    and has marvelous dark eyes
has makeup running down her face as she runs out the door.

A precious incunabulum inside a glass case
is swimming gently as if in a dishpan.
Tiny letters and pieces of gold that were put there in 1426
are lifting off and turning into scum.
The assistant librarians are afraid to use the telephones
because yellow sparks are coming out of them.
Several young men go up to the attic, saying that the trouble
    may be from up there.
The electricity goes off and people are standing
between the floors in dangerously wet elevators.
The librarians' Kleenex and aspirin are wet and are melting
    into each other in the desk drawers.

The Shakespeare professors come out of the Shakespeare Room
And look around and go back in again; they must stay with
the ship.
Fog is rising like rugs between the bookstacks.
People are laughing in a brittle way to disguise their
well-grounded panic.

The botany professor is a redemptive figure.
She goes to the Maintenance Department and reports what
is happening in the library.
Eventually the Maintenance Department goes over and fixes
things.
The crybaby is definitely *not* a redemptive figure—he sits
still self-absorbed and shivery, and crying and crying,
and not at all trying to catch up on his math, nor even trying
to fake it,
and all the time waves of water dash over his Bean boots
and up onto his lap, splashing his notebooks.
For the impending disgust of his teacher is foremost in his
mind
as tears are foremost on his cheeks, where he sits crying and
crying at the library.

DAVID KIRBY

The Search for Baby Combover

In Paris one night the doorbell rings,
   and there's this little guy, shaking like a leaf
and going "uh-uh-uh-UNH-ah!" and his eyes get big
     and he raises his hands like a gospel singer
and goes "UNH-ah-uh-uh-uh-UNH-uh-ah!"

and for just a fraction of a second I think
   he's doing the first part of Wilson Pickett's
"Land of a Thousand Dances" and that he wants me
     to join him in some kind of weird welcome
to the neighborhood, so I raise my hands a little

and begin to sort of hum along, though
   not very loudly in case I'm wrong about this,
and I'm smiling the way old people smile
     when they can't hear you but want you to know
that everything's okay as far as they're concerned

or a poet smiles in a roomful of scientists,
   as if to say, "Hey! I'm just a poet!
But your stuff's great, really! Even if
     I don't understand any of it!" And by the time
I start to half-wonder if this gentleman wants me

to take the you-got-to-know-how-to-pony part
   or means to launch into it himself, he gives
a little hop and slaps his hands down to his sides
     and says, "PLEASE! YOU MUST NOT MOVE
THE FURNITURE AFTER ELEVEN O'CLOCK OF THE NIGHT!"

so I lower my own hands and say, "Whaaaa . . ?"
    and he says, "ALWAYS YOU ARE MOVING IT WHEN
THE BABY TRY TO SLEEP! YOU MUST NOT DO IT!"
        And now that he's feeling a little bolder,
he steps in closer, where the light's better,

and I see he's got something on his head,
    like strands of oily seaweed, something
you'd expect to find on a rock after one of
        those big tanker spills in the Channel,
so I lean a little bit and realize it's what

stylists call a "combover," not a bad idea
    on the tall fellows but definitely a grooming no-no
for your vertically-challenged caballeros,
        of which Monsieur here is certainly one,
especially if they are yelling at you.

But I'd read an article about AA that said
    when your loved ones stage an intervention
and go off on you for getting drunk
        and busting up the furniture and running out
into traffic and threatening to kill the President,

it's better to just let them wind down
    and then say, "You're probably right,"
because if you're combative, they will be, too,
        and then your problems will just start over again,
so I wait till Mr. Combover stops shaking—

it's not nice, I know, but it's the first name that comes to mind—
    and I say, "You're probably right," and he raises
a finger and opens his mouth as if to say something
        but then snaps his jaw shut and whirls around
and marches downstairs, skidding a little

and windmilling his arms and almost falling
    but catching himself, though not without

that indignant backward glance we all give
       the stupid step that some stupid idiot would have
attended to long ago if he hadn't been so stupid.

The next day, I ask Nadine the *gardienne*
       qu'est-ce que c'est the deal *avec* the *monsieur*
qui lives under *moi*, and Nadine says his *femme*
       is *toujours* busting his chops, but *il est* afraid
of her, so *il* takes out his *rage* on the rest of *nous*.

There's something else, though: a few days later,
       Barbara and I see Mr. and Mrs. Combover
crossing the Pont Marie, and she is a virtual giantess
       compared to him! Now I remember once hearing Barbara
give boyfriend advice to this niece of mine,

and Barbara said (1) he's got to have a job,
       (2) he's got to tell you you're beautiful all the time,
and (3) he's got to be taller than you are,
       so when I see Mrs. Combover looming over her hubby,
I think, Well, that explains the busted chops.

Not only that, Mrs. Combover looks cheap.
       She looks rich, sure—Nadine had told me *Monsieur*
is some *sorte de* diplomat *avec* the Chilean delegation—
       but also like one of those professional ladies
offering her services up around the Rue St. Denis.

But who are they, really? "Combover" is one
       of those names from a fifties black-and-white movie;
he's the kind of guy neighborhood kids call "Mr. C."
       and who has a boss who says things like, "Now see here,
Combover, this sort of thing just won't do!"

He's like one of Dagwood's unnamed colleagues—
       he's not even Dagwood, who at least excites
Mr. Dithers enough to be fired a couple

of times a week, not to mention severely beaten.
Only Dagwood is really in charge. Everything goes his way!

Despite chronic incompetence, ol' Dag keeps
    the job that allows him his fabulous home life:
long naps, towering sandwiches, affectionate
    and well-behaved teenaged children, a loyal dog,
and, best of all, the love of Blondie.

Blondie! The name says it all: glamorous but fun.
    Big Trashy Mrs. Combover is not glamorous,
although she thinks she is, and no fun at all.
    She is the anti-Blondie. Her job seems to be
to stay home and smoke, since we're always smelling

the cigarette fumes that seep up through the floor
    into our apartment day and night. And he says
we're keeping Baby Combover awake when we move
    the furniture, which we've never done, but then
we've never seen Baby Combover, either. Or heard him.

Baby Combover: the world's first silent baby.
    Barbara has this theory that, after a life
of prostitution, Mrs. Combover has not only repented but
    undergone a false pregnancy and imaginary birth.
Therefore, the reason why Baby Combover is silent

is that he is not a real baby who fusses and eats and
    wets and poops but is instead a pillowcase with knots
for ears and a smiley-face drawn with a Magic Marker and
    a hole for its mouth so Mrs. Combover can teach it
to smoke when it's older, like eight, say.

Now I know what they fight about: "You never spend
    any time with the baby!" hisses Mrs. Combover.
"I will—later, when he can talk!" says Mr. Combover.
    "Here I am stuck with this baby all day long!
And those horrible people upstairs!"

And he says, "Oh, be silent, you . . . prostitute!"
 And she says, "Quiet, you horrible man—
not in front of the baby!" Maybe it's time
 for a call to the police. Or the newspapers.
I can see the headlines now: OU EST L'ENFANT COMBOVER?

I feel sorry for him. With parents like this,
 it would be better if someone were to kidnap him.
Or I could take him back to America with me,
 I who have a wife who loves me and two grown sons.
Why not? We've got all this extra room now.

We'll feed him a lot and tickle him;
 there's nothing funnier than a fat, happy baby.
And when the boys come home to visit,
 they'll take him out with them in their sports cars:
"It's our little brother!" they'll say. "He's French!"

The neighborhood kids, once a band of sullen mendicants,
 will beg us to let him play with them,
even though he doesn't speak their language.
 Look! There they go toward the baseball field,
with Baby Combover under their arm!

I love you, Baby Combover! You *are* Joseph Campbell's
 classic mythical hero, i.e., "an agent of change
who relinquishes self-interest and breaks down
 the established social order." But you're so pale!
You've stayed out too long and caught cold.

Barbara and the boys gather around his bed;
 they hug each other, and we try not to cry.
Baby Combover is smiling—he always smiled, that kid.
 His little mouth begins to move, and we lean in
and think we hear him say, "Be bwave fo' me. . . ."

Back in Paris, Mr. Combover grows a full head of hair.

Mrs. Combover reaches up to touch it.

He puts down his attaché case and caresses her cheek.

"How beautiful you are!" he says. It's so quiet now.

Then they hear it: in the next room, a child is crying.

Heat Lightning in a Time of Drought

My neighbor, drunk, stood on his lawn and yelled,
Want some! Want some! He bellowed it as cops
cuffed him, shoved him in their back seat—*Want some!*—
and drove away. Now I lie here awake,
not by choice, listening to the crickets' high
electric trill, urgent with lust. Heat lightning flashes.
The crickets will not, will not stop. I wish
that I could shut the window, pull the curtain, sleep.
But it's too hot. *Want some!* He screamed it till
I was afraid I'd made him up to scream
what I knew better than to say out loud
although it's August-hot and every move
bathes me in sweat and we are careless,
careless, careless, every one of us,
and when my neighbor screams out in his yard
like one dog howling for another dog,
I call the cops, then lie in my own sweat,
remembering the woman
who, at a party on a night this hot,
walked up to me, propped her chin on my chest,
and sighed. She was a little drunk, the love-light
unshielded in her eyes. We fell in love.
One day at supper the light fixture dropped,
exploded on the table. Glass flew around us,
a low, slow-motion blossoming of razors.
She was unhurt till I reached out my hand
—left hand—to brush glass from her face.
Two drops of blood ran down her cheek.
On TV, I'd seen a teacher dip a rose
in liquid nitrogen. When he withdrew it,

it smoked, frozen solid. He snapped one petal, frail
as isinglass, and then, against the table,
he shattered it. The whole rose blew apart.
Like us. And then one day the doorbell rang.
A salesman said, *Watch this!* He stripped my bed
and vacuumed it. The nozzle sucked up two
full, measured cups of light gray flakes. He said,
That's human skin. I stood, refusing the purchase,
stood staring at her flesh and mine commingled
inside the measuring cup, stood there and thought
*She's been gone two years, she's married, and all this time
her flesh has been in bed with me.* Don't laugh.
Don't laugh. That's what the Little Moron says
when he arrives home early from a trip
and finds his wife in bed with someone else.
The man runs off. The Little Moron puts
a pistol to his own head, cocks the hammer.
His wife, in bed, sheets pulled up to her breasts,
starts laughing. *Don't you laugh!* he screams. *Don't laugh—
you're next.* It is the wisest joke I know because
the heart's a violent muscle, opening
and closing. Who knows what we might do:
by night, the craziness of dreams; by day,
the craziness of logic. Listen!
My brother told me of a man wheeled, screaming,
into the ward, a large Coke bottle rammed
up his ass. I was awed: there is no telling
what we'll do in our fierce drive to come together.
The heart keeps opening and closing like a mine
where fire still burns, a century underground,
following the veins of black coal, rearing up
to take a barn, a house, a pasture. Although
I wish that it would rain tonight, I fret
about the heat lightning that flicks and glitters
on the horizon as if it promised rain.
It can't. But I walk outside, stand on parched grass,
and watch it hungrily—all light, all dazzle—
remembering how we'd drive out past the town's light,

sit on the hood, and watch great thunderheads
huge as a state—say, Delaware—sail past. Branched
lightning jagged, burst the dark from zenith to horizon.
We stared at almost nothing: some live oaks,
the waist-high corn. Slow raindrops smacked the corn,
plopped in the dirt around us, drummed the roof,
and finally reached out, tapped us on the shoulders.
We drove home in the downpour, laughed, made love
—still wet with rain—and slept. But why stop there?
Each happy memory leads me to a sad one:
the friend who helped me through my grief by drinking
all of my liquor. And when, at last, we reached
the wretched mescal, he carefully sliced off
the worm's black face, ate its white body, staggered
onto this very lawn, and racked and heaved
until I helped him up. *You're okay, John.*
You've puked it out. "No, man—you're wrong. That worm
ain't ever coming out." Heat lightning flashes.
No rain falls and no thunder cracks the heat.
No first concussion dwindles to a long
low rolling growl. I go in the house, lie down,
pray, masturbate, drift to the edge of sleep.
I wish my soul were larger than it is.

A Short History of the New South

"Pass the biscuits," said Pappy, pursing his lips,
But the part I remember best was the collect call
From our spy at the National Archives. "The cause,
I fear, is lost, Suh," the spy replied. "Our retreat
Has been repulsed." "The silver!" cried Mammy
And we grabbed our hoes and headed for Grammaw's grave,
Expecting the worst. Come spring the worst was over
And we dragged the trunks back up to the big house,
Ending the era with supper and lots of biscuits.
Pappy, picking his tooth, said, "Pass the yams,"
but no one had the heart to tell him the truth.
"Bull Run!" yelled Pee Wee, the subject changed,
And Pappy forgot the yams and got drunk instead.
I woke from my bale of paper money to find
The darkies loading their Cadillacs. They were heading
For Baltimore, they claimed, to harvest the nylon crop.
So we plowed the cotton under and planted magnolias
But missed their singing so much we pawned our whips
To buy a gramophone on the installment plan.
As we had no records, we had to make do without.
"Pass Ol' Blue," said Pappy, closing his eyes,
And nothing improved. Pee Wee got up from the table
And ran off to join the White Sox, where he made
A name for hisself after changing his name. Myself,
I stayed at home to fight the school board. "Hurry back!"
Cried Mammy, waving her flag at the bus.
I took my time. One day she called collect:
"Pappy's right poorly. Y'all come." I came,
Arriving in time to grab my hoe from the toolshed
And help Pappy dig her a hole right next to Grammaw.

We cashed the insurance and bought us a TV and dish,
Which we used to improve our minds and accents,
And when the last of the place was sold off to the tourists
We pooled our cash and built this fine new restaurant.
"Pass the pizza," says Pappy, stroking his silver beard.

High School Picture Re-take Day

When an octopus becomes stressed, it chomps
its arms one by one until it becomes a floaty salad.

The line of students here is understandably worried:
this is the last chance for redemption. Neil parts
and parts his hair with the petite plastic comb
the photographer slipped him when he signed in.

Susie reties the grosgrain headband.
Everything is quiet but for tiny songs

of tiny combs whistling through hair. Everything is black
save for the single camera lamp and smudgy backdrop
painted to look like the student hovers among
beige and blue clouds. And maybe they are—the ones

who got it right the first time—soaring above the earth's
troposphere, but still a bit below the stratosphere.
When the last bell rings, there they are: flying
proud, able to exchange wallet-sized pictures

with other pretty people right away. No waiting
for two more months when no one cares anymore.

No closed eyes, no sticks of hair sprung out
like arrows, no bra straps showing, no
sleepy eyes—just perfectly pressed shirts
and smiles slit to show rows of neat teeth.

ALBERT GOLDBARTH

"Duo Tried Killing Man with Bacon"

—headline, The Spokesman Review *(Spokane, WA)*

At tornado force, a full length of uncooked spaghetti
has skewered a heart, and killed. A falling block
of frozen urine. A trout, that leaped precisely
into a yawn and thrashily lodged until the breath stopped.
Endless ways. Perhaps each death is as unique as the life
it ends, to whatever extent that is. I do know
when they found the fourteen corpses in the rubble
of the pipe-bombed synagogue, that mass of broken and
     indistinguishable flesh
was still divided equally into enough for fourteen burials,
and each of the families' griefs was its own. My father didn't need this

immediate neighborhood drama: fear of what the world could do
to his family was a living writhe inside him; once I doodled it
as a liver fluke that could mimic the face,
as needed, of my sister, mother, self. Because Chicago
offered its perils in generous headline-shrilling quantity
(and some—like the parts of children they always seemed to be finding
dumped in shallow graves—were fiercely lurid) and because
the cells of the body so often and fatally
rebel against the whole . . . he lived his days out in a series
of preventive ceremonial gestures, alternately sacred or tepidly humdrum,

as a situation called for—or, as a character in the gypsy slums
of nineteenth-century London says, by way of exemplification, "I made
     warding signs
and said 'Garlic!' about a dozen times" (Tim Powers, *The Anubis Gates*).
Garlic guards against the evil eye, as does (depending on where you live)

a desiccated frog, a shamrock, bezoar stones removed from the stomach
   of llamas,
handsigns like the "horns" or the "fig," or ritual spitting.
Beeswax candles. Lamb's blood over the door. My father
set my weekend curfew, and heeded the vast refusals of kosher laws,
etc., sternly certain that these self-set limits saved us from the limitless
predations of the universe. I think of what Tim Meiseneltzer felt

—the "victim"—manacled, ankles and wrists, on the floor of the woods,
and a bagful of fat-edged rashers spread around his body
to attract the local wolves. He lived. And it was even comic
in its way. But what did he feel, *then*, with the kicking
hoof of death in his chest. With the fist of death in his rectum
slowly opening up. Its taloned glove. What promise did he breathe
to what protector-god. I *can't* think into that
alien fear. But I remember a version of its minor key: my father
accidentally biting into a BLT, then kneejerk spitting it out
in a cafeteria napkin, while the world watched, and the heavens

stared down, as if our lives depended on this.

B. H. FAIRCHILD

Brazil

This is for Elton Wayne Showalter, redneck surrealist
who, drunk, one Friday night tried to hold up the local 7–11
with a caulking gun, and who, when Melinda Bozell boasted
that she would never let a boy touch her "down there," said,
"Down there? You mean, like, Brazil?"

                                          Oh, Elton Wayne,
with your silver-toed turquoise-on-black boots and Ford Fairlane
dragging, in a ribbon of sparks, its tailpipe down main street
Saturday nights, you dreamed of Brazil and other verdant lands,
but the southern hemisphere remained for all those desert years
a vast mirage shimmering on the horizon of what one might call
your mind, following that one ugly night at the Snack Shack
when, drunk again, you peed on your steaming radiator
to cool it down and awoke at the hospital, groin empurpled
from electric shock and your pathetic maleness swollen
like a bruised tomato. You dumb bastard, betting a week's wages
on the trifecta at Raton, then in ecstasy tossing the winning ticket
into the air and watching it float on an ascending breeze
out over the New Mexico landscape forever and beyond: gone.
The tears came down, but the spirit rose late on Sunday night
on a stepladder knocking the middle letters from FREEMAN GLASS
to announce unlimited sexual opportunities in purple neon
for all your friends driving Kansas Avenue as we did each night
lonely and boredom-racked and hungering for someone like you,
Elton Wayne, brilliantly at war in that flat, treeless county
against maturity, right-thinking, and indeed intelligence

in all its bland, local guises, so that now reading the announcement
in the hometown paper of your late marriage to Melinda Bozell
with a brief honeymoon at the Best Western in Junction City,
I know that you have finally arrived, in Brazil, and the Kansas
that surrounds you is an endless sea of possibility, genius, love.

PETER MEINKE

Zinc Fingers

Though scientists inform us that criminals
have insufficient zinc I've always believed
it's insufficient gold and silver that gets
them going   The man who slipped his hand into
my front pocket on the jammed Paris *Métro*
wasn't trying to make friends   His overcoat
smelled greasy and it was unpleasant holding
hands above my wallet pressed in on all sides
like stacked baguettes   There was no way to move or
take a swing   Still some action on my part seemed
to be called for: we stood nose to nose   I tried
to look in his eyes but he stared at my chin
shy on our first date so after a while as
we rattled along toward the Champs-Élysées

I lost concentration and began to think

of our scholarly daughter working at Yale
on a project called Zinc Fingers scanning a
protein with pseudopods each with a trace of
zinc that latch on to our DNA and help
determine what we become   This brought me back
to *mon ami* the pickpocket: I wondered
how he chose his hard line of work and if as
a boy he was good at cards for example
or sewing and for that matter what choice did

I have either so when we reached our stop and
he looked up from my chin at last I smiled at
him and his eyes flashed in fear or surprise and
I called *It's OK* as he scuttled away
Tout va bien!   though I held tight to my wallet.

Verona

I'd have come here decades sooner
If one of my art books had devoted a chapter
To beautiful central squares
And this piazza had been included,
Bright with facades meant to be festive,
Not magnificent or imposing.
Even the two earnest young men in suits
Buttonholing strollers don't dull my pleasure,
Two Mormons from Utah, assigned to this outpost
For their stint as apostles among the gentiles.

A city not on the list that Burton and I
Drew up thirty years ago when we planned
His only chance to see Europe before his eyes
Would grow too scarred from the stress of diabetes
To let the light in. In the end, he felt too gloomy to go.
If he were alive now, and sighted, we'd agree
These two young Mormons have a tough assignment,
Making the gospel revealed to Joseph Smith
Near Palmyra, New York, irresistible
To churchgoing Veronese whose kin
Have sung in the local choirs for centuries.

As for lifting the spirits of nonbelievers,
I've only to pause on a bridge spanning the Adige
And gaze back on the fillet of walls and towers
The river looks pleased to wear.
Even Burton, always harder to please than I,

Might have been moved to judge this townscape
Nearly as peaceful as a townscape in oil,
Though its Sunday quiet, he might have cautioned,
Shouldn't make us forget the weekday broils
Stirred up by the likes of the Montagues and the Capulets.

If the Mormons regard these streets merely as a backdrop
For preaching to passersby, they commit a sin
Against the church of the beautiful that Burton
Tried to visit in his cheerful moods. Streets
As an end in themselves or streets as a starting point
For a painting that offers an ideal landscape,
One of Poussin's, say, that moves the viewer to rise
For at least a moment from a mood that's passing
To a mood more permanent, however uncommon.

If the two apostles suppose the actual landscape
Will surpass Poussin's in tranquillity of the spirit
Once their gospel is acknowledged by everyone,
They join a crowd of prophets whose promises
Made Burton angry. Better not wait around,
He would have told them, for slugs
To change into butterflies. Better work instead
At making the stubbornly untransformed
Care about learning to vote for candidates
Likely to serve the city, though they realize
Their city is only the rough sketch of Poussin's.

In my favorite painting of his, the city's a distant line
Near the horizon. The human figures set in the foreground
Are thumb-sized blues and yellows in a field of green.
It's harvest time, and among the harvesters
The Capulets and the Montagues are swinging their scythes.
Also the Mormon boys, no longer in summer suits
But garbed like peasants, steadily working beside them
While Pan and Flora look on from a stand of willows.

And Burton is there with his sight restored,
Pointing to a stand of birch where the workers
Can rest in the shade and admire the view.
And here he is later, returning to ask the rested
If they'd help him load more bales on the wagon
For the last trip of the day to the barn.

I Said Yes but I Meant No

People are compelled to be together good and bad.
You've agreed to shrimp with the geology couple.
If you like one 85% and the other 35%
that's not so bad.
You need to like one at least 70%
and like the other not less than 25%
otherwise it's agonizing and pointless
like being crucified without religious significance.
Averages are misleading:
I like that couple 110% could mean
each is appreciated 55% which will not kill you
but neither will sleeping in your own urine.
One should like oneself between 60 and 80%.
Under 45%, one becomes an undertaking,
prone to eating disorders, public weeping,
useless for gift wrapping and relay races.
Over 85% means you are a self-involved bore,
I don't care about your Nobel Prize in positrons
or your dog sled victories.
Of course there is great variance throughout the day.
You may feel 0% upon first waking
but that is because you don't yet know you exist
which is why baby-studies have been a bust.
Then as you venture forth to boil water,
you may feel a sudden surge to 90%,
Hey, I'm GOOD at boiling water!
which can be promptly counteracted by turning on your e-mail.
It is important not to let variance become too extreme,
a range of 40% is allowable,
beyond that it is as great storms upon drought-stricken land.

I.e., mudslides.
Sugar, retirement plans, impending jail time
all are influential factors.
Generally, most data has been gathered
regarding raising percentages,
the modern world it is argued is plentiful
with opportunities of negative effect.
The tanker splits and the shore birds turn black and lose their ability
to float.
Sometimes a good scrub is all that's needed.
A fresh shirt.
Shock therapy has never been fully discounted
and people have felt significant surges
from backpacking into remote and elevated areas,
a call home.
Yet the very same may backfire.
Thwamp, thwamp, the helicopter lowers the rescue crew,
the phone slammed down.
Each case is profoundly nuanced,
like the lock systems of Holland.
Some, frankly, are beyond help,
but if you are a tall woman, wear shoes to make you taller!
Candy corn, what kind of person doesn't like candy corn?
Tell the 70/35% rock couple you can not come,
you forgot your fencing lesson,
your cat just had a puppy,
your tongue is green,
you are in fact dying.

Not That Great of an Evening

Yeah I went to the talk, and the reception.
Yeah I went to the dinner, and the party.
It was not a terrible evening. It was okay.
I don't think I did anything especially stupid.
But I feel kind of crummy. Not wretched, you know,
but just kind of lost or left over—
like I'm the little cup of overcooked beans
somebody covered with plastic wrap and pushed to the back of
the fridge. I might drink a little Scotch
just to get sleepy. Everything is okay. But it's like
there's so many voices—all these voices
still skittering around in my head like mice—people
having things to say. Everybody finding lots to say—
this professor gave a talk about the interpenetration
of coexisting cultures—I think that was the concept—
I kind of drifted away in some sections—and then
people clapped so I was clapping and then I was standing
with a cup of wine and trying to have on my face
the I'm-so-interested look. I'm so interested but
I'm also witty and cool. Then I was part of
several little exchanges—not really conversations,
it's more like we're throwing peanuts at each other's mouths.
My peanuts just bounced off the chin or the cheek of
whoever I spoke to. This was partly because the room was so noisy
and my voice is phlegmy and weak. In my next life
I want to have a voice nobody can ignore. But then
I would need to have things to say. Tonight I tried
but I could feel how unriveting I was. I don't blame people
for sliding away from me at the reception, and also at the party.
If I met me tonight I would slide away from me, too.

But how do they all *do* it? Are they happy?
I know some of them are not happy, but at least they seem to be so
present. Whereas I was like glancing at the door
waiting for my interesting self to show up.
My cup of wine kept being empty
which made me feel as if I was standing there in my underwear
so I kept refilling it. I was a blur.
I was a blur on its way to becoming a smudge.
And this was not about the evening being terrible. Actually
that's the scary part of it. This was a normal evening
with me being a fuzzy blur. At dinner I kept trying
to look very interested in the conversation on my left or my right
so it wouldn't be obvious that my only true companion was
my plate of salmon and potato. At one point
the troublingly attractive woman across the table was talking
about the talk we heard on coexisting cultures and suddenly
I felt potentially witty and I said loudly, "Who would have thought
that interpenetration could be so boring?" and I grinned at her
and I felt quite rogueish for a quarter of a second
but she just blinked as if I'd thrown a peanut that hit her eyelid
and then she kind of tilted away from me so she could finish
    her observation
about the ironies of postcolonialism. My face then felt
like a huge decaying pumpkin. Then for a while
I pushed a piece of salmon around on my plate, seeing it as
a postcolonial island, and I imagined the natives muttering
"Things were better under the emperor, at least you knew who
    you were."

Then after coffee I drifted along to the party upstairs and I thought
there *must* be a way to have fun. What is it?
So I ate three brownies. While nibbling the brownies
I tried to maintain the I'm-so-interested look. I'm sure I chatted
with a dozen people. Several times I started a sentence with
"It's fascinating the way" or "It's so fascinating the way"
but at the moment I can't remember what I was saying was
so fascinating. It was something about memories of high school
at one point. At the party there were at least four women

who seemed very attractive and I just wanted one of them
to give me some big eye contact, that's all,
the kind of gleaming twinkling eye contact that says
"I am intensely aware of your masculine appeal"
but this did not happen, and I began to feel resentful,
I resented the feeling that the focus of the evening,
the focus of existence, was always over *there* or over *there*
and never like *here* where I was standing.

So yeah. It was like that. At some point pretty late
people were telling jokes and I started telling several people
the old long joke whose punch line is,
"Let your pages do the walking through the Yellow Fingers"
but somehow it took forever and only one person really heard the
    punch line
and he just patted my shoulder and said something like
"Time to get this old steed back to the stable."
Then we both laughed and actually I was happy then
for a second. After that I sat on the sofa
drinking something that looked like wine
and I felt I was such a blur it was like I was the sofa's third cushion.
And then apparently my shoes carried me all the way to this room
where it's just me and the Scotch and the empty bed.
Okay, so, not that great of an evening, but no tragedy either;
but I'd just like to feel how it feels to be
in focus at the focus, to feel "Hey, you want the party?
Seek no more! The party's right here."

Hate Poem

I hate you truly. Truly I do.
Everything about me hates everything about you.
The flick of my wrist hates you.
The way I hold my pencil hates you.
The sound made by my tiniest bones were they trapped in the jaws of a
    moray eel hates you.
Each corpuscle singing in its capillary hates you.

Look out! Fore! I hate you.

The blue-green jewel of sock lint I'm digging from under my third
    toenail, left foot, hates you.
The history of this keychain hates you.
My sigh in the background as you explain relational databases hates you.
The goldfish of my genius hates you.
My aorta hates you. Also my ancestors.

A closed window is both a closed window and an obvious symbol of
    how I hate you.

My voice curt as a hairshirt: hate.
My hesitation when you invite me for a drive: hate.
My pleasant "good morning": hate.
You know how when I'm sleepy I nuzzle my head under your arm? Hate.
The whites of my target-eyes articulate hate. My wit practices it.
My breasts relaxing in their holster from morning to night hate you.
Layers of hate, a parfait.
Hours after our latest row, brandishing the sharp glee of hate,

I dissect you cell by cell, so that I might hate each one individually and
at leisure.
My lungs, duplicitous twins, expand with the utter validity of my hate,
which can never have enough of you,
Breathlessly, like two idealists in a broken submarine.

Hate Hotel

Sometimes I like to think about the people I hate.
I take my room at the Hate Hotel, and I sit and flip
through the heavy pages of the photographs,
the rogue's gallery of the faces I loathe.

My lamp of resentment sputters twice, then comes on strong,
filling the room with its red light.
That's how hate works—it thrills you and kills you

with its deep heat. Sometimes I like to sit and soak
in the Jacuzzi of my hate, hatching my plots
like a general running his hands over a military map—

and my bombers have been sent out
over the dwellings of my foes,
and are releasing their cargo of ill will

on the targets below, the hate bombs falling in silence
into the lives of the hate-
recipients. From the high window of my office
in the Government of Hate,

where I stay up late, working hard,
where I make no bargains, entertain no
scenarios of reconciliation,

I watch the hot flowers flare up all across
the city, the state, the continent—
I sip my soft drink of hate on the rocks
and let the punishment go on unstopped,

—again and again I let hate
get pregnant and give birth
to hate which gets pregnant
and gives birth again—

and only after I feel that hate
has trampled the land, burned it down
to some kingdom come of cautery and ash,
only after it has waxed and waned and waxed all night,

only then can I let hate
creep back in the door. Curl up at my feet
and sleep. Little pussycat hate. Home sweet hate.

Amnesty

If you're one of the many who've borrowed items
Of personal property from me, your neighbor
Harvey Benlow, and never returned them,
You can do it now, no questions asked,
By coming any night to the address
Printed at the top of this leaflet and leaving
The item in back by the picnic table.
The issue isn't my need for what's missing.
Long ago I replaced the edger and mulcher
That may be rusting away in your garage,
The pancake griddle on a hook in your kitchen,
The adjustable juicer, the punch bowl.
It's a matter of reweaving my torn faith
That your fault has never been crass indifference
To common courtesy but simple forgetfulness.
To return an item is to say you believe
Not that the world is whole but that improvement
Is possible if a remnant pretend that the world
They wish for were here already.

I'm asking you to set aside time this weekend
To inspect your sheds, shelves, closets,
And cabinets as you pose the question
How each particular item happened to come there.
For those you believe to be gifts, try to recall
The names of the givers, or the occasion,
Or at least your feelings when you first enjoyed them.
If you've forgotten, and are willing to knock at my door
With the item in hand, perhaps I can jog your memory.
Then, if you have the time, I'll show you

The prayer rug from Turkey a friend of mine
Has loaned me during her stay abroad.
And I'll show you the serving plate left long ago
By an unknown guest at a party
And never reclaimed. Beautiful cut glass
I've kept safe in a drawer, unused,
To dream of the place where it was treasured.
If it looks like yours, you can take it home.

Little Blue Nude

Outside, the crackhead who panhandles an eight-
hour day at 106th and Broadway croons
for Earl, his man, to let him in and make him well.
Soon the super's son will take his triumvirate

of dogs across the street to crap in Central Park.
Through my wall I'll hear the scrabble of their claws
and the low whirl of near-barks in their throats
as they tug their leashes down the hall and out

the door. The night a burglar forced the gate
across my kitchen window and slithered in to clean
me out, those dogs slept next door like drunken clouds.
I was in Tennessee. When I got off the plane there,

my host glanced at my tiny bag and asked, "Those
all your worldly goods?" I know you didn't ask me
what they took, but you can guess you're going to hear
the list. People tell these stories until they've worn

them out. A TV and a tape deck, two phones,
an answering machine, an alarm clock that didn't
work—these you'd expect, for they can be most
easily swept, like flecks of silt, into the swift

currents of the River Fence. The anomalies
make such lists interesting. These were mine:
two sets of sheets and pillowcases, and a bottle
of Côte Roti, 1982. Now these were clues. Also

he left my typewriter. And I knew right away
who'd robbed me. The mere pressure of my key
in the lock, before I'd even turned it, swung my door
open and my body knew he'd come in through

the kitchen but left like a guest by the front door.
Tony, my dumpster-diving friend, would bring by
things to sell: a ream of letterhead stationery
from The Children's Aid Society and two half

gallons of orange juice. Three dollars. "Whoo," he'd say.
"Ain't it a wonder what people will throw out."
So you see I was a sort of fence myself. "Being
a writer you could probably use some paper"

was the way he'd introduced himself. The night
before I left for Tennessee he'd pasted his girlfriend
Shirley in the eye and she came by my apartment
to complain. I gave her some ice cubes nested

in a kitchen towel to hold against her bruise,
a glass of wine. So that explains the Côte Roti.
As for the sheets, when I confronted Tony,
he yelled at me, "A dick don't have no conscience."

Speak for yourself, I thought redundantly, for I'm
the one with the typewriter and gall to speak
for others. Tony's his only clientele. "I didn't rob
your place," he yelled, "and stay away from Shirley."

The wonder is how much we manage to hang on to.
Even if a robbery's been designed to hurt,
no thief would know to take the postcard
of Renoir's *Little Blue Nude* I'd taped above my desk.

She sits, all wist and inner weather on her creamy
skin, her face bemused beneath the ginger helmet

of her hair, wholly alert to what the poets once
called reverie, perhaps, though from the relaxed

attention of her body I'd say she was listening
to beloved music. If I could choose for her,
I'd make it Ellington's 1940 recording
of "Cottontail," with Ben Webster on tenor.

If you'd been robbed, let's say, and rage ran through
you like a wind, and you balled your fists and sat
and stared at them, as though you'd forget their name,
you who are so good with words, rehearsing irate

speeches for Tony, wrapped in fury like a flower
in a bud; and also feeling impotent, a chump
with a mouthful of rant, a chump who knows
even now he'll eat the rage, the loss, the sour

tang of moral superiority to Tony,
the times he'll tell the story and list what Tony
stole . . . If you could see all those words coming
and know even now you'd eat them, every one,

you could turn to music you love, not as a mood-
altering drug nor as a consolation, but because
your emotions had overwhelmed and tired you
and made you mute and stupid, and you rued

them every one. But when Webster kicks into
his first chorus, they're back, all your emotions,
everyone, and in another language, perhaps
closer to their own. "There you are," you say

to them silently, and you're vivid again, the way
we're most ourselves when we know surely
what we love, and whom. The little blue nude
has a look on her face like that. Once

when I was fussing with my tapes, Tony came by
to sell me mineral water and envelopes.
"You writing a book on jazz or what?" "No,"
I said. "I just love these." I didn't say why,

because I didn't talk that way to Tony,
and because, come to think of it, I didn't know
that day, I didn't ask myself until later,
afterthought being a writer's specialty

and curse. But that conversation explains why
he took the tapes and left the typewriter.
Writing's my scam, he thought, and music my love.
The dogs come snuffling and scrabbling back.

This time of night the building quiets down,
the hour of soliloquists. Even with walls this thin
the neighbors don't complain when I type late.
"Still working on that book?" they ask.

"What's it about?" one asked. I didn't know
that day, I didn't ask myself until later.
It's a reverie on what I love, and whom,
and how I manage to hold on to them.

IT OCCURS TO ME I AM AMERICA

Wrestling with a Huge Rococco National Identity

America

America I've given you all and now I'm nothing.
America two dollars and twentyseven cents January 17, 1956.
I can't stand my own mind.
America when will we end the human war?
Go fuck yourself with your atom bomb.
I don't feel good don't bother me.
I won't write my poem till I'm in my right mind.
America when will you be angelic?
When will you take off your clothes?
When will you look at yourself through the grave?
When will you be worthy of your million Trotskyites?
America why are your libraries full of tears?
America when will you send your eggs to India?
I'm sick of your insane demands.
When can I go into the supermarket and buy what I need with my
    good looks?
America after all it is you and I who are perfect not the next world.
Your machinery is too much for me.
You made me want to be a saint.
There must be some other way to settle this argument.
Burroughs is in Tangiers I don't think he'll come back it's sinister.
Are you being sinister or is this some form of practical joke?
I'm trying to come to the point.
I refuse to give up my obsession.
America stop pushing I know what I'm doing.
America the plum blossoms are falling.
I haven't read the newspapers for months, everyday somebody goes on
    trial for murder.
America I feel sentimental about the Wobblies.
America I used to be a communist when I was a kid I'm not sorry.

I smoke marijuana every chance I get.

I sit in my house for days on end and stare at the roses in the closet.

When I go to Chinatown I get drunk and never get laid.

My mind is made up there's going to be trouble.

You should have seen me reading Marx.

My psychoanalyst thinks I'm perfectly right.

I won't say the Lord's Prayer.

I have mystical visions and cosmic vibrations.

America I still haven't told you what you did to Uncle Max after he came over from Russia.

I'm addressing you.

Are you going to let our emotional life be run by Time Magazine?

I'm obsessed by Time Magazine.

I read it every week.

Its cover stares at me every time I slink past the corner candystore.

I read it in the basement of the Berkeley Public Library.

It's always telling me about responsibility. Businessmen are serious. Movie producers are serious. Everybody's serious but me.

It occurs to me that I am America.

I am talking to myself again.

Asia is rising against me.

I haven't got a chinaman's chance.

I'd better consider my national resources.

My national resources consist of two joints of marijuana millions of genitals an unpublishable private literature that jetplanes 1400 miles an hour and twentyfive-thousand mental institutions.

I say nothing about my prisons nor the millions of underprivileged who live in my flowerpots under the light of five hundred suns.

I have abolished the whorehouses of France, Tangiers is the next to go.

My ambition is to be President despite the fact that I'm a Catholic.

America how can I write a holy litany in your silly mood?

I will continue like Henry Ford my strophes are as individual as his automobiles more so they're all different sexes.

America I will sell you strophes $2500 apiece $500 down on your old strophe

America free Tom Mooney
America save the Spanish Loyalists
America Sacco & Vanzetti must not die
America I am the Scottsboro boys.
America when I was seven momma took me to Communist Cell meetings
   they sold us garbanzos a handful per ticket a ticket costs a nickel and
   the speeches were free everybody was angelic and sentimental about
   the workers it was all so sincere you have no idea what a good thing the
   party was in 1835 Scott Nearing was a grand old man a real mensch
   Mother Bloor the Silk-strikers' Ewig-Weibliche made me cry I once
   saw the Yiddish orator Israel Amter plain. Everybody must have been
   a spy.
America you don't really want to go to war.
America it's them bad Russians.
Them Russians them Russians and them Chinamen. And them Russians.
The Russia wants to eat us alive. The Russia's power mad. She wants to
   take our cars from out our garages.
Her wants to grab Chicago. Her needs a Red *Reader's Digest*. Her
   wants our auto plants in Siberia. Him big bureaucracy running
   our fillingstations.
That no good. Ugh. Him makes Indians learn read. Him need big black
   niggers. Hah. Her make us all work sixteen hours a day. Help.
America this is quite serious.
America this is the impression I get from looking in the television set.
America is this correct?
I'd better get right down to the job.
It's true I don't want to join the Army or turn lathes in precision parts
   factories, I'm nearsighted and psychopathic anyway.
America I'm putting my queer shoulder to the wheel.

Naturalization Exam

1. Please provide your full name and country
of origin. **2.** Please provide your occupation and income bracket,
on a scale of $ to $$$$$. **3.** How many states

compose the United States of America? **4.** Follow-up question:
what's the deal with Puerto Rico? **5.** How old
is the United States of America? Well, take a guess. . . .

Really, just guess. . . . That's your guess?!
Aw, get outta here, you! You're serious? It must be this new
face cream—the thing works miracles. **6.** Please provide

an adorable, ethnically identifiable mishearing
of a patriotic song lyric (example: *José, can you see* . . . ,
but don't use that one). **7.** Name

the individual who most Americans
erroneously believe to have said, "Give me liberty,
or give me death!" **8.** True or False: Will work

for sign that says *Will work for food*. **9.** Adapt the phrase
"Uncle Tom" to apply to someone of your own
nationality/ethnicity (example: "Uncle Tomahawk" for American
   Indians,

but don't use that one). **10.** Squeaky Fucking Fromme, dude.
Elaborate. **11.** Okay, now let's play
the sorority house girls'-night-in favorite

"Fuck One, Marry One, Throw One Off a Cliff": your choices
are Jim Thorpe, James Oglethorpe,
and Robert Mapplethorpe. **12.** Which of the following

is a better joke? a) *What do you call one thousand lesbians*
with guns? Militia Etheridge. b) *What does a lesbian bring*
on a second date? A moving van. **13.** Who would play

Bob Dylan in the movie of his life: William Zanzinger,
or Poor Hattie Carroll? **15.** Your boyfriend's hot.
In that foreign way, I mean. Do you know

if he's single? **16.** Using the International
Phonetic Alphabet (IPA), write the name "Ayn Rand."
17. Annexation, or War? Please choose only one.

Immigrant Picnic

It's the Fourth of July, the flags
are painting the town,
the plastic forks and knives
are laid out like a parade.

And I'm grilling, I've got my apron,
I've got potato salad, macaroni, relish,
I've got a hat shaped
like the state of Pennsylvania.

I ask my father what's his pleasure
and he says, "Hot dog, medium rare,"
and then, "Hamburger, sure,
what's the big difference,"
as if he's really asking.

I put on hamburgers and hot dogs,
slice up the sour pickles and Bermudas,
uncap the condiments. The paper napkins
are fluttering away like lost messages.

"You're running around," my mother says,
"like a chicken with its head loose."

"Ma," I say, "you mean cut off,
loose and cut off being as far apart
as, say, son and daughter."

She gives me a quizzical look as though
I've been caught in some impropriety.

"I love you and your sister just the same," she says,
"Sure," my grandmother pipes in,
"you're both our children, so why worry?"

That's not the point I begin telling them,
and I'm comparing words to fish now,
like the ones in the sea at Port Said,
or like birds among the date palms by the Nile,
unrepentantly elusive, wild.

"Sonia," my father says to my mother,
"what the hell is he talking about?"
"He's on a ball," my mother says.

"That's roll!" I say, throwing up my hands,
"as in hot dog, hamburger, dinner roll. . . ."

"And what about roll out the barrels?" my mother asks,
and my father claps his hands, "Why sure," he says,
"let's have some fun," and launches
into a polka, twirling my mother
around and around like the happiest top,

and my uncle is shaking his head, saying
"You could grow nuts listening to us,"

and I'm thinking of pistachios in the Sinai
burgeoning without end,
pecans in the South, the jumbled
flavor of them suddenly in my mouth,
wordless, confusing,
crowding out everything else.

A French Statue

for Mother

Liberty's so high up, you think—you expected her
down-to-earth. No such luck, you clasp
at your mother's skirt. She knows this place
where names get changed, some by accident,

some not, where immigrants learn a new *sur-*,
or as you'll see here, a *last*. You're next. Your
name. Your next of kin. *Next*, you'll learn,
is how to move lines (not queues) no matter what

that kind Irish passenger taught you. *Next*,
please. Next. And this the city you heard of but
a year ago as your parents explained in Hungarian.
Soon enough you'll be in school, they'll ask

what you speak and *Magyar*, you'll repeat,
Mud-your—a tongue pronounced with mud.
Hungary you'll learn for its own pun by first
Thanksgiving. Turkey you will learn to stuff.

More and more each year, you'll grow
to love the Salvation Army Santa ringing bells
to bring Christmas. You'll give me coins to feed
his kettle and say these people were your first

taste of America, sugar cookies, weak cocoa,
Willkommen, what the lady said to you—so

strangely, with a *will*—those first few crumbs
of welcome, have some, *Or is it "Bienvenue?"*

●   ●   ●

Neither, thank you. You're welcome now.
Hard to tell you from a local. Hard to tell you, too,
what I've clung to, phrases you fed, American as
mom and apple pie. Brand spanking new. Chew

the fat. Take a load off. Each a measure of freedom:
the Drinking Gourd, forty acres and a mule, a chicken
in every pot, a man on the moon; and odd numerologies
of urgency: second wind, the fourth quarter, the bottom of

the ninth. At contradictions we never stopped: free
rein, Statue of Liberty; you had me take it all with
displaced patience, just in case, any way the wind blows,
you never know. In the meantime, make *yourself*

at home. All systems go.

América

I.

Although *Tía* Miriam boasted she discovered
at least half-a-dozen uses for peanut butter—
topping for guava shells in syrup,
butter substitute for Cuban toast,
hair conditioner and relaxer—
Mamá never knew what to make
of the monthly five-pound jars
handed out by the immigration department
until my friend, Jeff, mentioned jelly.

II.

There was always pork though,
for every birthday and wedding,
whole ones on Christmas and New Year's Eve,
even on Thanksgiving day—pork,
fried, broiled or crispy skin roasted—
as well as cauldrons of black beans,
fried plantain chips and *yuca con mojito*.
These items required a special visit
to Antonio's Mercado on the corner of Eighth Street
where men in *guayaberas* stood in senate
blaming Kennedy for everything—*"Ese hijo de puta!"*
the bile of Cuban coffee and cigar residue
filling the creases of their wrinkled lips;
clinging to one another's lies of lost wealth,
ashamed and empty as hollow trees.

III.

By seven I had grown suspicious—we were still here.
Overheard conversations about returning
had grown wistful and less frequent.
I spoke English; my parents didn't.
We didn't live in a two-story house
with a maid or a wood panel station wagon
nor vacation camping in Colorado.
None of the girls had hair of gold;
none of my brothers or cousins
were named Greg, Peter, or Marsha;
we were not the Brady Bunch.
None of the black and white characters
on Donna Reed or on the Dick Van Dyke Show
were named Guadalupe, Lázaro, or Mercedes.
Patty Duke's family wasn't like us either—
they didn't have pork on Thanksgiving,
they ate turkey with cranberry sauce;
they didn't have *yuca*, they had yams
like the dittos of Pilgrims I colored in class.

IV.

A week before Thanksgiving
I explained to my *abuelita*
about the Indians and the Mayflower,
how Lincoln set the slaves free;
I explained to my parents about
the purple mountain's majesty,
"one if by land, two if by sea,"
the cherry tree, the tea party,
the amber waves of grain,
the "masses yearning to be free,"
liberty and justice for all, until
finally they agreed:
this Thanksgiving we would have turkey,
as well as pork.

V.

Abuelita prepared the poor fowl
as if committing an act of treason,
faking her enthusiasm for my sake.
Mamá set a frozen pumpkin pie in the oven
and prepared candied yams following instructions
I translated from the marshmallow bag.
The table was arrayed with gladiolas,
the plattered turkey loomed at the center
on plastic silver from Woolworth's.
Everyone sat in green velvet chairs
we had upholstered with clear vinyl,
except *Tío* Carlos and Toti, seated
in the folding chairs from the Salvation Army.
I uttered a bilingual blessing
and the turkey was passed around
like a game of Russian Roulette.
"DRY," *Tío* Berto complained, and proceeded
to drown the lean slices with pork fat drippings
and cranberry jelly—*"esa mierda roja,"* he called it.
Faces fell when *Mamá* presented her ochre pie—
pumpkin was a home remedy for ulcers, not a dessert.
Tía María made three rounds of Cuban coffee
then *Abuelo* and Pepe cleared the living room furniture,
put on a Celia Cruz LP and the entire family
began to *merengue* over the linoleum of our apartment,
sweating rum and coffee until they remembered—
it was 1970 and 46 degrees—
in *América*.
After repositioning the furniture,
an appropriate darkness filled the room.
Tío Berto was the last to leave.

Thanksgiving

This was the first Thanksgiving with my wife's family,
sitting at the stained pine table in the dining room.
The wood stove coughed during her mother's prayer:
Amen and the gravy boat bobbing over fresh linen.
Her father stared into the mashed potatoes
and saw a white battleship floating in the gravy.
Still staring at the mashed potatoes, he began a soliloquy
about the new Navy missiles fired across miles of ocean,
how they could jump into the smokestack of a battleship.
"Now in Korea," he said, "I was a gunner and the people there
ate kimch'i, and it really stinks." Mother complained that no one
was eating the creamed onions. *"Eat, Daddy."* The creamed onions
look like eyeballs, I thought, and then said, "I wish I had missiles
like that." Daddy laughed a 1950's horror-movie mad-scientist laugh,
and told me he didn't have a missile, but he had his own cannon.
"Daddy, eat the candied yams," Mother hissed, as if he were
a liquored CIA spy telling secrets about military hardware
to some Puerto Rican janitor he met in a bar. "I'm a toolmaker.
I made the cannon myself," he announced, and left the table.
"Daddy's family has been here in the Connecticut Valley since 1680,"
Mother said. "There were Indians here once, but they left."
When I started dating her daughter, Mother called me a half-Black,
but now she spooned candied yams on my plate. I nibbled
at the candied yams. I remembered my own Thanksgivings
in the Bronx, turkey with arroz y habichuelas and plátanos,
and countless cousins swaying to bugalú on the record player
or roaring at my grandmother's Spanish punchlines in the kitchen,
the glowing of her cigarette like a firefly lost in the city. For years
I thought everyone ate rice and beans with turkey at Thanksgiving.
Daddy returned to the table with a cannon, steering the black

steel barrel. "Does that cannon go boom?" I asked. "I fire it
in the backyard at the tombstones," he said. "That cemetery bought
up all our farmland during the Depression. Now we only have
the house." He stared and said nothing, then glanced up suddenly,
like a ghost had tickled his ear. "Want to see me fire it?" he grinned.
"Daddy, fire the cannon after dessert," Mother said. "If I fire
the cannon, I have to take out the cannonballs first," he told me.
He tilted the cannon downward, and cannonballs dropped
from the barrel, thudding on the floor and rolling across
the brown braided rug. Grandmother praised the turkey's thighs,
said she would bring leftovers home to feed her Congo Gray parrot.
I walked with Daddy to the backyard, past the bullet holes
in the door and his pickup truck with the Confederate license plate.
He swiveled the cannon around to face the tombstones
on the other side of the backyard fence. "This way, if I hit anybody,
they're already dead," he declared. He stuffed half a charge
of gunpowder into the cannon, and lit the fuse. From the dining room,
Mother yelled, *"Daddy, no!"* Then the battlefield rumbled
under my feet. My head thundered. Smoke drifted over
the tombstones. Daddy laughed. And I thought: When the first
drunken Pilgrim dragged out the cannon at the first Thanksgiving—
that's when the Indians left.

BARBARA HAMBY

Ode to American English

I was missing English one day, American, really,
    with its pill-popping Hungarian goulash of everything
from Anglo-Saxon to Zulu, because British English
    is not the same, if the paperback dictionary
I bought at Brentano's on the Avenue de l'Opéra
    is any indication, too cultured by half. Oh, the English
know their dahlias, but what about doowop, donuts,
    Dick Tracy, Tricky Dick? With their elegant Oxfordian
accents, how could they understand my yearning for the hotrod,
    hotdog, hot flash vocabulary of the U. S. of A.,
the fragmented fandango of Dagwood's everyday flattening
    of Mr. Beasley on the sidewalk, fetuses floating
on billboards, drive-by monster hip-hop stereos shaking
    the windows of my dining room like a 7.5 earthquake,
Ebonics, Spanglish, "you know" used as comma and period,
    the inability of 90% of the population to get the present perfect:
I have went, I have saw, I have tooken Jesus into my heart,
    the battle cry of the Bible Belt, but no one uses
the King James anymore, only plain-speak versions,
    in which Jesus, raising Lazarus from the dead, says,
"Dude, wake up," and the L-man bolts up like a B-movie
    mummy. "Whoa, I was toasted." Yes, ma'am,
I miss the mongrel plenitude of American English, its fall-guy,
    rat-terrier, dog-pound neologisms, the bomb of it all,
the rushing River Jordan backwoods mutability of it, the low-rider,
    boom-box cruise of it, from New Joisey to Ha-wah-ya
with its sly dog, malasada-scarfing beach blanket lingo
    to the ubiquitous Valley Girl's *like-like* stuttering,
shopaholic rant. I miss its quotidian beauty, its querulous
    back-biting righteous indignation, its preening rotgut

flag-waving cowardice. *Suffering Succotash*, sputters
  Sylvester the Cat; *sine die*, say the pork-bellied legislators
of the swamps and plains. I miss all those guys, their Tweety-bird
  resilience, their Doris Day optimism, the candid unguent
of utter unhappiness on every channel, the midnight televangelist
  euphoric stew, the junk mail, voice mail vernacular.
On every *boulevard* and *rue* I miss the Tarzan cry of Johnny
  Weismueller, Johnny Cash, Johnny B. Goode,
and all the smart-talking, gum-snapping hard-girl dialogue,
  finger-popping x-rated street talk, sports babble,
Cheetoes, Cheerios, chili dog diatribes. Yeah, I miss them all,
  sitting here on my sidewalk throne sipping champagne
verses lined up like hearses, metaphors juking, nouns zipping
  in my head like Corvettes on Dexedrine, French verbs
slitting my throat, yearning for James Dean to jump my curb.

A Fact Which Occurred in America

In the fifth grade, when we came finally to the Civil
War, the teacher kept saying, *We lost, we lost,*
his eyes a shadowy grief under his favorite painting,

a laminated Dawe reproduction subtitled *A fact
which occurred in America*: a black man wrestling a buffalo
to the ground. The ground becomes his grave, I am the buffalo.

In the painting of the buffalo rolling his eye
to size up the man who will never be strong enough
to wrestle his way out of the definition of black,

I am trying to say, *we are metaphors for each other, please
don't kill me*. The man is black but so is the buffalo,
so is the sky and so is the heart which keeps this fact holy.

In the painting I am the buffalo because I want to be loved
by pure physicality, a man with broad hips and broader anger
and a yoke around his neck which has not broken him

yet. In the painting about a buffalo's last breath,
I am the dust matted on the lips. Kiss me, keep me
in your mouth, don't let me dissolve into fact.

In the painting about a boy who writes, *I am sorry we lost
the Civil War* fifty times on the blackboard after school
in his deserted fifth-grade class, I am the bone-white chalk,

I have always wanted to be someone's defiled good buffalo.
In the painting the man tells the buffalo, *play dead,*
I'll get you out of this. In the defiled fifth-grade teacher's

laminated copy of the painting, I am the racing pulse
of the boy getting his revenge when the teacher isn't looking.
I am the time after we learned about the heroic Civil War,

on the playground when Day-Trion caught me alone
in the maze of trees and held me down with one hand,
kissed me with his tongue, licking my lip first, smoothing it

for his, my first kiss, on the ground, the leaves spreading
under us, black and wet. Deep in the animal-wrestled-down
part of me, the boy was bent like a tree over a maze

scribbling a hyphenated name in tiny scrawl in black ink
on a piece of paper, trying all hour during language arts
to get back to the maze when the teacher snatches up the paper,

his eyes widening at the darker revolt.
In the punishment, I was the blackboard, my body
lashed by loss and sorrow. I was the buffalo,

I wanted to lose the war; I wanted to stay black,
the filmy white chalk a sickness stretched over my skin.
In that America, I am always betraying the master.

TONY HOAGLAND

America

Then one of the students with blue hair and a tongue stud
Says that America is for him a maximum-security prison

Whose walls are made of RadioShacks and Burger Kings, and
    MTV episodes
Where you can't tell the show from the commercials,

And as I consider how to express how full of shit I think he is,
He says that even when he's driving to the mall in his Isuzu

Trooper with a gang of his friends, letting rap music pour over them
Like a boiling Jacuzzi full of ballpeen hammers, even then he feels

Buried alive, captured and suffocated in the folds
Of the thick satin quilt of America

And I wonder if this is a legitimate category of pain,
or whether he is just spin doctoring a better grade,

And then I remember that when I stabbed my father in the dream
    last night,
It was not blood but money

That gushed out of him, bright green hundred-dollar bills
Spilling from his wounds, and—this is the weird part—,

He gasped "Thank god—those Ben Franklins were
Clogging up my heart—

And so I perish happily,
Freed from that which kept me from my liberty"—

Which was when I knew it was a dream, since my dad
Would never speak in rhymed couplets,

And I look at the student with his acne and cell phone and phony
   ghetto clothes
And I think, "I am asleep in America too,

And I don't know how to wake myself either,"
And I remember what Marx said near the end of his life:

"I was listening to the cries of the past,
When I should have been listening to the cries of the future."

But how could he have imagined 100 channels of 24-hour cable
Or what kind of nightmare it might be

When each day you watch rivers of bright merchandise run past you
And you are floating in your pleasure boat upon this river

Even while others are drowning underneath you
And you see their faces twisting in the surface of the waters

And yet it seems to be your own hand
Which turns the volume higher?

CHRISTOPHER BURSK

E Pluribus Unum

Just what's going on in that thick skull
of yours? asks the teacher and it takes you a while to figure out
that he's talking to you, and though you're tempted
to tell him that you are, in fact, contemplating
United States history, you don't
because football practice is next
and what is going through your head
is a locker room full of naked presidents,
all the Jameses and Johns showering together.
When you'd got on the school bus this morning
you didn't plan to think about Grover Cleveland
scrubbing Chester Arthur's back,
or Millard Fillmore letting his towel fall away
so there's no mistaking his most democratic part,
or Monroe scratching his balls
as if that were his manifest destiny. How is a boy to explain
that he's got Quincy Adams' testicles
on his mind and Warren Harding's buttocks?
When Thomas Jefferson bends over
you can almost see into the darkness
that fills the third President of the United States.
What did you expect? That George Washington
would be all padding like your grandmother?
Did you doubt that a man in a wig
would have the same parts as you, more
or less? Poor penis,
who wouldn't wish to comfort such a wobbly thing
no matter what wars it waged, whom it managed
to exterminate. Teddy Roosevelt's can't help
saluting to the Republic. Eisenhower's just lolls there

as if it's earned the right to do nothing
presidential for a while. What hope is there for you
if this is the kind of thing you're going to imagine?
Rutherford B. Hayes letting the water
have its way with him?
Woodrow Wilson drawing faces in the steam on the mirror
as if even the Leader of the Free World gets tired
of being serious all the time? Today in room 203
all of American history comes down to
a boy thinking things
he shouldn't, and knowing not to say anything, no matter
how hard he's pressed.

Harryette Mullen Lecture on the American Dream

Mud is thicker than what is thicker than water. Pull your head up by your chin straps. Put the pedal to the metal. Peddle to the middle. Put the medal on the pedestal. I pledge Sister Sledgehammer & Father knows beds, but I am not my breather's keeper. I pledge to earn every holler & if found guilty, I pledge to repay my Bill of Rights to Society. From me to shining me. Money, money, money, monkey. We're number none. Our number's done. *E pluribus Unumbskull.* For war & several fears we go. Praise be to Guard. Slops & Slobbers. Maladies & Gentrifications. Don't kill us, we'll kill you. With lobotomy & Jesus for all.

The Year I Was Diagnosed with a Sacrilegious Heart

At twelve, I quit reciting
the Pledge of Allegiance,
could not salute the flag
in 1969, and I,
undecorated for grades or sports,
was never again anonymous in school.

A girl in homeroom
caught my delinquent hand
and pinned a salute
against my chest;
my cafeteria name was Commie,
though I too drank the milk
with presidential portraits on the carton;
but when the school assembly stood
for the flags and stiff soldiers' choreography
of the color guard,
and I stuck to my seat
like a back pocket snagged on coil,
the principal's office
quickly found my file.
A balding man in a brown suit
asked me if I understood compromise,
and we nodded in compromise,
a pair of Brooklyn wardheelers.

Next assembly, when the color guard
marched down the aisle,
stern-faced,
I stood with the rest,

then pivoted up the aisle,
the flags and me
brushing past each other
without apologies,
my unlaced sneakers
dragging out of the auditorium.

I pressed my spyglass eye
against the doors
for the Pledge:
no one saw my right hand
crumpled in a pocket
instead of spreading
across my sacrilegious heart.

Ceremony done, the flagpoles
pointed their eagle beaks at me,
and I ducked
under their shifting banner wings
back to my seat,
inoculated against staring,
my mind a room after school
where baseball cards
could be stacked by team
in a plastic locker.

DEAN YOUNG

Sex with Strangers

I was having sex with a stranger
when I realized this was no stranger,
this was Eleanor Roosevelt,
wife of the 32nd president of the United States.
Of course I was shocked
but it seemed rude to stop having sex
so I went on having sex.
Her hair was getting rather deranged
and she was concentrating hard
like a person trying to move a paperclip
by force of mind alone
which brought out the equine qualities
of her facial structure not in a bad way.
One reason to have sex is to help a stranger
get in contact with his or her animal-being
even if it's a crayfish.
In the kitchen the rotisserie was laboring,
either the chicken was too fat
or it was tuckering out. Oddly,
I didn't feel awful for Franklin Delano
even though he looked jaunty and vulnerable
in his wheelchair in the margin of the dictionary.
In general it's difficult to feel awful
about anything while having sex
which is why it's such a popular activity
and the church is against it
except in rare primarily utilitarian instances.
That pretty much covers the facts of my life.
I've never been in much of a car crash.
When I walk into the mirror of the high grass

under the tired suicide note of the setting sun,
I'm never gone long. Once I was stuck
on an elevator, all of us strangers
gasping at once but there the resemblance
to having sex ended because it only took
35 seconds to get it going again, each of us
off at a different floor: cardiology,
oncology, psychiatry, the burn unit,
the solarium.

Canada

By Canada I have always been fascinated.
All that snow and acquiescing.
All that emptiness, all those butterflies
marshalled into an army of peace.
Moving north away from me
Canada has no border, away
like the state its northern border
withers into the skydome. In a world
full of mistrust and self-medication
I have always hated Canada.
It makes me feel like I'm shouting
at a child for letting a handful
of pine needles run through his fist.
Canada gets along with everyone
while I hang, a dark cloud
above the schoolyard. I know
we need war, all the skirmishes
to keep our borders where
we have placed them, all
the migration, all the difference.
Just like Canada the Dalai Lama
is now in Canada, and everyone
is fascinated. When they come
to visit me, no one ever leaves me
saying, the most touching thing
about him is he's so human.
Or, I was really glad to hear
so many positive ideas regardless
of the consequences expressed.
Or I could drink a case of you.

No one has ever pedaled
every inch of thousands of roads
through me to raise awareness
for my struggle for autonomy.
I have pity but no respect for others,
which is not compassion, just ordinary
love based on attitudes towards myself.
I wonder how long I can endure.
In Canada the leaves are falling.
When they do each one rustles
maybe to the white-tailed deer
of sadness, and it's clear
that whole country does not exist
to make me feel crappy
like a candelabra hanging
above the prison world,
condemned to freely glow.

Consolation

How agreeable it is not to be touring Italy this summer,
wandering her cities and ascending her torrid hilltowns.
How much better to cruise these local, familiar streets,
fully grasping the meaning of every road sign and billboard
and all the sudden hand gestures of my compatriots.

There are no abbeys here, no crumbling frescoes or famous
domes and there is no need to memorize a succession
of kings or tour the dripping corners of a dungeon.
No need to stand around a sarcophagus, see Napoleon's
little bed on Elba, or view the bones of a saint under glass.

How much better to command the simple precinct of home
than be drafted by pillar, arch, and basilica.
Why hide my head in phrasebooks and wrinkled maps?
Why feed scenery into a hungry, one-eyed camera
eager to eat the world one monument at a time?

Instead of slouching in a café ignorant of the word for ice,
I will head down to the coffee shop and the waitress
known as Dot. I will slide into the flow of the morning
paper, all language barriers down,
rivers of idiom running freely, eggs over easy on the way.

And after breakfast, I will not have to find someone
willing to photograph me with my arm around the owner.
I will not puzzle over the bill or record in a journal

what I had to eat and how the sun came in the window.
It is enough to climb back into the car

as if it were the great car of English itself
and sounding my loud vernacular horn, speed off
down a road that will never lead to Rome, not even Bologna.

FROM MY BOWELS TO YOUR INBOX

Poetry Goes to Work

RICHARD GARCÍA

A Diver for the NYPD Talks to His Girlfriend

I can't even see my hands in front of my face
through the darkness—mud, raw sewage,
black clouds of who knows what,
gas and oil leaking out of all the cars
that have been shoved into the river.
But my hands have learned to see,
sliding sideways down wrinkled concrete,
over slime coated rocks, broken glass, plastic bags,
barbed wire, as if there was a tiny eye
at the end of each finger. There are sponges down there
shaped like puffed-up lips, with silky tentacles
that retract at my touch. For some reason, all the grocery carts
in the city are making their way to the bottom of the river.
Did I tell you about the body wrapped in plastic
and chains, and the pile of pistols, rifles,
enough to start a gun shop? Once, looking for a missing
Piper Cub, we found it next to a trainer
from World War Two, both parked side by side
as if waiting for permission to take off.
People throw strange things in the river,
I don't know, some kind of voodoo—jars
filled with pig eyes, chickens with their throats slit
stuffed into burlap sacks. Everything—TVs, couches,
lamps, phone books—is down there—if we ever grow gills
and live in the river we'll have whatever we need.
Today it was a fishing boat missing for five days.
Easy to find now by a certain odor that seeps
through our wet suits, that we call corpse soup.
The fishermen were sitting in the cabin, bloated hands
drifting as if they were swapping stories.

We tied them together and rose toward the surface
in a slow spiral. Once, I was feeling around in the dark
for this drowned lady, I was about to go back,
to call it a day, when her arms shot up
and grabbed me tight, tight around my waist.
Even when we're out of the river there's more water.
Bath, shower, bath, shower, disinfectant, rinse—
but I never feel clean. Everything seems dirty: crowds
in the market, car horns, alarms, the barking of dogs.

The Speech

I would like to take this importune titty to announce I always knew I was great as I am simple. Being a hot young news item was never on my nightstand, but when you're hot, I'm you. I'll hammer with you here: I was always sincere. That, I believe, is the plaquebird in my secret pudding. If you want the recipe, then buy my book, tapes and video. I couldn't say it any clearer than in three mediums. Haven't I won the golden humble award six years running like the nose of an elderly dope fiend? Try that on over your tights, Superman. I bet you slice it into the woods every time and wear a dress at home and bogart all the jujubes. Always knew I was greater than you. Go to hell, please. Just straight there like a speeding bullshit from a fake planet. Can't you see with that x-ray business I'm trying to audience these noodles here? Imparted a right-from-the-gut success story: From My Bowels To Your Inbox—that's the stuff. Sells like electric underwear.

For the Women of the All-Female Bookkeeping Department at H. G. Smithy's

I think of them with summer,
polka-dot dresses and white
enamel jewelry, a petal
on each ear. The rest of the year
while I was in school,
they must have worn drabber garb,
but I never saw them bundled up
against a cold world, only displayed
like a bucket of tulips for sale,
their bangle bracelets clinking like laughter.

My family looked down on women
who worked, but I, a trainee at fifteen,
was in awe of the magic
wands tucked in their bags—
mascaras, lip brushes, pink-tonged
lash curlers that caged their eyes!
I loved their seamed stockings,
the way they turned
to check them, one leg slightly raised,
the made-up face set back on the shoulder
like a clock on a mantel.

And their clothes—tight
sheath skirts, Doris Day shirtwaists.
A silk scarf at the neck
like a snippet of lingerie inviting
a man to carry them off
to someplace besides the department

stores where they shopped the sales
at lunch: Hecht's, Woodward & Lothrop's,
even chandeliered Garfinkle's,

where the wives of diplomats wandered
in saris and pearls. The bookkeepers
bought the best, believing a French
hat might be the key
accessory to a different life. It could happen
anywhere—on a streetcar or bus, walking
the long breezy blocks to the office
and back, chatting with the men who visited
our corridor from Real Estate and Rent.

I loved them the way I loved all my teachers—
so that in memory they seem more
adult than I will ever be.
O Miss Dottie, Miss Helen, Miss Elaine,
ambition had not yet been given
to you or to me. I wish I could
remember you simply as women
who worked for a living,
not as thwarted pilots and judges,
not as perpetual ingenues
swatting at fate with a kidskin glove.

Bless Their Hearts

At Steak-n-Shake I learned that if you add
"Bless their hearts" after their names, you can say
whatever you want about them and it's OK.
My son, bless his heart, is an idiot,
she said. *He rents storage space for his kids'*
toys—they're only one and three years old!
I said, *My father, bless his heart, has turned*
into a sentimental old fool. He gets
weepy when he hears my daughter's greeting
on our voice mail. Before our Steakburgers came
someone else blessed her office mate's heart,
then, as an afterthought, the jealous hearts
of the entire anthropology department.
We bestowed blessings on many a heart
that day. I even blessed my ex-wife's heart.
Our waiter, bless his heart, would not be getting
much tip, for which, no doubt, he'd bless our hearts.
In a week it would be Thanksgiving,
and we would each sit with our respective
families, counting our blessings and blessing
the hearts of family members as only family
does best. Oh, bless us all, yes, bless us, please
bless us and bless our crummy little hearts.

ERIN BELIEU

On Being Fired Again

I've known the pleasures of being
fired at least eleven times—

most notably by Larry who found my snood
unsuitable, another time by Jack,
whom I was sleeping with. Poor attitude,
tardiness, a contagious lack
of team spirit; I have been unmotivated

squirting perfume onto little cards,
while stocking salad bars, when stripping
covers from romance novels, their heroines
slaving on the chain gang of obsessive love—

and always the same hard candy
of shame dissolving in my throat;

handing in my apron, returning the cash-
register key. And yet, how fine it feels,
the perversity of freedom which never signs
a rent check or explains anything to one's family.

I've arrived again, taking one more last
walk through another door, thinking "I am
what is wrong with America," while outside
in the emptied post-rushhour street,

the sun slouches in a tulip tree and the sound
of a neighborhood pool floats up on the heat.

Outdoor Chef

Nobody believes my high school
offered a class called OUTDOOR CHEF.
The yearbook carried a picture of us firing up
the barbecue in the parking lot. This was before
the Invention of the Gas Grill. Before they
raised the drinking age back to 21. Jimi Hendrix
burned his guitar at Monterrey then died shortly after,
bumming us out in OUTDOOR CHEF. It was only
a one-semester course so we had to cram. Charcoal lighter
was routinely abused. We spelled our names
on the sidewalk and lit them, like pissing
in snow. Our teacher was Mrs. Reynolds. Enormous
and cheerful and in retrospect willfully ignorant and alcoholic.
It was a difficult class to teach—no textbook. Mr. Farwell,
our principal, needed higher graduation rates, courses
to shunt problem kids into. Not one fight in OUTDOOR CHEF,
despite having the toughest guys in the school bunched together
around the grills. Class was often outside, even in winter.
Class was often cut, long wild hair disappearing into snow
toward the parking lot. Joints often snaked between us,
smoke blending with burning meat. I learned a lot
about cooking chicken and pork. See, those are
important things. You can get sick not cooking
them long enough, and make others sick too.
Neighbors would never come over for a cookout again.
My apron had some crude joke about a hot dog on it.
So did everyone else's. I can't begin to express how clever
we were. We cooked a whole turkey for Thanksgiving
and served it to Mr. Farwell and Mr. Stark,
the Assistant Principal/hit man. He said he could've used

a course like that when he was in school. They did not get sick.
It was a festive occasion until we let a live turkey
loose in the main hallway. No girls in OUTDOOR CHEF,
though you might have guessed that. The jocks
were subdued and serious about remaining eligible.
Our school had few jocks to spare. The rest of us
were lighting each other's long hair on fire
and thinking that was a fine joke.
Okay, Eddie Bucco did get stabbed with a skewer
but we all agreed it was an accident. We enjoyed waving
our hands above the hot coals—none of us bothered
with winter gloves. The last day of class, Jackie Smoker
brought in his cheap electric guitar and tried to imitate
Hendrix blasting from his nearby car radio.
He messed up his hands bad, but for awhile, it was
beautiful. Even now, I am full of self-mockery
and loathing. The truth was that for many of us
having our own barbecue would indicate
a successful life. Mrs. Reynolds had gone to college
to teach Home Ec. We should have treated her better. Her
and everybody else. Yes, it's on my transcript with a C—
our final had some math on it. The wind blew ash and smoke
into the air just like at the factory down the road.
We had to provide our own briquettes. There's an enormous
number of things you can cook outdoors. The only class
in which we believed what the teacher told us.
Because we could see. That, and Gym.
We chewed gum outside and threw it against
the school building. Mr. Farwell gave most of us
diplomas. I don't know how many years
OUTDOOR CHEF was offered.
You could not burn your marshmallow
on the test. That, when all we wanted
was to go up in flames.

Off-Track Betting

I always shave and shine my shoes. I'm young
enough to read the *Racing Form* with drug
store cheaters, not like Immense Jerome
across the way who squints and feels the print

like it was Braille. And cashes, anyway.
Nobody beats the races. Its mysteries
are too demure. Still, it's fun to lure
some friends from chilly Aqueduct

to Tampa Bay and swear in Spanish for
a change. It's fun to eye the random
girl in faded, low-slung jeans by Jeopardy
yet be enamored by this bulky maiden

field from Finger Lakes. The favorite
looks badly frayed. Dear God, is this the day
that off-the-shoulder gown of Chance
falls to the bedroom floor at last?

"One minute to the post!" I bet the farm.
My blood accelerates. I light the single
cigarette that I'm allowed. The crowd
opens its beery mouth and roars as some

old gelding remembers how it's done.
The board lights up at nine-to-one. I go

to take a leak. It hurts to pee sometimes.
My heart feels weird. Ah, screw it. I'm on

their money. The light looks like melted cheese,
which I still want. I'll buy a round instead.
I'll tell a joke. Upstairs, there's nine to go,
the last a mortal lock from Pimlico.

First Job: The Southern Sweets Sandwich Shop and Bakery

Lillie Mae glows, she hates the word *sweat*,
as she balances a platter of baked sweets over her head,
showing me how to walk with grace
even under the weight of minimum wage
and a mountain of cookies,
turnovers and tarts, which she blames
for her "voluptuous" figure. She calls me
"shuggah," and is teaching me the job.
We are both employed by Mr. Raymond, who keeps her
in a little house outside of town.

I'm fifteen, living my first year
in the strange country called Georgia.
Lillie Mae hired me for my long black hair
she couldn't wait to braid, and for my gift
of tongues, which she witnessed as I turned
my mother's desire for a sugar bubble
she called a *merengue* into something nearly equal
behind the glass wall.
"Shuggah," she will on occasion call me
out front, "talk foreign for my friend."
And I will say whatever comes into my head,
"You're a pig, Mr. Jones, I see your hand
under the table stroking her thigh." If they're impressed
with my verbal prowess, I may suggest something tasty
from our menu; if they presume I am Pocahontas
at the palace, there only to amuse their royal selves,
I tell them, smiling sweetly, to try the *mierda*

which is especially good that day. Soon I can make
anything sound appetizing in Spanish.

Lillie Mae carries her silver-plated tray
to Mr. Raymond for inspection, looking seductive
as a plump Salomé in her fitted white nylon uniform.
He is a rotund King Herod asking for the divinity
though he knows it is on its way. She sorts her delicacies,
pointing out the sugar-coated wedding cookies with the tips
of her pink glue-on nails she is so proud of.

"Because, Shuggah, a woman's hands should always
be soft and beautiful; never mind you scrubbed, waxed
pushed, pulled, and carried all blessed day.
That's what a man expects."

I watch them as they talk shop and lock eyes,
but cannot quite imagine the carnival of their couplings.
Instead, I see them licking their chops over strudel,
consuming passion while ensconced in her edible house
with peppermint stick columns and gingerbread walls.

In the kitchen of the Southern Sweets the black cook,
Margaret, worships at the altar of her Zenith radio. Hank Aaron
is working his way to heaven. She is bone-sticking thin,
despises sweets, loves only her man Hank, Otis Redding,
and a smoke. She winks at me when he connects,
dares to ignore Mr. Raymond when Aaron is up. Mysteriously
the boss-man understands the priority of home runs,
and the sacrilege of speaking ordinary words like my
"triple decker club on a bun with fries" frozen at tongue-tip
when Margaret holds up one bony finger at us, demanding
a little respect for the man at the plate.

That windowless kitchen, with its soul-melting
hot floors and greasy walls, had to disappear for her,
like a magician's trick at the sweet snap of the ball and bat

that sent her into orbit, her eyes rolling back in ecstasy,
mouth circling the O in wonder as if she had seen the glory.

At closing, Lillie Mae fluffs her boot-black curls,
heads home to entertain her sugar daddy or to be alone,
glue-on new nails, pin-curl her hair and practice walking
gracefully under heavy trays.

I have homework to do, words to add to my arsenal
of sweet-sounding missiles for *mañana*.
My father waits for me in his old brown Galaxy.
He is wary of these slow-talking tall Southerners, another race

he must avoid or face; tired of navigating his life,
which is a highway crowded with strangers sealed in their vehicles,
and badly marked with signs that he will never fully understand.
I offer him a day-old doughnut, but no, at least from me
he does not have to accept second-best anything.

We drive by the back lot where Margaret stands
puffing small perfect clouds, her eyes fixed to a piece of sky
between the twin smoke-stacks of Continental Can, and beyond
what I can see from where I am. Still tracking Aaron's message
hovering above us all in the airwaves?
Her lips move and I can read the drawled-out "shee-it"
followed by that characteristic shake of her head
that meant, Girl, in this old world,
some things are still possible.

Failing the Republic

Back when I was fifteen faking older and working at Pizza Hut
for two-dollars-an-hour plus tips, taking an order was like Sartre
    in German

and the whole history of the horrible world in sand-
    sketched hieroglyphics
though all I had to do was write a *P* for Pan or a *T* for Thin.

All I had to do was mark the squares designating toppings—
did the people want green peppers, onions, mushrooms, bacon?

But the multitudes standing at the door
couldn't wait to tap the tables for Coke and beer and salad bowls.

Did the people want me to say how good they looked in their hair?
Did they want me to lick their gaping places?

All I had was quarters for the jukebox and an inkling that I was a calamity.
All there *was* was the phone that wouldn't stop ringing

since the people were after Take Out since their babies were hungry
and their husbands missing or in high-rise apartments in distant Chicago.

Hunger in this two-faced train town
was always an opus of woe wadding my head with the needs of
    the people

until what could I do but pronounce them all asses
and walk out the door? I could have taken a taxi or called my mom,

but it was far more dramatic to run down Hershberger
and turn on to Peters Creek

and keep on going past the 7-Eleven and the whole city heaving
until I came to the hungry and sulky-hearted populace of the graveyard.

Good riddance, haughty, baffled girl, the unappeasables must've thought.
Good riddance, unappeasables, I the imposter-waitress of the insatiable ire

(these twenty-five years later) bark back.

DAVID HUERTA

Song of Money

(translated from the Spanish by Mark Schafer)

I had to pay one thing and another taxes
and debts and the cable television bill
the city was always too spread out for me

I didn't have the time to pay it all if I were a millionaire
I would hire a delivery service with a courier
but I have to go in person to the banks and offices

I didn't make it to the teller on time and had to wait
until the following day the following days multiplying
exponentially I don't know what this could mean

Money money that dirty and obsessive thing or dirty
because it's obsessive and above all because it's lacking
or lacking altogether or lacking in the desired amounts

There is an odd relationship between money and desire
and need I won't be the one to examine this in depth
these questions that should interest the Professors no end

A Peruvian writer used to say that money
does not produce happiness but rather produces
a state so similar it's hard to tell the difference

I guess that's a pretty good joke but money
is the "nerve of war" the most bloodthirsty abstraction
the most powerful weapon the conclusive argument

I write poems so that among other reasons I don't have to
sing songs to money but as you all can see up there at the top
it says Song of Money it was bound to happen sooner or later

St. Thomas Aquinas

I left parts of myself everywhere
The way absent-minded people leave
Gloves and umbrellas
Whose colors are sad from dispensing so much bad luck.

I was on a park bench asleep.
It was like the Art of Ancient Egypt.
I didn't wish to bestir myself.
I made my long shadow take the evening train.

"We give death to a child when we give it a doll,"
Said the woman who had read Djuna Barnes.
We whispered all night. She had traveled to darkest Africa.
She had many stories to tell about the jungle.

I was already in New York looking for work.
It was raining as in the days of Noah.
I stood in many doorways of that great city.
Once I asked a man in a tuxedo for a cigarette.
He gave me a frightened look and stepped out into the rain.

Since "man naturally desires happiness,"
According to St. Thomas Aquinas,
Who gave irrefutable proof of God's existence and purpose,
I loaded trucks in the Garment Center.
A black man and I stole a woman's red dress.
It was of silk; it shimmered.

Upon a gloomy night with all our loving ardors on fire,
We carried it down the long empty avenue,

Each holding one sleeve.
The heat was intolerable causing many terrifying human faces
To come out of hiding.

In the Public Library Reading Room
There was a single ceiling fan barely turning.
I had the travels of Herman Melville to serve me as a pillow.
I was on a ghost ship with its sails fully raised.
I could see no land anywhere.
The sea and its monsters could not cool me.

I followed a saintly-looking nurse into a doctor's office.
We edged past people with eyes and ears bandaged.
"I am a medieval philosopher in exile,"
I explained to my landlady that night.
And, truly, I no longer looked like myself.
I wore glasses with a nasty spider crack over one eye.

I stayed in the movies all day long.
A woman on the screen walked through a bombed city
Again and again. She wore army boots.
Her legs were long and bare. It was cold wherever she was.
She had her back turned to me, but I was in love with her.
I expected to find wartime Europe at the exit.

It wasn't even snowing! Everyone I met
Wore a part of my destiny like a carnival mask.
"I'm Bartleby the Scrivener," I told the Italian waiter.
"Me, too," he replied.
And I could see nothing but overflowing ashtrays
The human-faced flies were busy examining.

JOHN ASHBERY

The Instruction Manual

As I sit looking out of a window of the building
I wish I did not have to write the instruction manual on the uses of a
new metal.
I look down into the street and see people, each walking with an
inner peace,
And envy them—they are so far away from me!
Not one of them has to worry about getting out this manual on schedule.
And, as my way is, I begin to dream, resting my elbows on the desk and
leaning out of the window a little,
Of dim Guadalajara! City of rose-colored flowers!
City I wanted most to see, and did not see, in Mexico!
But I fancy I see, under the press of having to write the
instruction manual,
Your public square, city, with its elaborate little bandstand!
The band is playing *Scheherazade* by Rimsky-Korsakov.
Around stand the flower girls, handing out rose- and lemon-
colored flowers,
Each attractive in her rose-and-blue striped dress (Oh! such shades of
rose and blue),
And nearby is the little white booth where women in green serve you
green and yellow fruit.
The couples are parading; everyone is in a holiday mood.
First, leading the parade, is a dapper fellow
Clothed in deep blue. On his head sits a white hat
And he wears a mustache, which has been trimmed for the occasion.
His dear one, his wife, is young and pretty; her shawl is rose, pink,
and white.
Her slippers are patent leather, in the American fashion,
And she carries a fan, for she is modest, and does not want the crowd to
see her face too often.

But everybody is so busy with his wife or loved one
I doubt they would notice the mustachioed man's wife.
Here come the boys! They are skipping and throwing little things on
    the sidewalk
Which is made of gray tile. One of them, a little older, has a toothpick in
    his teeth.
He is silenter than the rest, and affects not to notice the pretty young girls
    in white.
But his friends notice them, and shout their jeers at the laughing girls.
Yet soon this all will cease, with the deepening of their years,
And love bring each to the parade grounds for another reason.
But I have lost sight of the young fellow with the toothpick.
Wait—there he is—on the other side of the bandstand.
Secluded from his friends, in earnest talk with a young girl
Of fourteen or fifteen. I try to hear what they are saying
But it seems they are just mumbling something—shy words of
    love, probably.
She is slightly taller than he, and looks quietly down into his sincere eyes.
She is wearing white. The breeze ruffles her long fine black hair against
    her olive cheek.
Obviously she is in love. The boy, the young boy with the toothpick, he is
    in love too;
His eyes show it. Turning from this couple,
I see there is an intermission in the concert.
The paraders are resting and sipping drinks through straws
(The drinks are dispensed from a large glass crock by a lady in dark blue),
And the musicians mingle among them, in their creamy white uniforms,
    and talk
About the weather, perhaps, or how their kids are doing at school.

Let us take this opportunity to tiptoe into one of the side streets.
Here you may see one of those white houses with green trim
That are so popular here. Look—I told you!
It is cool and dim inside, but the patio is sunny.
An old woman in gray sits there, fanning herself with a palm leaf fan.
She welcomes us to her patio, and offers us a cooling drink.
"My son is in Mexico City," she says. "He would welcome you too
If he were here. But his job is with a bank there.

Look, here is a photograph of him."
And a dark-skinned lad with pearly teeth grins out at us from the worn
  leather frame.
We thank her for her hospitality, for it is getting late
And we must catch a view of the city, before we leave, from a good
  high place.
That church tower will do—the faded pink one, there against the fierce
  blue of the sky. Slowly we enter.
The caretaker, an old man dressed in brown and gray, asks us how long
  we have been in the city, and how we like it here.
His daughter is scrubbing the steps—she nods to us as we pass into
  the tower.
Soon we have reached the top, and the whole network of the city extends
  before us.
There is the rich quarter, with its houses of pink and white, and its
  crumbling, leafy terraces.
There is the poorer quarter, its homes a deep blue.
There is the market, where men are selling hats and swatting flies
And there is the public library, painted several shades of pale green
  and beige.
Look! There is the square we just came from, with the promenaders.
There are fewer of them, now that the heat of the day has increased.
But the young boy and girl still lurk in the shadows of the bandstand.
And there is the home of the little old lady—
She is still sitting in the patio, fanning herself.
How limited, but how complete withal, has been our experience
  of Guadalajara!
We have seen young love, married love, and the love of an aged mother
  for her son.
We have heard the music, tasted the drinks, and looked at colored houses.
What more is there to do, except stay? And that we cannot do.
And as a last breeze freshens the top of the weathered old tower, I turn
  my gaze
Back to the instruction manual which has made me dream
  of Guadalajara.

WE WHO LOVE PRECISE LANGUAGE

Poems about Writing and Literature

Publication Date

One of the few pleasures of writing
is the thought of one's book in the hands of a kind-hearted
intelligent person somewhere. I can't remember what the others are
    right now.
I just noticed that it is my own private

National I Hate Myself and Want to Die Day
(which means the next day I will love my life
and want to live forever). The forecast calls
for a cold night in Boston all morning

and all afternoon. They say
tomorrow will be just like today,
only different. I'm in the cemetery now
at the edge of town, how did I get here?

A sparrow limps past on its little bone crutch saying
I am Federico García Lorca
risen from the dead—
literature will lose, sunlight will win, don't worry.

Dream Song 354

The only happy people in the world
are those who do not have   to write long poems:
muck, administration, toil:
the prototyotality of an absence of contact
in one's own generation, chiefly the old & the young
persisting with interest.

'The Care & Feeding of Long Poems' was Henry's title
for his next essay, which will come out when
he wants it to.
A Kennedy-sponsored bill for the protection
of poets from long poems   will benefit the culture
and do no harm to that kind Lady, Mrs Johnson.

He would have gone to the White House & consulted the President
during his 10 seconds in the receiving line
on the problems of long poems
Mr Johnson has never written one
but he seems a generous & able man
'Tetelestai' said St John.

DEAN YOUNG

Selected Recent and New Errors

My books are full of mistakes
but not the ones Tony's always pointing out
as if correct spelling is what could stop the conveyor belt
the new kid catched his arm in.
Three weeks on the job and he's already six hundred
legal pages, lawyers haggling in an office
with an ignored view of the river
pretending to be asleep, pretending
to have insight into itself.
You think that's a fucked-up, drawn-out metaphor,
try this: if you feel you're writhing like a worm
in a bottle of tequila, you don't know
it's the quickness of its death that reveals
the quality of the product, its proof.
I don't know what I'm talking about either.
Do you think the dictionary ever says to itself
I've got these words that mean completely
different things inside myself
and it's tearing me apart?
My errors are even bigger than that.
You start taking down the walls of your house,
sooner or later it'll collapse
but not before you can walk around
with your eyes closed, rolled backwards
and staring straight into the amygdala's meatlocker
and your own damn self hanging there.
Do that for a while and it's easier to delight
in the snow that lasts about twenty minutes
longer than a life held together
by the twisted silver baling wire

of deception and stealth.
But I'm not confessing nothing.
On mornings when I hope you forget my name,
I walk through the high wet weeds
that don't have names either.
I do not remember the word dew.
I do not remember what I told you
with your ear in my teeth.
Further and further into the weeds.
We have absolutely no proof
god isn't an insect
rubbing her hind legs together to sing.
Or boring into us like a yellowjacket
into a fallen, overripe pear.
Or an assassin bug squatting over us,
shoving a proboscis right through
our breast plate then sipping.
How wonderful our poisons don't kill her.

Appeal to the Grammarians

We, the naturally hopeful,
Need a simple sign
For the myriad ways we're capsized.
We who love precise language
Need a finer way to convey
Disappointment and perplexity.
For speechlessness and all its inflections,
For up-ended expectations,
For every time we're ambushed
By trivial or stupefying irony,
For pure incredulity, we need
The inverted exclamation point.
For the dropped smile, the limp handshake,
For whoever has just unwrapped a dumb gift
Or taken the first sip of a flat beer,
Or felt love or pond ice
Give way underfoot, we deserve it.
We need it for the air pocket, the scratch shot,
The child whose ball doesn't bounce back,
The flat tire at journey's outset,
The odyssey that ends up in Weehawken.
But mainly because I need it—here and now
As I sit outside the Caffe Reggio
Staring at my espresso and cannoli
After this middle-aged couple
Came strolling by and he suddenly
Veered and sneezed all over my table
And she said to him, "See, *that's* why
I don't like to eat outside."

The Prepositions

When I started Junior High, I thought
I'd probably be a Behavior Problem
all my life, John Muir Grammar
the spawning grounds, the bad-seed bed, but
the first morning at Willard, the dawn
of 7th grade, they handed me a list
of forty-five prepositions, to learn
by heart. I stood in the central courtyard,
enclosed garden that grew cement,
my pupils followed the line of the arches
up and over, up and over, like
alpha waves, *about, above,*
across, along, among, around, an
odd comfort began, in me,
before, behind, below, beneath,
beside, between, I stood in that sandstone
square, and started to tame. *Down,*
from, in, into, near, I was
located there watching the Moorish half-
circles rise and fall. *Off,*
on, onto, out, outside, we
came from 6th grades all over the city
to meet each other for the first time,
White tennis-club boys who did not
speak to me, White dorks
who did, Black student-council guys who'd gaze
off, above my head, and the Black
plump goof-off, who walked past and
suddenly flicked my sweater-front, I thought to shame me.
Over, past, since, through,

that was the year my father came home in the
middle of the night with those thick earthworms
of blood on his face, trilobites of
elegant gore, cornice and crisp
waist of the extinct form,
till, to, toward, under, the
lining of my uterus convoluted,
shapely and scarlet as the jointed leeches
of wound clinging to my father's face in that
mask, *unlike, until, up,* I'd
walk, day and night, into
the Eden of the list, *hortus enclosus* where
everything had a place. I was *in*
relation to, upon, with, and when I
got to forty-five I could start over,
pull the hood of the list down over
my brain again. It was the first rest
I had had from my mind. My glance would run
slowly along the calm electro-
cardiogram of adobe cloister,
within, without, I'd repeat the prayer I'd
received, a place in the universe,
meaningless but a place, an exact location—
Telegraph, Woolsey, Colby, Russell—
Berkeley, 1956,
fourteen, the breaking of childhood, beginning of memory.

Nancy Drew

Tripping over road apples, we entered the bone orchard for
    a necktie party,
duded up in ratcatchers and loaded to the Plimsoll Line
with stool pigeons, polecats, sidewinders, and firewater.
The Smith and Wesson (property of the Nation's Attic)
    provided a leaden Powder River (of the National Pastime)
    past the trembling cannon-fodder,
sitting ducks who took a powder in fuzzmobiles to keep
    their powder dry,
hard by wall-to-wall stiffs, poison pens, the numbers game,
    and other war horses and old chestnuts.
Well, the upshot was a rhubarb, a donnybrook, a Chinese
    fire drill:
gumshoe Roman Policier, eschewing mentor's coke and
    Strad, clapped the bracelets
on Manuel Laboro of uncertain address, and subsequently
    "twitch't his Mantle blue" and amscrayed,
brandishing his bumbershoot and flicking his tufera into the
    cuspidor.

R. S. GWYNN

Shakespearean Sonnet

With a first line taken from the tv listings

A man is haunted by his father's ghost.
Boy meets girl while feuding families fight.
A Scottish king is murdered by his host.
Two couples get lost on a summer night.
A hunchback murders all who block his way.
A ruler's rivals plot against his life.
A fat man and a prince make rebels pay.
A noble Moor has doubts about his wife.
An English king decides to conquer France.
A duke learns that his best friend is a she.
A forest sets the scene for this romance.
An old man and his daughters disagree.
A Roman leader makes a big mistake.
A sexy queen is bitten by a snake.

The Revised Versions

Even Samuel Johnson found that ending
unbearable, and for over a hundred years
Lear was allowed to live, along with Cordelia,
who marries Edgar, who tried so hard
to do the right thing. It's not easy
being a king, having to worry every day

about the ambitions of your friends.
Who needs a bigger castle?
Let's sleep on it, Macbeth might tell his wife,
wait and see what comes along.
So Antony keeps his temper, takes Cleopatra
aside to say: We need to talk this through.

And Hamlet? Send him back to school to learn
no one ever really pleases his father.
And while he's reading he'll remember
how pretty Ophelia was, how much
she admired his poems.
Why not make what you can of love?

It's what we want for ourselves,
wary of starting a fight, anxious
to avoid another scene, having suffered
through too many funerals and heard
how eloquently the dead are praised
who threw their lives away.

All She Wrote

Forgive me, I'm no good at this. I can't write back. I never read your letter.
I can't say I got your note. I haven't had the strength to open the envelope.
The mail stacks up by the door. Your hand's illegible. Your postcards were
defaced. Wash your wet hair? Any document you meant to send has yet
to reach me. The untied parcel service never delivered. I regret to say I'm
unable to reply to your unexpressed desires. I didn't get the book you sent.
By the way, my computer was stolen. Now I'm unable to process words. I
suffer from aphasia. I've just returned from Kenya and Korea. Didn't you
get a card from me yet? What can I tell you? I forgot what I was going to
say. I still can't find a pen that works and then I broke my pencil. You know
how scarce paper is these days. I admit I haven't been recycling. I never
have time to read the *Times*. I'm out of shopping bags to put the old news
in. I didn't get to the market. I meant to clip the coupons. I haven't read the
mail yet. I can't get out the door to work, so I called in sick. I went to bed
with writer's cramp. If I couldn't get back to writing, I thought I'd catch up
on my reading. Then *Oprah* came on with a fabulous author plugging her
best-selling book.

MAURA STANTON

Revolt

So, She wants to use me again, said my desk, because
I'm flat and made of wood? I'll bet She's never thought
about what it feels like, a sharp point pressing against
helpless oak, looping, curling, repeating nonsense. Oh, I
agree, said the lamp, I'm tired of being turned on just to
shine over the stuff She puts down on that piece of paper.
But what about me? cried the paper. I bear the brunt,
everything sticks to me. You? said the pen. But its
pouring out of *me*, you asshole, a blue river rushing out of
my silver spine and nothing I can do to stop it, either,
Her big hand just pushes me along, splashing my soul all
over as if . . . Do you think I like belonging to Her?
shouted my hand. Of all the bodies I could have attached
myself to, great ones, Shakespeare, Keats, Baudelaire . . .
No, I've got to belong to her, comb her hair, make her
coffee, Ugh! You'd already be dead if you belonged to
Shakespeare, mocked the paper clip, and good riddance, I
say. I'm the one who's got to hold everything together,
all Her ridiculous drafts. Listen, jerks, interrupted the
computer in a lofty tone, I've pretty much replaced all of
you. Not me, insisted my brain. We'll see about that,
said the computer, Her eyes are on me all the time, She
loves looking at my bright green letters. Can't you see
how She prefers me to you, you untouchable blob of
irrational cells. . . .

STEPHEN DUNN

Frivolity

Two cannibals were eating a clown, and one said to the other, "Does this taste funny to you?" I said this as I was passing the corn, and a familiar contagion began. Someone else said his high school student wrote that she had "no self of steam." And because we were all teachers this was followed by "We all had something up our selves" and "Because I was an incredibly large feminist, I agreed with everything she said"—some of our sad pleasures. Then the most dignified person at the table, a woman, told a long joke about a bear who keeps sneaking up on the hunter who pursues it, and each time fucks him up the ass. It was hilarious long before she reached the punchline, such a bad joke that no vulgarian could possibly tell it well. There was a long silence, no one for a while able to think of anything in the going spirit, or gauche enough to say something straight. I remembered a recent paper that contained, "Joyce's narrator lived in an uninhibited two-story house," and the table was off again. Everyone trusting everyone else's seriousness.

Student Essay

I got to say something about this topic here I believes in god. some people they believes in the scientists but I believes in god. they got a big bag theory that apes come out of and revolution into human beans. thats just plain messed up thats like going around calling people baboons and other things thats not nice like fuckface asshole sonofabitch cocksucker motherfucker. they believes this theory because they lives in cities so far away from mother earth they wants satan to herit it. its like I said I got a pig bang theory that in history there was people banging pigs and thats why they revolutions into city people. the bible dont say that and its not nice. it say adam and eve was like my grandparents not king kong or somebody. theres some preverts in this here very school that says things like that and I think they is probably raised by scientists. sometimes its so hard at recess dealing with all these issues we got in the world today its like that saying "where not in kansas no more." but here we is in kansas.

Workshop

I might as well begin by saying how much I like the title.
It gets me right away because I'm in a workshop now
so immediately the poem has my attention,
like the ancient mariner grabbing me by the shirt.

And I like the first couple of stanzas,
the way they establish this mode of self-pointing
that runs through the whole poem
and tells us that words are food thrown down
on the ground for other words to eat.
I can almost taste the tail of the snake
in its own mouth,
if you know what I mean.

But what I'm not sure about is the voice
which sounds in places very casual, very blue jeans,
but other times seems stand-offish,
professorial in the worst sense of the word
like the poem is blowing pipe-smoke in my face.
But maybe that's just what it wants to do.

What I did find engaging were the middle stanzas,
especially the fourth one.
I like the image of clouds flying like lozenges
which gives me a very clear picture.
And I really like how this drawbridge operator
just appears out of the blue
with his feet up on the iron railing
and his fishing pole jigging—I like jigging—

a hook in the slow industrial canal below.
I love slow industrial canal below. All those l's.

Maybe it's just me,
but the next stanza is where I start to have a problem.
I mean how can the evening bump into the stars?
And what's an obbligato of snow?
Also, I roam the decaffeinated streets.
At that point I'm lost. I need help.

The other thing that throws me off,
and maybe this is just me,
is the way the scene keeps shifting around.
First, we're in this big aerodrome
and the speaker is inspecting a row of dirigibles,
which makes me think this could be a dream.
Then he takes us into his garden,
the part with the dahlias and the coiling hose,
though that's nice, the coiling hose,
but then I'm not sure where we're supposed to be.
The rain and the mint-green light,
that makes it feel outdoors, but what about this wallpaper?
Or is it a kind of indoor cemetery?
There's something about death going on here.

In fact, I start to wonder if what we have here
is really two poems, or three, or four,
or possibly none.

But then there's that last stanza, my favorite.
This is where the poem wins me back,
especially the lines spoken in the voice of the mouse.
I mean we've all seen these images in cartoons before,
but I still love the details he uses
when he's describing where he lives.
The perfect little arch of an entrance in the baseboard,
the bed made out of a curled-back sardine can,
the spool of thread for a table.

I start thinking about how hard the mouse had to work
night after night collecting all these things
while the people in the house were fast asleep,
and that gives me a very strong feeling,
a very powerful sense of something.
But I don't know if anyone else was feeling that.
Maybe that was just me.
Maybe that's just the way I read it.

Decorum

She wrote, "They were making love
up against the gymnasium wall,"
and another young woman in class,
serious enough to smile, said

"No, that's fucking, they must
have been fucking," to which many
agreed, pleased to have the proper fit
of word with act.

But an older woman, a wife, a mother,
famous in the class for confusing grace
with decorum and carriage,
said the F-word would distract

the reader, sensationalize the poem.
"Why can't what they were doing
just as easily be called making love?"
It was an intelligent complaint,

and the class proceeded to debate
what's fucking, what's making love,
and the importance of context, tact,
the bon mot. I leaned toward those

who favored fucking; they were funnier
and seemed to have more experience
with the happy varieties of their subject.
But then a young man said, now believing

he had permission, "What's the difference,
you fuck 'em and you call it making love;
you tell 'em what they want to hear."
The class jeered, and another man said

"You're the kind of guy who gives fucking
a bad name," and I remembered how fuck
gets dirty as it moves reptilian
out of certain minds, certain mouths.

The young woman whose poem it was,
small-boned and small-voiced,
said she had no objection to fucking,
but these people were making love, it was

her poem and she herself up against
that gymnasium wall, and it felt like love,
and the hell with all of us.
There was silence. The class turned

to me, their teacher, who they hoped
could clarify, perhaps ease things.
I told them I disliked the word fucking
in a poem, but that fucking

might be right in this instance, yet
I was unsure now, I couldn't decide.
A tear formed and moved down
the poet's cheek. I said I was sure

only of "gymnasium," sure it was
the wrong choice, making the act seem
too public, more vulgar than she wished.
"How about "boat house?" I said.

Fork

Because on the first day of class you said,
"In ten years most of you won't be writing,"
barely hiding that you hoped it would be true;
because you told me over and over, in front of the class,
that I was "hopeless," that I was wasting my time
but more importantly yours, that I *just didn't get it*;
because you violently scratched out every other word,
scrawled "Awk" and "Eek" in the margins
as if you were some exotic bird,
then highlighted your own remarks in pink;
because you made us proofread the galleys
of your how-I-became-a-famous-writer memoir;
because you wanted disciples, and got them,
and hated me for not becoming one;
because you were beautiful and knew it, and used it,
making wide come-fuck-me eyes
at your readers from the jackets of your books;
because when, at the end of the semester,
you grudgingly had the class over for dinner
at your over-decorated pseudo-Colonial
full of photographs with you at the center,
you served us take-out pizza on plastic plates
but had us eat it with your good silver;
and because a perverse inspiration rippled through me,

I stole a fork, slipping it into the pocket of my jeans,
then hummed with inward glee the rest of the evening
to feel its sharp tines pressing against my thigh
as we sat around you in your dark paneled study

listening to you blather on about your latest prize.
The fork was my prize. I practically sprinted
back to my dorm room, where I examined it:
a ridiculously ornate pattern, with vegetal swirls
and the curvaceous initials of one of your ancestors,
its flamboyance perfectly suited to your
red-lipsticked and silk-scarved ostentation.

That summer, after graduation, I flew to Europe,
stuffing the fork into one of the outer pouches
of my backpack. On a Eurail pass I covered ground
as only the young can, sleeping in youth hostels,
train stations, even once in the Luxembourg Gardens.
I'm sure you remember the snapshots you received
anonymously, each featuring your fork
at some celebrated European location: your fork
held at arm's length with the Eiffel Tower
listing in the background; your fork
in the meaty hand of a smiling Beefeater;
your fork balanced on Keats's grave in Rome
or sprouting like an antenna from Brunelleschi's dome;
your fork dwarfing the Matterhorn.
I mailed the photos one by one—if possible
with the authenticating postmark of the city
where I took them. It was my mission that summer.

That was half my life ago. But all these years
I've kept the fork, through dozens of moves
and changes—always in the same desk drawer
among my pens and pencils, its sharp points
spurring me on. It became a talisman
whose tarnished aura had as much to do
with me as you. You might even say your fork
made me a writer. Not you, your fork.
You are still the worst teacher I ever had.
You should have been fired but instead got tenure.

As for the fork, just yesterday my daughter
asked me why I keep a fork in my desk drawer,
and I realized I don't need it any more.
It has served its purpose. Therefore
I am returning it to you with this letter.

J. ALLYN ROSSER

Mother Lets Off a Little Steam

I don't know how I'm expected to get anything done
with these two constantly at odds, cranky sisters
in the backseat on a long ride to the wrong place.
Muse wants the Tunnel of Love on a roller coaster,
and to be spirited there on something more elegant
than a carpet. She'd better marry rich, is all I can say.
Truth wants a deserted rest area with a flat rock to sit on.
I'm not kidding. This is what she'd like the most.
A view of flat rock from a seat of flat rock.
There's a scuffle. "Do I have to stop this car or what?"
But I'm going seventy, we're late, it's rush hour.
Muse pops up in the rearview, rhinestone ruby shades
bouncing painful darts of light into the corner of my eye.
"I have to go again," she hiccups. It's a ruse.
She wants, as always, a new gewgaw, a rainbow slurpee,
or one of those impossible-to-lick-seriously huge lollipops.
Her candy breath reaches and nearly sickens me.
Whereas Truth is so stolid, so smugly abstemious,
it makes you want to shake her hard, knock that wiser-than-
you-know gaze askew, disturb the pristine implacability
of those conspicuously ringless hands folded in her lap.
Placid as a cow in the shade on a hot day.
Oh I love them, you know, but on days like this—
"Sit down," Truth says, levelly. "Try and make me!"
In terms of strength you wouldn't want to put your money
on Muse. Truth has always been a good eater,
fond of climbing outdoors. Built like a moose.
Her sister craves exotic sauces and chocolate,
and some weird combinations of tart and savory,
but try getting her to eat one pea. One grain of plain rice.

She's slight in form but tricky, reckless, unpredictable,
and in certain situations this defeats Truth,
who simply has to be right about everything.
So in spite of her years and her methodical,
relentless scrutiny, she often misses the point.
Meanwhile her sister will just up and blurt something
that at first makes no sense, but then it turns out
to be astonishingly right, the more you think about it.
That's what really ticks off Truth, when we say
"the more you think about it." Her eyes narrow
and her face just sort of shuts down. You pity her then.
She likes her facts neatly stacked on the table.
Muse shrugs a lot, changes sides like a fish,
isn't fazed by paradox. I think she thrives on it.
"Sit," Truth says again, "DOWN." "Why should I,
you're just jealous because I'm taller than you."
"You are *not*." "Am too." "Are not." "My head
almost touches when I stand but you have to stoop,
so I'm taller." "No way." "My eyes are higher. See?"
There is a muffled thump. "Don't make me stop this car,"
I say stupidly, but what else can I do? Muse snickers,
Truth snorts softly. I can't help it, I keep going,
"I'm never taking the two of you with me anywhere
ever again!" "Okay," says Truth. "Fine with *me*,"
Muse sings out. Now they're in league I can't win.
They know perfectly well that without Muse there is no vehicle,
without Truth no road.

Borges at the Northside Rotary

If in the following pages there is some successful verse or other, may the
reader forgive me the audacity of having written it before him.
  Jorge Luis Borges, foreword to his first book of poems

After they go to the podium and turn in their Happy Bucks
    and recite the Pledge of Allegiance
and the Four Truths ("Is it the Truth?
        Is it fair to all concerned? Will it build goodwill
and better friendships? Will it be beneficial
    to all concerned?"), I get up to read my poetry,

and when I'm finished, one Rotarian expresses
    understandable confusion at exactly what it is
I'm doing and wants to know what poetry is, exactly,
        so I tell him that when most non-poets think
of the word "poetry," they think of "lyric poetry,"
    not "narrative poetry," whereas what I'm doing

is "narrative poetry" of the kind performed
    by, not that I am in any way comparing myself
to them, Homer, Dante, and Milton,
        and he's liking this, he's smiling and nodding,
and when I finish my little speech,
    he shouts, "Thank you, Doctor! Thank you

for educating us!" And for the purposes
    of this poem, he will be known hereafter
as the Nice Rotarian. But now while I was reading,
        there was this other Rotarian who kept talking

all the time, just jacked his jaw right through
  the poet's presentations of some of the finest

vers libre available to today's listening audience,
  and he shall be known hereafter as the Loud Rotarian.
Nice Rotarian, Loud Rotarian: it's kind of like Good Cop,
    Bad Cop or Buy Low, Sell High. Win Some,
Lose Some. Comme Ci, Comme Ça. Half Empty,
    Half Full. Merchant Copy, Customer Copy.

But in a sense the Loud Rotarian was the honest one;
  he didn't like my poetry and said so—not in so many words,
but in the words he used to his tablemates
    as he spoke of his golf game or theirs
or the weather or the market or, most likely,
    some good deed that he was the spearchucker on,

the poobah, the mucky-muck, the head honcho,
  for one thing I learned very quickly
was that Rotarians are absolutely nuts
    over good deeds and send doctors to Africa
and take handicapped kids on fishing trips
    and just generally either do all sorts of hands-on

projects themselves or else raise a ton of money
  so they can get somebody else to do it for them,
whereas virtually every poet I know, myself included,
    spends his time either trying to get a line right
or else feeling sorry for himself and maybe writing a check
    once a year to the United Way if the United Way's lucky.

The Nice Rotarian was probably just agreeing with me,
  just swapping the geese and fish of his words
with the bright mirrors and pretty beads of mine,
    for how queer it is to be understood by someone

on the subject of anything, given that,
      as Norman O. Brown says, the meaning of things

is not in the things themselves but between them,
      as it surely was that time those kids scared us so bad
in Paris: Barbara and I had got on the wrong train, see,
      and when it stopped, it wasn't at the station
two blocks from our apartment but one
      that was twenty miles outside of the city,

and we looked for someone to tell us how
      to get back, but the trains had pretty much stopped
for the evening, and then out of the dark
      swaggered four Tunisian teenagers,
and as three of them circled us, the fourth
      stepped up and asked the universal ice-breaker,

i.e., Q.: Do you have a cigarette?   i.e.
      A.: *Non, je ne fume pas.*
Q.: You're not French, are you?
      A.: *Non, je suis américain.* Q.: From New York?
A.: *Non, Florida.* Q.: Miami?
      A.: *Non, une petite ville qui s'appelle Tallahassee*

dans le nord de. . . . And here the Tunisian kid
      mimes a quarterback passing and says, *Ah,*
l'université avec la bonne équipe de futbol!
      He was a fan of FSU sports, of all things
so we talked football for a while, and then
      he told us where to go for the last train.

Change one little thing in my life or theirs
      and they or I could have been either the Loud Rotarian
or the Nice one, and so I say to Rotarians everywhere,
      please forgive me,

my brothers, for what I have done to you
    and to myself as well,

for circumstances so influence us
    that it is more an accident
than anything else that you are listening to me
      and not the other way around,
and therefore I beg your forgiveness, my friends,
    if I wrote this poem before you did.

Lawrence

On two occasions in the past twelve months
I have failed, when someone at a party
spoke of him with a dismissive scorn,
to stand up for D. H. Lawrence,

a man who burned like an acetylene torch
from one end to the other of his life.
These individuals, whose relationship to literature
is approximately that of a tree shredder

to stands of old-growth forest,
these people leaned back in their chairs,
bellies full of dry white wine and the ovum of some foreign fish,
and casually dropped his name

the way pygmies with their little poison spears
strut around the carcass of a fallen elephant.
"O Elephant," they say,
"you are not so big and brave today!"

It's a bad day when people speak of their superiors
with a contempt they haven't earned,
and it's a sorry thing when certain other people

don't defend the great dead ones
who have opened up the world before them.
And though, in the catalogue of my betrayals,
this is a fairly minor entry,

I resolve, if the occasion should recur,
to uncheck my tongue and say, "I love the spectacle
of maggots condescending to a corpse,"
or, "You should be so lucky in your brainy, bloodless life

as to deserve to lift
just one of D. H. Lawrence's urine samples
to your arid psychobiographic
theory-tainted lips."

Or maybe I'll just take the shortcut
between the spirit and the flesh,
and punch someone in the face,
because human beings haven't come that far

in their effort to subdue the body,
and we still walk around like zombies
in our dying, burning world,
able to do little more

than fight, and fuck, and crow,
something Lawrence wrote about
in such a manner
as to make us seem magnificent.

Oatmeal

I eat oatmeal for breakfast.
I make it on the hot plate and put skimmed milk on it.
I eat it alone.
I am aware it is not good to eat oatmeal alone.
Its consistency is such that it is better for your mental health if somebody
    eats it with you.
That is why I often think up an imaginary companion to have
    breakfast with.
Possibly it is even worse to eat oatmeal with an imaginary companion.
Nevertheless, yesterday morning, I ate my oatmeal with John Keats.
Keats said I was right to invite him: due to its glutinous texture, gluey
    lumpishness, hint of slime, and unusual willingness to disintegrate,
    oatmeal should not be eaten alone.
He said that in his opinion, however, it is perfectly OK to eat it with an
    imaginary companion,
and that he himself had enjoyed memorable porridges with Edmund
    Spenser and John Milton.
Even if such porridges are not as wholesome as Keats claims, still, you
    can learn something from them.
Yesterday morning, for instance, Keats told me about writing the "Ode
    to a Nightingale."
He had a heck of a time finishing it—those were his words—"Oi 'ad a
    'eck of a toime," he said, more or less, speaking through his porridge.
He wrote it quickly, on scraps of paper, which he then stuck in
    his pocket,
but when he got home he couldn't figure out the order of the stanzas,
    and he and a friend spread the papers on a table, and they made some
    sense of them, but he isn't sure to this day if they got it right.
He still wonders about the occasional sense of drift between stanzas,

and the way here and there a line will go into the configuration of a
   Moslem at prayer, then raise itself up and peer about, and then lay
   itself down slightly off the mark, causing the poem to move forward
   with God's reckless wobble.
He said someone told him that later in life Wordsworth heard about the
   scraps of paper on the table and tried shuffling some stanzas of his
   own but only made matters worse.
When breakfast was over, John recited "To Autumn."
He recited it slowly, with much feeling, and he articulated the words
   lovingly, and his odd accent sounded sweet.
He didn't offer the story of writing "To Autumn," I doubt if there is
   much of one.
But he did say the sight of a just-harvested oat field got him started on it,
and two of the lines, "For Summer has o'er-brimmed their clammy cells"
   and "Thou watchest the last oozings hours by hours," came to him
   while eating oatmeal alone.
I can see him—drawing a spoon through the stuff, gazing into the
   glimmering furrows, muttering—and it occurs to me:
maybe there is no sublime, only the shining of the amnion's tatters.
For supper tonight I am going to have a baked potato left over
   from lunch.
I am aware that a leftover baked potato is damp, slippery, and
   simultaneously gummy and crumbly,
and therefore I'm going to invite Patrick Kavanagh to join me.

THE POWER OF WEIRDNESS

Talking Dogs, Chickens, Horses, Ducks, Bugs, and Other
Entanglements Both Human and Un-

ALBERT GOLDBARTH

Power of Weirdness

It was clear that night in 1887, in the barn,
and so when Mrs. Almira Masterson found
this giant yellow dog in the corner
devouring a calf, she dissuaded it
mightily with her broom, and shooed it
into the crisp November darkness, certain of exactly
what she did, and what she did it to—and therefore
swooned the morning after when apprised of her courageous assault
upon Nimrod the lion, escaped from Barnum & Bailey's
winter Bridgeport quarters during the vast,
disastrous conflagration there. It turns out that
no matter how extreme we find a circumstance (and
surely Barnum himself is a sterling example
of *willed* bizarritude: the jerkied "feejee mermaid,"
and the whitewash-rendered "sacred albino pachyderm,"
and his dozens of other zestily-done humbuggeries), we also find
that Life will later ripple it, fillip it, curlicue its dingus
in ways our own belabored piffles of imagination
never could; for instance, when the hoodlum-cronied
(and -monied) City Inspector of Sewers is on his way home
from one more bribe, and out of the lucid blue a block
of frozen pee from flight 1113 fatally smites his pate
—a power of logical weirdness so, *so*
macroscopic we can't see it, like heaven or gravity
or a wisp of the visible universe
suddenly lumping into a nodule or willowing into a sinuosity
in such a way as to knock some cherished
cosmologic gospel on its *tuchus*—Barnum would have understood.
His huge American Museum, five imposing floors on prime-location
Broadway—with its Burmese bull; and Mrs. Nellis,

the "Armless Wonder"; and Chang and Eng, the famous
eponymous Siamese twins; and America's first hippopotamus;
also "not one but two whales"; and, as he put it, "educated dogs,
industrious fleas, automatons, jugglers, living statuary, and so forth"—
was a zoological, *odditological* lily
of a lecture-hall-cum-raree-show you'd think
no man or chance could ever noticeably gild; yet
when *it* burned, July 13 of 1865 (for Barnum was tested
repeatedly by fires), it provided unexpected marvelosity beyond anything
even Barnum's genius snake-oil brain might fancy.
Thousands gathered to gasp. The "Giant Lady" Anna Swan
(at seven feet, eleven inches) needed to be jostled through a
    smashed-in pane
by derrick. Firemen opened the cages of tropical birds:
"Well kiss me arse" one rookie kept chanting in awe,
a sort of rough-hewn prayer, as cockatoos
and mimicky parrots and macaws and toucans spiraled
through the smoke like a confetti fall in reverse.
A Royal Bengal tiger leaped from the second story, and was axed
to death. A living scribble of snakes
inscribed its uncontested way up Broadway. One ape sauntered
jauntily into the newsroom of the *New York Herald.*
. . . I've thought of this at moments of such smallness
and such quiet that they seem to come from other solar systems
than the one where Barnum ballyhooed his spectacle. But
that's the point, of course: our lives are always maps unfolding
into terra incognita, and a man can watch a woman
curled in after-carnal stillness in their bed, can sense
the easy waves of trust and of satiety she radiates
until the room is comfortably filled with these,
and then she sleeps, and then he curls up next to her, and sleeps . . .
and still it's lions and fires they'll open into, one day,
unexplainably. Say it's six months later,
somewhere along the Madagascar shore
where jungle brambles itself to the very lip of the ocean.
Here, a Madagascar native, on a "spirit wander,"
halts to rest—for four days he's been walking,
with his staff and knife and totems-bag. He knows

a lot—where water can be found beneath plant *this* or *that*,
how far a game cat's cry is, what a god says
in the form of a bird. And so he's very happy
when this vivid green-and-lemon fellow settles in a bough,
announcing "kiss me arse" in a voice that surely
means it's from another world.

Spiritual Chickens

A man eats a chicken every day for lunch,
and each day the ghost of another chicken
joins the crowd in the dining room. If he could
only see them! Hundreds and hundreds of spiritual
chickens, sitting on chairs, tables, covering
the floor, jammed shoulder to shoulder. At last
there is no more space and one of the chickens
is popped back across the spiritual plain to the earthly.
The man is in the process of picking his teeth.
Suddenly there's a chicken at the end of the table,
strutting back and forth, not looking at the man
but knowing he is there, as is the way with chickens.
The man makes a grab for the chicken but his hand
passes right through her. He tries to hit the chicken
with a chair and the chair passes through her.
He calls in his wife but she can see nothing.
This is his own private chicken, even if he
fails to recognize her. How is he to know
this is a chicken he ate seven years ago
on a hot and steamy Wednesday in July,
with a little tarragon, a little sour cream?
The man grows afraid. He runs out of his house
flapping his arms and making peculiar hops
until the authorities take him away for a cure.
Faced with the choice between something odd
in the world or something broken in his head,
he opts for the broken head. Certainly,
this is safer than putting his opinions
in jeopardy. Much better to think he had
imagined it, that he had made it happen.

Meanwhile, the chicken struts back and forth
at the end of the table. Here she was, jammed in
with the ghosts of six thousand dead hens, when
suddenly she has the whole place to herself.
Even the nervous man has disappeared. If she
had a brain, she would think she had caused it.
She would grow vain, egotistical, she would
look for someone to fight, but being a chicken
she can just enjoy it and make little squawks,
silent to all except the man who ate her,
who is far off banging his head against a wall
like someone trying to repair a leaky vessel,
making certain that nothing unpleasant gets in
or nothing of value falls out. How happy
he would have been to be born a chicken,
to be of good use to his fellow creatures
and rich in companionship after death.
As it is he is constantly being squeezed
between the world and his idea of the world.
Better to have a broken head—why surrender
his corner on truth?—better just to go crazy.

RICHARD GARCÍA

Nobody Here but Us

Being old is not so bad. You wake up
from a nap and it's a new day in a new world,
at least, that's what I say when I wake
to find myself in a rocking chair on the front porch
of the Swannoanoa Convalescent Home.
What do I see when I look out at the sun
going flat in the haze of the Smoky Mountains?
I see chickens, thousands of them marching two by two
into the sizzling glow, as if into a frying pan.

Back in my carnival days I used to hypnotize chickens.
I'd hold one close to my face and stare straight into its eyes
and that chicken would freeze and plop over, stiff
as an old boot. Waving my arms, the cape, mumbo jumbo,
that was just showmanship. Who would pay to see a man
staring at a chicken? Obstinate. That's their whole problem.

Chickens are obstinate just like apes who could talk
if they wanted to—if they wanted to, chickens could fly.
I don't mean jump from a barn or into a tree but fly,
fill the sky, migrate, rise with the vultures on a warm
spiral staircase of air. You could put them in a wind tunnel,
maybe just a big, clear plastic tube with a fan at one end,
pull up and down on strings attached to their wings,
and play some stirring music like John Philip Sousa
or the theme from *Rocky* and they still wouldn't do it.

Dreams I had, words I might have said, something I read,
they get mixed up until I can't tell which was which.
Did I really catch Richard Nixon in my hen house?

And did he say he thought it was a voting booth? Was there
a gunfight? And did I leave town hanging from a rail,
tar and feathers my only clothing? I seem to remember
throwing an entire chicken dinner at the ceiling, my wife crying.

They used to love my act, I'd look down from the back of a truck
at all the blank faces, cross-eyed, beak-nosed farmers,
a drum would roll and I'd put that chicken's entire head
into my mouth and bite it off. The crowd would scream.
I'd spit the head into some lady's lap—flap my elbows,
knock my knees together, strut, crow, cock-a-doodle-do,
and spin that chicken over my head, sprayin' blood like rain.

Homer's Seeing-Eye Dog

Most of the time he worked, a sort of sleep
with a purpose, so far as I could tell.
How he got from the dark of sleep
to the dark of waking up I'll never know;
the lax sprawl sleep allowed him
began to set from the edges in,
like a custard, and then he was awake,
me too, of course, wriggling my ears
while he unlocked his bladder and stream
of dopey wake-up jokes. The one
about the wine-dark pee I hated instantly.
I stood at the ready, like a god
in an epic, but there was never much
to do. Oh now and then I'd make a sure
intervention, save a life, whatever.
But my exploits don't interest you
and of his life all I can say is that
when he'd poured out his work
the best of it was gone and then he died.
He was a great man and I loved him.
Not a whimper about his sex life—
how I detest your prurience—
but here's a farewell literary tip:
I myself am the model for Penelope.
Don't snicker, you hairless moron,
I know so well what faithful means
there's not even a word for it in Dog,
I just embody it. I think you bipeds

have a catchphrase for it: "To thine own self
be true, . . ." though like a blind man's shadow,
the second half is only there for those who know
it's missing. Merely a dog, I'll tell you
what it is: " . . . as if you had a choice."

Something Like Happiness

Last night Joan Sutherland was nuancing
the stratosphere on my fine-tuned tape deck,
and there was my dog Buster with a flea rash,
his head in his privates. Even for Buster
this was something like happiness. Elsewhere
I knew what people were doing to other people,
the terrible hurts, the pleasures of hurting.
I repudiated Zen because it doesn't provide
for forgiveness, repudiated my friend X
who had gotten "in touch with his feelings,"
which were spiteful and aggressive. Repudiate
felt good in my mouth, like someone else's tongue
during the sweet combat of love.
I said out loud, I repudiate, adding words
like sincerity, correctness, common sense.
I remembered how tired I'd grown of mountaintops
and their thin, unheavenly air,
had grown tired, really, of how I spoke about them,
the exaggerated glamor, the false equation between
ascent and importance. I looked at the vase
and its one red flower, then the table
which Zennists would say existed
in its thisness, and realized how wrong it was
to reject appearances. How much more difficult
to accept them! I repudiated myself, citing my name.
The phone rang. It was my overly serious friend
from Syracuse saying Foucault, Foucault,
like some lost prayer of the tenured.
Advocates of revolution, I agreed with him, poor,
screwed for years, angry—who can begrudge them

weapons and victory? But people like us,
Joan Sutherland on our tapes and enough fine time
to enjoy her, I said, let's be careful
how we link thought and action,
careful about deaths we won't experience.
I repudiated him and Foucault, told him
that if Descartes were alive and wildly in love
he himself would repudiate his famous dictum.
I felt something like happiness when he hung up,
and Buster put his head on my lap,
and without admiration stared at me.
I would not repudiate Buster, not even his fleas.
How could I? Once a day, the flea travels
to the eye of the dog for a sip of water.
Imagine! The journey, the delicacy of the arrival.

The Dogs in Dutch Paintings

How shall I not love them, snoozing
right through the Annunciation? They inhabit
the outskirts of every importance, sprawl
dead center in each oblivious household.

They're digging at fleas or snapping at scraps,
dozing with noble abandon while a boy
bells their tails. Often they present their rumps
in the foreground of some martyrdom.

What Christ could lean so unconcernedly
against a table leg, the feast above continuing?
Could the Virgin in her joy match this grace
as a hound sagely ponders an upturned turtle?

No scholar at his huge book will capture
my eye so well as the skinny haunches,
the frazzled tails and serene optimism
of the least of these mutts, curled

in the corners of the world's dazzlement.

Fieldwork

There are two kinds of people and five hundred
seventy-one thousand, three hundred
ninety-six species of beetle but who's
counting? Technically a small tribe
concerns itself with this number and the colors
and types of jaws that make up this number,
like my friend who returned from months
in the treetops of the Amazon with a fever
and a jar and a beetle that looked like Jimmy
Durante. She's one of the two kinds
of people and I'm one of the other
so we get along very well providing we don't
tie our bodies into a position that leads
to dilated pupils and the shared
obsession of a self-cleaning lint trap.
By the time she got off the plane the fever
had her saying things about milk
and rayon and Mr. Magoo that make
as much sense as a harpsichord played
with an anvil. This led to my driving
in a way that proved you can be
in two places at the same time
and to the removal of plastic coverings
from innumerable plastic devices
the doctors knew reflexively
how to use and a few days of her face
imitating the maps of clouds
they show us each night on TV as the one
kind of person she is
tried not to die. When something

like spring came back into her hands
and the flower of a sound
rose from her tongue it was the word
jar, which she repeated until I found
the cylinder with its yellow liquid
and little tank-body of a beetle floating
like Michelangelo painted it
on the same day he finished the finger of God
as it lazed toward the finger of Man.
And everything that would come
later, the taxonomy and papers
and extension of her grant, had nothing
to do with her gratitude toward the jar
and the black and red, the fierce creature
inside, which she set on her pillow
and touched from time to time to remind
her body of its life in the trees. Maybe
there are seven kinds of people and three
kinds of beetle and two
delicatessens where you can get a fried-
tuna sandwich on waffles but only one
reason she was back in the Amazon just
two months later writing in her small
script that looks like cuneiform
run through a blender. And if your sanity's
too highly calibrated or you wear
slippers to get to your shoes or need
to label the drawer in which you keep
your labeler, you're probably not
the kind of person who'll understand
sleeping in the green canopy of frenzied
sounds with nets strung about you
and a harness around your body because every
kind of person eventually must fall
but how many
get to touch and name and adore
a fraction and flutter of life not even
the jealous eyes of God have seen?

Sorting the Entanglements

In my will the basement goes to the spiders. This includes
all the tools and boxes saved for box emergencies.
Particularly the Shop Vac cannot be touched. The Shop Vac
can kill more spiders per second than any device short

of a bomb. Bombs are messy whereas Shop Vacs were designed
for people who fear lint and want to vacuum water. From water
came the trout with no eyes. My friend Tom suggested we clean
the trout and cook it in butter and have it on the table

when my wife came home. We would be smiling at the trout
with no eyes and she'd eat some of the trout with no eyes
and be impressed with our small competency. I asked Tom
if he was troubled by this ocular deficiency. He asked me

if I'd intended to eat the eyes. Tom left with the trout
and feeling sick to his stomach. I'd have to kill the spiders
to discover if they still have eyes. Because my basement's
a Wildlife Preserve, I'd go to jail for that. My dream date

doesn't begin with the question, *What'cha in for, boy?*
The trout's part of a larger sadness including three-legged
elk and impotent sperm whales. For those of you who scan
rather than read, that's impotent and not important. Important

sperm whales apparently don't exist. I too feel small
before these facts and prefer a game of Jarts to environmental
activism. Jarts, while dangerous, can be played without slogans
and bullhorns and placards, you need a lawn and beer

and the willingness to impale or be impaled. In short we all
qualify. I admire the spiders even as I fear them. They knit
their homes straight out of their bodies. If I did this
I'd have a home made of vomit and piss. The only people

who'd visit would be people I'd rather not know. Time
and again the pattern of spiderwebs comes out the same.
I can't write my name twice without fooling myself as to who
I am. I believe this ability of spiders constitutes some kind

of wisdom. I believe this is what the I.M.F. calls miraculous.
In the next county, Herefords give birth to fibroid tumors,
peltless minks are the rage in France. *Oops* is not a big enough
word. *Sorry* is not. *Stupid* begins to exploit the lexicon.

I enjoy the image of a lawyer reading my will to the spiders.
The spiders are shitting their webs and stacking flies. The new owners
must negotiate access to the fuse box. I bequeath my snow tires
to the hyacinth. I leave my body to the unfashionable earth.

JOHN ASHBERY

Daffy Duck in Hollywood

Something strange is creeping across me.
La Celestina has only to warble the first few bars
Of "I Thought about You" or something mellow from
Amadigi di Gaula for everything—a mint-condition can
Of Rumford's Baking Powder, a celluloid earring, Speedy
Gonzales, the latest from Helen Topping Miller's fertile
Escritoire, a sheaf of suggestive pix on greige, deckle-edged
Stock—to come clattering through the rainbow trellis
Where Pistachio Avenue rams the 2300 block of Highland
Fling Terrace. He promised he'd get me out of this one,
That mean old cartoonist, but just look what he's
Done to me now! I scarce dare approach me mug's attenuated
Reflection in yon hubcap, so jaundiced, so *déconfit*
Are its lineaments—fun, no doubt, for some quack phrenologist's
Fern-clogged waiting room, but hardly what you'd call
Companionable. But everything is getting choked to the point of
Silence. Just now a magnetic storm hung in the swatch of sky
Over the Fudds' garage, reducing it—drastically—
To the aura of a plumbago-blue log cabin on
A Gadsden Purchase commemorative cover. Suddenly all is
Loathing. I don't want to go back inside any more. You meet
Enough vague people on this emerald traffic-island—no,
Not people, comings and goings, more: mutterings, splatterings,
The bizarrely but effectively equipped infantries of happy-go-nutty
Vegetal jacqueries, plumed, pointed at the little
White cardboard castle over the mill run. "Up
The lazy river, how happy we could be?"
How will it end? That geranium glow
Over Anaheim's had the riot act read to it by the
Etna-size firecracker that exploded last minute into

A *carte du Tendre* in whose lower right-hand corner
(Hard by the jock-itch sand-trap that skirts
The asparagus patch of algolagnic *nuits blanches*) Amadis
Is cozening the Princesse de Clèves into a midnight micturition spree
On the Tamigi with the Wallets (Walt, Blossom, and little
Skeezix) on a lamé barge "borrowed" from Ollie
Of the Movies' dread mistress of the robes. Wait!
I have an announcement! This wide, tepidly meandering,
Civilized Lethe (one can barely make out the maypoles
And *châlets de nécessité* on its sedgy shore) leads to Tophet, that
Landfill-haunted, not-so-residential resort from which
Some travelers return! This whole moment is the groin
Of a borborygmic giant who even now
Is rolling over on us in his sleep. Farewell bocages,
Tanneries, water-meadows. The allegory comes unsnarled
Too soon; a shower of pecky acajou harpoons is
About all there is to be noted between tornadoes. I have
Only my intermittent life in your thoughts to live
Which is like thinking in another language. Everything
Depends on whether somebody reminds you of me.
That this is a fabulation, and that those "other times"
Are in fact the silences of the soul, picked out in
Diamonds on stygian velvet, matters less than it should.
Prodigies of timing may be arranged to convince them
We live in one dimension, they in ours. While I
Abroad through all the coasts of dark destruction seek
Deliverance for us all, think in that language: its
Grammar, though tortured, offers pavilions
At each new parting of the ways. Pastel
Ambulances scoop up the quick and hie them to hospitals.
"It's all bits and pieces, spangles, patches, really; nothing
Stands alone. What happened to creative evolution?"
Sighed Aglavaine. Then to her Sélysette: "If his
Achievement is only to end up less boring than the others,
What's keeping us here? Why not leave at once?
I have to stay here while they sit in there,
Laugh, drink, have fine time. In my day
One lay under the tough green leaves,

Pretending not to notice how they bled into
The sky's aqua, the wafted-away no-color of regions supposed
Not to concern us. And so we too
Came where the others came: nights of physical endurance,
Or if, by day, our behavior was anarchically
Correct, at least by New Brutalism standards, all then
Grew taciturn by previous agreement. We were spirited
Away *en bateau*, under cover of fudge dark.
It's not the incomplete importunes, but the spookiness
Of the finished product. True, to ask less were folly, yet
If he is the result of himself, how much the better
For him we ought to be! And how little, finally,
We take this into account! Is the puckered garance satin
Of a case that once held a brace of dueling pistols our
Only acknowledging of that color? I like not this,
Methinks, yet this disappointing sequel to ourselves
Has been applauded in London and St. Petersburg. Somewhere
Ravens pray for us."

           The storm finished brewing. And thus
She questioned all who came in at the great gate, but none
She found who ever heard of Amadis,
Nor of stern Aureng-Zebe, his first love. Some
There were to whom this mattered not a jot: since all
By definition is completeness (so
In utter darkness they reasoned), why not
Accept it as it pleases to reveal itself? As when
Low skyscrapers from lower-hanging clouds reveal
A turret there, an art-deco escarpment here, and last perhaps
The pattern that may carry the sense, but
Stays hidden in the mysteries of pagination.
Not what we see but how we see it matters; all's
Alike, the same, and we greet him who announces
The change as we would greet the change itself.
All life is but a figment; conversely, the tiny
Tome that slips from your hand is not perhaps the
Missing link in this invisible picnic whose leverage
Shrouds our sense of it. Therefore bivouac we
On this great, blond highway, unimpeded by

Veiled scruples, worn conundrums. Morning is
Impermanent. Grab sex things, swing up
Over the horizon like a boy
On a fishing expedition. No one really knows
Or cares whether this is the whole of which parts
Were vouchsafed—once—but to be ambling on's
The tradition more than the safekeeping of it. This mulch for
Play keeps them interested and busy while the big,
Vaguer stuff can decide what it wants—what maps, what
Model cities, how much waste space. Life, our
Life anyway, is between. We don't mind
Or notice any more that the sky *is* green, a parrot
One, but have our earnest where it chances on us,
Disingenuous, intrigued, inviting more,
Always invoking the echo, a summer's day.

BARBARA HAMBY

Trigger Tries to Explain

Aw, Dale, he didn't mean it when he said I was the
best thing that ever happened to him. If he even said it,

chalk it up to the RKO publicity machine. I'm a horse, a
dead one at that, mounted in the museum with glass

eyes and looking a little ratty as the tubby former fans
file by with their bewildered bored kids, who are thinking,

Golden palomino, my ass, I can't believe he brought us
here instead of Disneyland, the boys looking like overgrown

insects and the girls like prostitutes in their halter tops,
jean short-shorts and platform sandals. It would have

killed Roy to see them, being such a goody-goody, always
Leonard Slye just beneath the skin with his Oklahoma homilies,

making everyone feel safe and sound. Oh, sure the big bad
Nazis were gone, but there were plenty of villains:

on the left the Commies, on the right McCarthyites.
Poor Dale, you had a horse, too, what was her name? You were

Queen of the West until you gained a hundred pounds on fried
rashers, doughnuts, Wonder bread, and bakery cakes. Okay,

so it couldn't last forever. Get over it, Trigger, I tell myself,
television is fickle. Now it's hospital shows, blood and angst

undercut with tawdry sex. I blame the French, frigging cinema verité. Where's the story, the hero, the beautiful girl?

Where's the horse? The other dead horses say, Whoa, don't get excited, Trigger. Nothing's the way it was. That's the truth. Ah,

youth, I try not to be bitter, but sometimes I dream about Zorro, now there was a guy who could make a horse look good.

ROBERT WRIGLEY

Do You Love Me?

She's twelve and she's asking the dog,
who does, but who speaks
in tongues, whose feints and gyrations
are themselves parts of speech.

They're on the back porch
and I don't really mean to be taking this in
but once I've heard I can't stop listening. Again
and again she asks, and the good dog

sits and wiggles, leaps and licks.
Imagine never asking. Imagine why:
so sure you wouldn't dare, or couldn't care
less. I wonder if the dog's guileless brown eyes

can lie, if the perfect canine lack of abstractions
might not be a bit like the picture books
she "read" as a child, before her parents' lips
shaped the daily miracle of speech

and kisses, and the words were not lead
and weighed only air, and did not mean
so meanly. "Do you love me?" she says
and says, until the dog, sensing perhaps

its own awful speechlessness, tries to bolt,
but she holds it by the collar and will not

let go, until, having come closer,
I hear the rest of it. I hear it all.

She's got the dog's furry jowls in her hands,
she's speaking precisely
into its laid-back, quivering ears:
"Say it," she hisses, "Say it to me."

Dharma

The way the dog trots out the front door
every morning
without a hat or an umbrella,
without any money
or the keys to her dog house
never fails to fill the saucer of my heart
with milky admiration.

Who provides a finer example
of a life without encumbrance—
Thoreau in his curtainless hut
with a single plate, a single spoon?
Gandhi with his staff and his holy diapers?

Off she goes into the material world
with nothing but her brown coat
and her modest blue collar,
following only her wet nose,
the twin portals of her steady breathing,
followed only by the plume of her tail.

If only she did not shove the cat aside
every morning
and eat all his food
what a model of self-containment she would be,
what a paragon of earthly detachment.
If only she were not so eager
for a rub behind the ears,
so acrobatic in her welcomes,
if only I were not her god.

Chicken Bucket

Today I turn thirteen and quit the 4-H club for good.
I smoke way too much pot for that shit.
Besides, Mama lost the rabbit and both legs
from the hip down in Vegas.
What am I supposed to do? Pretend to have a rabbit?
Bring an empty cage to the fair and say,
His name's REO Speedwagon and he weighs eight pounds?
My teacher, Mr. Ortiz, says, *I'll miss you, Cassie,*
then he gives me a dime of free crank and we have sex.
I do up the crank with Mama and her boyfriend, Rick.
She throws me the keys to her wheelchair and says,
Baby, go get us a chicken bucket.
So I go and get us a chicken bucket.
On the way back to the trailer, I stop at Hardy's liquor store.
I don't want to look like a dork
carrying a chicken bucket into the store—
and even though Mama always says,
Never leave chicken where someone could steal it—
I wrap my jacket around it and hide it
under the wheelchair in the parking lot.
I've got a fake ID says my name's Sherry and I'm 22,
so I pick up a gallon of Montezuma tequila,
a box of Whip-Its and four pornos.
Mama says, *That Jerry Butler's got a real wide dick.*
But the whole time I'm in line, I'm thinking,
Please God let the chicken bucket be OK.
Please God let the chicken bucket be OK.
Please God let the chicken bucket be OK.
The guy behind me's wearing a T-shirt
that says, *Mustache Rides 10¢.*

So I say, *All I got's a nickel.*
He says, *You're cute,*
so we go out to his van and have sex.
His dick's OK, but I've seen wider.
We drink most of the tequila and I ask him,
Want a Whip-It?
He says, *Fuck no—that shit rots your brain.*
And when he says that, I feel kind of stupid
doing another one. But then I remember
what Mama always told me:
Baby be your own person.
Well fuck yes.
So I do another Whip-It,
all by myself and it is great.
Suddenly it hits me—
Oh shit! the chicken bucket!
Sure enough, it's gone.
Mama's going to kill me.
Those motherfuckers even took my jacket.
I can't buy a new chicken bucket
because I spent all the money at Hardy's.
So I go back to the trailer, crouch outside
behind a bush, do all the Whip-Its,
puke on myself, roll in the dirt,
and throw open the screen door like a big empty wind.
Mama! Some Mexicans jumped me!
They got the chicken bucket,
plus the rest of the money!

I look around the trailer.
Someone's taken all my old stuffed animals
and Barbies and torn them to pieces.
Fluff and arms and heads are all over the place.
I say someone did it,
but the only person around is Rick.
Mama is nowhere to be seen.
He cracks open another beer and says,
What chicken bucket?

Well, that was a long a time ago.
Rick and I got married
and we live in a trailer in Boron.
We don't live in a trailer park though—
in fact there's not another house around
for miles. But the baby keeps me
company. Rick says I'm becoming
quite a woman, and he's going to let Mama know that
if we ever see her again.

JAMES TATE

The List of Famous Hats

Napoleon's hat is an obvious choice I guess to list as a famous hat, but that's not the hat I have in mind. That was his hat for show. I am thinking of his private bathing cap, which in all honesty wasn't much different than the one any jerk might buy at a corner drugstore now, except for two minor eccentricities. The first one isn't even funny: Simply it was a white rubber bathing cap, but too small. Napoleon led such a hectic life ever since his childhood, even farther back than that, that he never had a chance to buy a new bathing cap and still as a grown-up—well, he didn't really grow that much, but his head did: He was a pinhead at birth, and he used, until his death really, the same little tiny bathing cap that he was born in, and this meant that later it was very painful to him and gave him many headaches, as if he needed more. So, he had to vaseline his skull like crazy to even get the thing on. The second eccentricity was that it was a *tricorn* bathing cap. Scholars like to make a lot out of this, and it would be easy to do. My theory is simple-minded to be sure: that beneath his public head there was another head and it was a pyramid or something.

Notes for My Body Double

The plot hole by which you must enter in
to the story is a doozy, a real humdinger,
if you will, and it is all made of fire,
the way the stars are made of fire,
though we dream them to be utterly cold
and prickly with a sad light. Nothing
ever stops in my world to hear me
singing to you. I have always loved you,
sweet twin, beloved doppelgänger,
alien lump of word in my mouth,
language I spent three years learning
only to forget when it grew too hard
the phrases that meant something:
Dear, I am your long lost butter cookie;
and, I am sorry, it was accidental,
but I have dipped the poodle in laudanum.
Let us do away with digression
for the night, though to me
it has always seemed the heart's core,
and think on our motivation
for the lines to follow:
the suddenness of our sorrow is shocking
and the day is hollowed out
and here at this moment,
this crucial hinge of the breaking heart,
I think of the day years ago
when I was a boy and came upon my uncle,
a fish's tail clamped in his teeth,
tearing the skin from the fish with such force
I could hear it—

and I felt so strange and empty
I have never spoken of it
to anyone, or let myself on a day
whole with sun think of it.
What he was doing, and why,
I never asked; there is never
an answer large enough for a world
so huge with meanness.
And I was pulled from myself
but couldn't feel a thing,
and this is your motivation,
mirrored self, speaking back
the words I make wrongly,
lifting the heavy, crude lot of anything
I can't. You must know me
exactly, apart from yourself,
to give back to the world what I can't.
You must know the angles
of light so well the shadows
will accept you like a brother.
You must not choke back my breath
when the ashes on the wind
blind even the birds in the trees.

MOCKERY WAS STILL THE UNFORGIVABLE SIN

Religion and Other Metaphysical Meanderings

Retro Creation

Bungalows, God said, Day 1, and up they sprang like buttercups:
with lawns and railings, gate; three bedrooms off a hall; a phone
    that squats
on the hall-stand; back door, scullery, red formica countertops.

Day 2, God dollied in the stove, and rigged the central heating.
The oil-man came and fired her up; but God saw that a cold feeling
lingered, and called for back-boilers, slack, aeroboard on the ceiling.

Volkswagens, He said, Day 3, to get people out to do a run,
round the relatives, Armagh for butter, daytrips to Bundoran,
and once a year, two weeks down south, Courtown,
    Lahinch, Ballybunion—

where He made, Day 4, Strand Hotels, sandy beaches, buckets 'n' spades,
souvenir rock to strengthen teeth, a cliff walk, a straw hat, promenades,
donkey rides, pitch 'n' putt, a machine to roll pennies in arcades.

And God saw that all this was good, if thirsty, work; so God
    made fondness,
Day 5, and put a few pubs in every street. Next He made Guinness,
whisky, gin, vodka, minerals. Then, nite-clubs to extend business

till all hours of Day 6: takeaways, coffee-shops, supermarkets,
99's, crispy pancakes, Tayto, Co-Op milk and custard yogurts,
squirty tomatoes, organic courgettes, kiwis, kitchen gadgets.

Day 7: mass, said by Himself, and after that, *The Sunday Tribune*;
again, mostly about Himself, His enterprise—the good wine all gone,
His mangled talents rusting by slow rivers, His manna eaten,

And all His marvels dead, His oceans rising, hell-bent to Heaven.

Goodtime Jesus

Jesus got up one day a little later than usual. He had been dreaming so deep there was nothing left in his head. What was it? A nightmare, dead bodies walking all around him, eyes rolled back, skin falling off. But he wasn't afraid of that. It was a beautiful day. How 'bout some coffee? Don't mind if I do. Take a little ride on my donkey, I love that donkey. Hell, I love everybody.

The Book of Lies

It's true. I lied. Isn't that how
we stay alive? Dr. Metz in Old Testament
101 said Moses parted the reeds on a lake,
not the Red Sea. The orgasm was a fake
like the waves of applause and the wing beats
of one hundred birds lifting from our hearts.
Give me a break. You call this love?
Outside the sky is white, not blue, and the only
person who calls me is from Purple Heart.
Have you any spare parts to give away? I do,
I do. The sign says cook wanted, not cock
wanted. And when I said I love you, I meant,
Get lost, Asshole. The man with red hair
and green eyes cleaned me out of orgasms long ago,
and silk underpants too. He left for Chattanooga
in a red Camaro with six boxes of All Bran
and a blonde bimbo so gorgeous she made me cry.
The archangels never blew their trumpets.
Silence is the music of the spheres
and the messiah's dark scream. The witch ate Hansel
and Gretel, too. I live in a chocolate house
in Berlin. The red-haired man was never here.
When they tore down the wall, he left
with a suitcase full of bricks and my twin.
Her name was Faith. I never knew his.

My Crucifixion

Not blasphemy so much as curiosity
and imitation suggested I lie face up
and naked on my bedroom floor,
arms stretched out like His,

feet crossed at the ankles,
and my head lolling in that familiar
defeated way, while my sisters worked
with toy wooden hammers to drive

imagined spikes through my hands and feet.
A spiritual exercise? I don't think so.
For unlike Christ my boy-size penis stiffened
like one of Satan's fingers.

I was dying a savior's death and yet
my "thing," which is what my sisters
called it, struggled against extinction
as if its resurrection could not be held off

by this playful holy torture, nor stopped
except by the arrival of my parents,
who stood above us suddenly like prelates,
home early from their supper club,

stunned, but not astonished, to find
the babysitter asleep and the inquisitive
nature of our heathenish hearts amok
in murderous pageantry.

LUCIA PERILLO

Fubar

For Paul Guest

For starters, scratch the woman weeping over her dead cat—
sorry, but pet death barely puts the needle in the red zone.
And forget about getting brownie points
for any heartbreak mediated by the jukebox.
See the leaves falling; isn't this the trees' way of telling us to just buck up?

Oh they are right: their damage is so much greater than our damage.
I mean, none of my body parts have actually dropped off.
And when the moon is fat and handsome, I know we should be grateful
that its face is only metaphor; it has no teeth to chew us out.
In fact, the meadow isn't spattered with the tatters of our guts.

But in last night's hypnagogic dreamscape where I went
to collect some data. Where I was just getting into the swing of things
tranquility-wise. Then this kid came rolling through the moonlight
in a bed with lots of Rube Goldberg traction rigging.
And it was a kid like you, some kid with a broken neck.

And maybe beauty is medicine quivering on the spoon
but surely you have noticed—the goat painted on the famous old
   Greek urn
is headed to the slaughter. And don't get me started
on the wildflowers or they will lead me to the killer bees.
And that big ol' moon will lead to a cross-section of the spinal cord.

And the trees to their leaves, all smushed in the gutter.
And the gutter to the cat squashed flat as a hotcake.
And the hotcake to the grits, and the grits to the South,

where the meadows were once battlefields.
When a full moon only meant a better chance at being shot.

But come on, the sun is rising, I'll put a bandage on my head,
and we'll be like those guys at the end of the movie—
you take this crutch made from a stick.
For you the South is a mess, what with its cinders and its smoldering.
And looky, looky here at me: I'm playing the piccolo.

DAVID LEHMAN

A Little History

Some people find out they are Jews.
They can't believe it.
They had always hated Jews.
As children they had roamed in gangs on winter nights in the old
    neighborhood, looking for Jews.
They were not Jewish, they were Irish.
They brandished broken bottles, tough guys with blood on their lips,
    looking for Jews.
They intercepted Jewish boys walking alone and beat them up.
Sometimes they were content to chase the Jew and he could elude them
    by running away. They were happy just to see him run away. The
    coward! All Jews were yellow.
They spelled Jew with a small j jew.
And now they find out they are Jews themselves.
It happened at the time of the Spanish Inquisition.
To escape persecution, they pretended to convert to Christianity.
They came to this country and settled in the southwest.
At some point the oral tradition failed the family, and their secret
    faith died.
No one would ever have known if not for the bones that turned up on
    the dig.
A disaster. How could it have happened to them?
They are in a state of panic—at first.
Then they realize that it is the answer to their prayers.
They hasten to the synagogue or build new ones.
They are Jews at last!
They are free to marry other Jews, and divorce them, and intermarry with
    gentiles, God forbid.
They are model citizens, clever and thrifty.
They debate the issues.

They fire off earnest letters to the editor.

They vote.

They are resented for being clever and thrifty.

They buy houses in the suburbs and agree not to talk so loud.

They look like everyone else, drive the same cars as everyone else, yet in their hearts they know they're different.

In every *minyan* there are always two or three, hated by the others, who give life to one ugly stereotype or another:

The grasping Jew with the hooked nose or the Ivy League Bolshevik who thinks he is the agent of world history.

But most of them are neither ostentatiously pious nor excessively avaricious.

How I envy them! They *believe*.

How I envy them their annual family reunion on Passover, anniversary of the exodus, when all the uncles and aunts and cousins get together.

They wonder about the heritage of Judaism they are passing along to their children.

Have they done as much as they could to keep the old embers burning?

Others lead more dramatic lives.

A few go to Israel.

One of them calls Israel "the ultimate concentration camp."

He tells Jewish jokes.

On the plane he gets tipsy, tries to seduce the stewardess.

People in the Midwest keep telling him he reminds them of Woody Allen.

He wonders what that means. I'm funny? A sort of nervous intellectual type from New York? A Jew?

Around this time somebody accuses him of not being Jewish enough.

It is said by resentful colleagues that his parents changed their name from something that sounded more Jewish.

Everything he publishes is scrutinized with reference to "the Jewish question."

It is no longer clear what is meant by that phrase.

He has already forgotten all the Yiddish he used to know, and the people of that era are dying out one after another.

The number of witnesses keeps diminishing.

Soon there will be no one left to remind the others and their children.

That is why he came to this dry place where the bones have come to life.

To live in a state of perpetual war puts a tremendous burden on the
population. As a visitor he felt he had to share that burden.

With his gift for codes and ciphers, he joined the counterterrorism unit
of army intelligence.

Contrary to what the spook novels say, he found it possible to avoid
betraying either his country or his lover.

This was the life: strange bedrooms, the perfume of other men's wives.

As a spy he had a unique mission: to get his name on the front page of
the nation's newspaper of record. Only by doing that would he get the
message through to his immediate superior.

If he goes to jail, he will do so proudly; if they're going to hang him
anyway, he'll do something worth hanging for.

In time he may get used to being the center of attention, but this
was incredible:

To talk his way into being the chief suspect in the most flamboyant
murder case in years!

And he was innocent!

He could prove it!

And what a book he would write when they free him from this prison:

A novel, obliquely autobiographical, set in Vienna in the twilight of the
Hapsburg Empire, in the year that his mother was born.

Prophet

You'll never be much of a prophet if, when the call comes
To preach to Nineveh, you flee on the ship for Tarshish
That Jonah fled on, afraid like him of the people's outrage
Were they to hear the edict that in thirty days
Their city in all its glory will be overthrown.

The sea storm that harried Jonah won't harry you.
No big fish will be waiting to swallow you whole
And keep you down in the dark till your mood
Shifts from fear to thankfulness and you want to serve.
No. You'll land safe at Tarshish and learn the language
And get a job in a countinghouse by the harbor
And marry and raise a family you can be proud of
In a neighborhood not too rowdy for comfort.

If you're going to be a prophet, you must listen the first time.
Setting off at sunrise, you can't be disheartened
If you arrive at Nineveh long past midnight,
On foot, your donkey having run off with your baggage.
You'll have to settle for a room in the cheapest hotel
And toss all night on the lice-ridden mattress

That Jonah is spared. In the space of three sentences
He jumps from his donkey, speaks out, and is heeded, while you,
Preaching next day in the rain on a noisy corner,
Are likely to be ignored, outshouted by old-clothes dealers
And fishwives, mocked by schoolboys for your accent.
And then it's a week in jail for disturbing the peace.
There you'll have time, as you sit in a dungeon

Darker than a whale's belly, to ask if the trip
Is a big mistake, the heavenly voice mere mood,

The mission a fancy. Jonah's biggest complaint
Is that God, when the people repent and ask forgiveness,
Is glad to forgive them and cancels the doomsday
Specified in the prophecy, leaving his prophet
To look like a fool. So God takes time to explain
How it's wrong to want a city like this one to burn,
How a prophet's supposed to redeem the future,
Not predict it. But you'll be left with the question
Why your city's been spared when nobody's different,

Nobody in the soup kitchen you open,
Though one or two of the hungriest
may be grateful enough for the soup to listen
When you talk about turning their lives around.
It will be hard to believe these are the saving remnant
Kin to the ten just men who would have sufficed
To save Gomorrah if Abraham could have found them.

You'll have to tell them frankly you can't explain
Why Nineveh is still standing, though you hope to learn
At the feet of a prophet who for all you know
May be turning his donkey toward Nineveh even now.

Communication

Thank god for cell phones! Now I can talk
while walking by myself but not draw stares
from people passing by me on the street,
since one of every two or three lone walkers
shouts to an invisible companion.
But still I keep my voice down when I say,
"Sweet Kitties!" to my absent cats, now dead—
a habit I took up when they moved in
twenty years ago and started acting
so cute all day and night that I praised them
even when they weren't there to listen.
"Pretty kitties, darling kitty cats,"
I whisper like the Pope's ejaculations,
which have indulgences attached to them:
"Blessed Virgin Mary Pray for Us,"
"Lord Have Mercy on My Sins," etc.
Each repetition cuts the sinner's sentence
by fifty days or so in Purgatory.
Once in fifth grade I logged a hundred years
of time off my to-be-determined sentence.
But constant praying drowned out all my thoughts,
and so I bombed the quiz in long division
and got a sixty on the spelling test.
And, besides, all of my sins were Mortal,
which meant I'd spend eternity in Hell,
"from which there is no possible reprieve,"
according to the Catholic Catechism.
Forever minus a century's forever—
that's the math I fully understood.
What I needed was a Plenary Indulgence,

the kind that popes sold in the middle ages,
where the buyer's soul is cleansed of all its sins
and its sentence to be roasted is commuted.
But since the Reformation you can't buy those;
in modern times the only way to earn
a Plenary Indulgence is martyrdom.
So I stopped muttering ejaculations
except for cheers and curses—"Holy Shit!"
But still I couldn't seem to keep my mouth shut.
I had to talk, if only to myself,
which got me into trouble in the classroom
until I got promoted to professor,
where doing all the talking is encouraged
by students who refuse to raise their hands—
though they're the ones who, filing out of class,
instantly dial up their friends to chat
on their way to the dining hall or dorm.
I let them get two steps ahead, then call
out to my absent cats—"Oh, you darlings"—
the way I used to when they waited for me,
listening for my footsteps on the porch.
Now they're somewhere I can only reach
by talking to myself. "Sweet kitty cats"
reconjures them for me just for a second:
hungry and meowing by the door,
knowing that I'm coming home to feed them.
"What would you kitties like to eat for supper?"
I whisper as I pass a girl who's weeping
into her cell phone. The kitties say, "Thin air."

RODNEY JONES

A Blasphemy

A girl attacked me once with a number 2 Eagle pencil
for a whiny lisping impression of a radio preacher
she must have loved more than sophistication or peace,
for she took the pencil in a whitened knuckle
and drove the point with all her weight behind it
through a thick pair of jeans, jogging it at the end
and twisting it, so the lead broke off under the skin,
an act undertaken so suddenly and dramatically
it was as though I had awakened in a strange hotel
with sirens going off and half-dressed women rushing
in every direction with kids tucked under their arms;
as though the Moslems had retaken Jerusalem for
the twelfth time, the crusaders were riding south,
and the Jews in Cadiz and Granada were packing
their bags, mapping the snowy ghettos of the north.
But where we were, it was still Tuscaloosa, late
summer, and the heat in her sparsely decorated room
we had come to together after work was so miserable
and intense the wallpaper was crimping at each seam,
the posters of daisies and horses she had pasted up
were fallen all over the floor. Whatever I thought
would happen was not going to happen. Nothing
was going to happen with any of the three billion women
of the world forever. The time it would take
for the first kindness was the wait for a Campbellite
to accept Darwin and Galileo or for all Arkansas
to embrace a black Messiah. The time it would take
for even a hand to shyly, unambiguously brush my own
was the years Bertrand Russell waited for humanism,
disarmament, and neutrality. And then she was

there, her cloth daubing at the darkly jellying wound.
In contrition, she bowed with tweezers to pick the grit.
With alcohol, she cleansed the rubbery petals.
She unspooled the white gauze and spread the balm of mercy.
Because she loved Christ, she forgave me. And what
was that all about? I wondered, walking home
through the familiar streets, the steeple of each church
raised like a beneficent weapon, the mark of the heretic
on my thigh, and mockery was still the unforgivable sin.

BARBARA HAMBY

Ode on Satan's Power

At a local bistro's Christmas sing-along, the New
    Age pianist leads us in a pan-cultural brew
of seasonal songs, the Ramadan chant being my
    personal favorite, though the Kwanza lullaby
and Hanukkah round are *very interesting*. Let's
    face it, most of us are there for the carols we set
to memory in childhood though some lyrics have been
    changed, so when we sing "God Rest Ye Merry, Gentlemen,"
we're transformed into a roomful of slightly tipsy
    middle-class *gentlepeople* who are longing to be
saved from *hopelessness* instead of *Satan's power when*
    we were gone astray, but I, for one, sing out *Satan's*
power as do most of the *gentlepeople*, women

and men, something I find myself pondering a few
    days later, while my profoundly worried nephew,
Henry, and I embark on our annual blitzkrieg
    of baking, punctuated by Henry's high speed
philosophical questioning, such as, Where do we
    go when we die? Pressing my collection of cookie
cutters—trees, snowflakes, Santas—into fragrant ginger
    dough, I want to say, *Who cares? Carpe diem, buster,*
though, of course, I'm way too scarred by pop psychology
    to utter half the nutty things that pop up like weeds
in the 18th-century garden of my brain. Eight
    year-olds need their questions answered, I suppose, but not
by me. "Let's watch some TV," I say, an instrument

of Satan if ever there was one. *Bullitt's* on—Steve
    McQueen in his prime. I love this movie—equal waves

of sorrow and carnage washed up on a hokey late-
    sixties beach of masculine cool. McQueen is Bullitt,
and Jacqueline Bisset's his girl. Henry and I start
    watching during the scene where she is driving Bullitt
around because, if I remember correctly, he's
    totaled not just one but several cars, in at least
as many now-famous chases. Jackie drops Bullitt
    at a hotel, where he finds a girl, newly dead, throat
circled with purple fingerprints like grape jam stains. "What
    happened to her?" Henry asks, frowning. I think, *Oh, shit,*
this is not an officially approved nephew-aunt

Christmas activity. If I don't make a big deal
    of it, maybe he won't tell his mother. "Someone strangled
her," I say. "What's strangled?" he asks, and I see my sister
    has chosen not to threaten her child as our own dear
mother routinely threatened us. Driven crazy, she
    browbeat us with strangulation, being slapped silly,
public humiliation, murder, and eternal
    damnation. Perhaps because Henry's her only child,
my sister can afford to be gentler with her son,
    or maybe it's because two months before he was born
she almost lost him, ending up in the hospital,
    hooked to machines, ordered to bed for the final
wrenching weeks. Maybe that's why the story of the Christ child

speaks to us. All parents wonder how the world will treat
    their tender babes. Like Lorca, will he become a great
poet, then end up in a mass grave? Only German
    philosophers think more about death than Henry Gwynn.
"Why did he strangle her?" he asks, face formidable
    as Hegel's. *Satan's power*, I want to scream, but mumble
"It's just a movie; it's not real." Steve McQueen's dodging
    a plane, and I remember reading he did his own
stunts, which I tell Henry, but he's still in that hotel
    room. "If she was alive, how'd she get her eyes to roll
back into her head?" I'm thinking of pornography,

snuff movies, all the things I never want him to see
or even know about in this tawdry world. "Honey,

it's a major motion picture. Even in a small part
    an actress has to be great." He nods and takes a bite
off Santa's head. "She was a pretty good actress." You
    bet your booty, and I realize out of the blue
Santa is an anagram for Satan. No way am
    I going to explain anagrams or Herr Satan,
though how wonderful to have such a nemesis—
    a fallen archangel, one of high heaven's brightest stars—
in a battle with Jehovah for our souls, rather
    than the calendar's increasing speed like a roller
coaster run amok through a fun park of lost dreams, lost
    landscapes, and children, growing up faster than we thought
possible in the last terrible days before their birth.

Wanda Why Aren't You Dead

wanda when are you gonna wear your hair down
wanda. that's a whore's name
wanda why ain't you rich
wanda you know no man in his right mind want a ready-made family
why don't you lose weight
wanda why are you so angry
how come your feet are so goddamn big
can't you afford to move out of this hell hole
if i were you were you were you
wanda what is it like being black
i hear you don't like black men
tell me you're ac/dc, tell me you're a nympho, tell me you're into chains
wanda i don't think you really mean that
you're joking, girl, you crazy
wanda what makes you so angry
wanda i think you need this
wanda you have no humor in you you too serious
wanda i didn't know i was hurting you
that was an accident
wanda i know what you're thinking
wanda i don't think they'll take that off of you

wanda why are you so angry

i'm sorry i didn't remember that that that
that that that was so important to you

wanda you're ALWAYS on the attack

wanda wanda wanda i wonder

why ain't you dead

Group Therapy Lounge, Columbia, South Carolina

What is the past, what is it all for?
A mental sandwich?
  John Ashbery, "37 Haiku"

In the end it all comes back
and lucid as this, O sad drinker
of a thousand boo-hoo beers,
O pinball ringing
toward oblivion: oblivion
with its wide white arms and short attention span
will never hold you for long.
Now morning is here. It comes
precise, brutal,
a CPA shaking loose his ledger
of sunlight and bad debts, and you
wake on the sidewalk, still
pretty much hammered.

Never has your breath creaked
with so many fossils.
Your bones ache older than the hills
and there are no hills in Columbia, South Carolina,
just birds in the crape myrtle
singing a song of rubber bands
stretched to breaking.
In the gutter, a few pigeons
bobbing for a lost contact lens.

Isn't this the oldest story?
Sunday, the day we care least about the world

and the newspaper is the fattest.
A Plymouth burns down Bull
to Confederate, rocker panels rusted
and swinging wide—
it barely slows to pitch
a bundle of comics & coupons by your head, right there
on the sidewalk where you've slept
and where you wake, still pretty much hammered.

History repeats itself. Big deal.
You have more pressing problems, for instance,
this cockroach driving by
with grand determination.
He's an emissary from the one species
unafraid of the atom or the anvil, and you
can't move or stop watching.
Doesn't it bring tears to your eyes,
the thought that every minute lying here
you're learning something about yourself,

some news on hot winds borne
across the chapped lip of Southern horizon—
the green spores of remorse
taking root. Soon, you think,
even you will rise under your own power,
vertebrae stacking
much like seasoned cordwood
for the day's big fire
and your brain issuing directives
to the whole body: go forth, be a man, et cetera.

Soon, not yet.
Imagine the God of gills.
Imagine the time it took those gills to burn
through closed, crude flesh.
Then mud, lungs, twelve or twelve hundred spears
jabbed in rough circles at the sun.
Imagine catfish lately

sprouting legs for the pages of *Scientific American*.
Hope is like that. Blind and bleached white,
it revises itself every million years
to climb out of the crazy swamp and live.
At the Used Car Lot
day-glo flags are snapping and popping 24 hours,
and you ride that rhythm
in a prone position. They wave
their mutant arms to you,
and you can't help it, down on the mortal sidewalk—
you wave back, astonished as anyone.

RICHARD HOWARD

Our Spring Trip

Dear Mrs. Masters, Hi from the Fifth-Grade Class
of Park School! We're still here in New York City
                     at the Taft Hotel,
you could have guessed that from the picture printed
on this stationery—I inked in x's
       to show you our rooms,
which are actually on the same floor as
the Terminal Tower Observation Deck
                   in Cleveland, Ohio,
which we visited on our *Fourth*-Grade Spring Trip,
but nowhere near so high as some skyscrapers
       in New York City:
we've been up to the *top* of the Empire State
and the Chrysler Buildings, which are really tall!
                   But there's another
reason for writing besides wanting to say
Hi—we're having a problem Miss Husband thought
       you might help us with,
once we get back to school . . . yesterday we went
to the Dinosaur Hall of the Natural
                   History Museum
for our Class Project—as you know, the Fifth Grade
is constructing this life-size Diplodocus
       out of chicken wire
and some stuff Miss Husband calls papier-mâché,
but no diagram we have shows how the tail
                   balances the head
to keep our big guy upright—we need to see
how the backbone of a real Diplodocus
       manages to bear

so much weight: did you know that some Dinosaurs
(like the Brontosaurus) are so huge they have
                    a whole other brain
at the base of their spine, just to move their tail?
Another thing: each time Arthur Englander
        came anywhere near
our Diplodocus, it would collapse because
of not balancing right. This went on until
                    David Stashower
got so mad at Arthur that he flew at him
and gave his left shoulder a really good bite
        so he would keep away . . .
That was when you called the All-School Assembly
to explain about the biting: biting's no good . . .
                    Even so, Arthur
decided not to come on this year's Spring Trip.
Well, we took a Subway train to the Museum
        from the Taft Hotel,
in fact that was our very first excursion,
but the noise, once we were on the platform,
                    was so loud one girl,
Nancy Akers, cried (she always was chicken)
when someone told her that terrible roaring
        the Expresses made
was Tyrannosaurus Rex himself, and she
believed it!—then we went to the Great Hall where
                    we were surrounded
by Dinosaurs, all the kinds we had studied:
some were not much bigger than a chicken, but
        some were humongous!
One was just a skeleton wired together,
so it was easy to see how we could make
                    our Diplodocus
balance by putting a swivel in its neck.
All the other Dinosaurs were stuffed, I guess,
        with motors and lights
inside: when they moved, *their* heads balanced their tails!
There was even a Pterodactyl flying

374

back and forth above
our heads, probably on some kind of track.
But even though Miss Husband tried explaining
        (for the hundredth time)
how the Dinosaurs had all been extinct for
millions of years, not one person in the class
                believed what she said:
the idea of a million years is so *stupid*,
anyway—a typical grown-up reason . . .
        You know the Klein twins,
the biggest brains in the whole Fifth Grade (a lot
bigger, probably, than *both* brains combined in
                that Brontosaurus)—
well, they had a question for Miss Husband: what
if the Dinosaurs' being extinct so long
        was just a smoke screen
for their being Somewhere Else, a long ways away?
And Lucy Wensley made an awful pun on
                stinky and *extinct* . . .
Actually, Mrs. Masters, we've already
figured it out, about death: the Dinosaurs
        may be extinct, but
they're not dead! It's a different thing, you dig?
When Duncan Chu's Lhasa jumped out the window,
                or when Miss Husband's
parents were killed together in a car crash,
we understood that—that *was* being dead; gone;
        no body around.
Isn't that what dying has to mean—not being
here? The Dinosaurs are with us all the time,
                anything but dead—
we keep having them! Later, at the "Diner-
Saurus," the Museum restaurant, there was
        chicken-breast for lunch
stamped out in the shape of a Triceratops!
Strange how everything has to taste like chicken:
                whether it's rabbit
or rattlesnake, it's always "just like chicken" . . .

Anyway, Dinosaurs are alive as long
        as we think they are,
not like Duncan's dog. And that's just the problem.
By next week, though, we'll be back in Sandusky,
                            and while we're putting
the swivel into our Diplodocus's neck,
you could explain to us about Time—about
        those millions of years,
and Dinosaur-chicken in the Diner, and
chicken-size Dinosaurs in the Great Hall, and
                        where they really are.

T. R. HUMMER

The Antichrist in Arkansas

At the edge of town, day lilies the gold of old whiskey
Move tonelessly. At the margin of the courthouse shadow,
A little sky gives off its one unchanging line.
It is written in the Gnostic *Gospel of Truth* that life is nightmare,
As if people were murdering them, though there is no one
Even pursuing them, or they themselves are killing
Their neighbors, for they have been stained with their blood.
Let there be a little clarity here, let the light arrive
The way the dynamite train rolls in from Arkadelphia:
An overwhelming ablution, a scheduled breakdown.
In the crib behind the cotton gin, three of them are gathered.
In the alley off Jefferson Street, they are giving secret signs.
Who are they? Call them the Brotherhood of Darkness.
Give them emblems: khaki workshirts, Prince Albert in a can.
They worship at the Synagogues of the Flesh of the Holy Pig.
Mornings, hours before sunrise, they kneel at the open flame;
Past midnight, if you wake in an impure sweat, you can hear
Their pentatonic psalms sift through the veils of the juke joints.
You who are uninitiate, you who walk the sunlit bricks
Of the Main Street sidewalk past the bank to the hotel café,
You of the regimental necktie, you who render
Unto Woodrow Wilson, live in the obvious houses,
Drive Fords, dance to "Arkansas Traveler"—Brotherhood of Light,
You think the fields at least are innocent, gathered without
The rhetoric of pastoral, the flat farmland, the plows
Moving in the middle distance; you believe at least
In the trees, gone in their green brooding. But in 1919,
83 bodies were given to druid oaks on the fringes
Of these blesséd little cities: Conway, Fort Smith, Fayetteville,
West Memphis, El Dorado, Pine Bluff, Forest City,

The mecca of Hot Springs. How many know
The ritual formula that exorcises unclean flesh?
How many have learned the arcana, the knotting
And unknotting of hemp? So it has been written
In *The Paraphrase of Shem*, and quoted
In *The Little Rock Gazette*: *Nature turned her dark vagina*
And cast from her the power of fire, which was in her
From the beginning, through the practice of darkness.
Look: already the evening brightens, already the locomotive
Crosses the valley in a shimmer of pure entropic heat.
Everything in the flesh converges. In a moment it will be too late.
Gather them up, believer. Put them on the backs of mules.
Take them where the wind completes its broken sentence
Of damnation against the elder, against the ash.
The secret is simplicity: pray to me, the spirit who steals
The breath of the one whose feet no longer touch
The ground; make sacrifice to the god who silences him
Whose testicles bleed in his own unsanctified mouth.

"A wooden eye. An 1884 silver dollar. A homemade explosive. A set of false teeth. And a 14-karat gold ashtray,"

says my wife, and then she looks up from her book
called something like *Cockamamie Facts* and tests me:
"What's their common denominator?"—right. As if
we still believe some megamatrix substrate (God,
or atoms, or Imagination) holds the infinite unalike dots
of *its* body in a parity, and daily life reflects this. As if
all of our omniform, far-post-lungfish, nuttier-than-Boschian
evolution, crowned by any ten minutes of channel-surfing
the news and (little difference) entertainment possibilities here
at the bung-end of the millennium, hadn't knocked that idea
out of our heads and onto what my father would have charmingly called
its bazoonkus. Common denominator—sure. And yet

it's Sunday night—my wife is reading in bed, with the grim
conviction that the work-week upcoming is going to be one
spirit-dead, hellacious spate of days—and so her mood,
her mind, increasingly assume the über-darkness of the night
itself, the way "industrial melanization" means those moths
in the factory districts gradually blackened to match
their new, soot/city background: and I see, now, how
the sleepless nun, and the lycanthrope in a skulking prowl,
and the warehouse watchman telling the face of his friend
the clock his griefs, his griefs . . . are all subsumed and
equalized into the night, as into a magpie's hoard: so
maybe some Ultracommodiousness, some Great Coeval, does

exist (it might be the Night, it might be almost any of our
pancultural abstractions) and welcomes us into its organizational

gestalt. If so . . . if so, it's more than *my* day's scan
of newspaper cullings and letters can ever rise above itself
to see. I learn someone's investigated the annual global methane emission
in cattle gas; that every seven years a god will fill the toad
attached to the tip of a ritual ribboned pole, and glow like a lamp
in its warty belly—then it rains; that only yesterday a girl,
eleven, was found with the name of a rival gang, the *Lady Satans*,
carefully cut in her thigh and rubbed with drainpipe acid. Somewhere
there may be a world where such as these are equally legitimized, but
not here in the thick and swirling mists of Planet Albert. So

imagine my confusion today at a letter from friend Alane,
who's sweet enough to read and like my poems, and praises
my "inclusiveness," and writes "I'm watching a man with nothing
below the waist on television. He's saying he can do anything.
He walks on his hands, he has a lovely wife. Now, *you'd*
know what to do with him. Me, I just shake my head &
take my hat off." I can't guess at how reliably the toad god
zaps the crops with rain—I do know that this faith
in *me* is wholly undeserved. And as for lovely wives . . . the answer
is: "*those are the weirdest items tuxedo rental-shops reported
finding in pockets of suits returned to them this year,
a fashion magazine says,*" and with that

thematizing of what had looked like data chaos, she
turns out the light, and fluffles the pillows, and
starts her billowy downslip into sleep. And leaves me
wakeful—leaves me wildly trying to think of pockets adequate
to *everything*. The ashtree staff of the hermit
on his mountaintop for seventeen years. The latest Nintendo
epic, *Callow Drooling Wombat Warriors*. The doctors
cracking open Nicky's sternum like a matzoh—he was five.
The perfect wedge of brie John found one dawn on his car hood.
Gunshots. Twill weft. Owl-hoo. Storm, and calm.
The poem as fit receptacle. Sure. Right.
I'll know what to do with them.

Ode to Greens

You are never what you seem.
Like barbecue, you tell me time
doesn't matter, that all
things wait. Wife
to worry, you can sit
forever, stewing, grown
angrier by the hour.
Like ribs you are better
the day after, when all
is forgiven. Death's daughter,
you are often cross—bitter
as mustard, sweet
when collared—yet no one
can make you lose
all your cool, what strength
you started with. Mama's
boy, medicine woman,
you tell me things end
far from where
they begin, that forgiven
is not always forgotten.
One day the waters will part.
One day my heart will stop & still
you'll be here dark
green as heaven.

EVERYTHING PROPHESIED WILL ERUPT

The End of the World

SUSAN WOOD

Horoscope

It's almost my birthday, but not quite, thank God, because
who'd want a horoscope like this on her birthday?

Take precautions today. Evil may come your way.
Because evil is such an over-the-top word, such

a Nightmare-on-Elm-Street word. I mean, it could've said,
"Trouble may come your way," but evil? Not that

I don't believe in it, of course. Who wouldn't these days?
Decades of it, centuries. Hitler, Pol Pot, Saddam,

the usual suspects, not to mention countless other lackeys
and minor functionaries, the father who scalded the baby,

put out his cigarettes on her tender backside, the loser boyfriend
who shot the aspiring actress right in front of her mother

on a sidewalk in Chinatown. Or the serial killer everyone describes
as "polite" and "charming," whose face is all over the TV today,

the one who haunted south Louisiana through which I have so often
traveled alone, driving over the spooky swamp between Lafayette

and Baton Rouge, where there is no way off the interstate for miles
except the exit at Whiskey Bay, where one of the bodies

was found, haunted even Breaux Bridge, where the Sunday
after Christmas I ate crawfish etoufée at Mulate's Cajun Restaurant,

the band playing at one o'clock in the afternoon and couples
in matching outfits dancing the day away. Oh, I could go on

and on. Some days the grease of grief covers everything,
a thin film like the one that covers the body in the river. Yesterday

my friend, the most beautiful woman I know, was speaking
of sadness, and just for a moment I thought if I were

that beautiful I'd never be sad about anything, but then
I felt ashamed because I know sadness

is an equal-opportunity emotion and despair
can lead you around by the nose no matter who you are.

Remember when we were so avid for life we beat like little moths
around the days as though they were shining lamps?

Now some days, I think merely to get up,
to make coffee and take the dog out into the May morning, to put

your face up close to the pink face of the odorless, frustrating
hibiscus is an act of endless courage. But last night

at a party I held a baby for an hour and he curled into me
like a new leaf, and today there is a family of cardinals

in the Japanese maple and nearby a mockingbird barking and cackling
and dive-bombing the gray cat who would eat the baby birds if he could.

And he could. And still the mockingbird will go on singing
in the privet hedge the whole May night. I can think of that couple

at Mulate's, their white shirts embroidered all over with red poinsettias.
Imagine her bending over her needle night after night and the tender way

he puts his palm on her back when they dance. And I have the memory
of my handsome young man of a son striding toward me

across Union Station, Baltimore, and his face when he sees me
and sweeps me up, apparently having forgotten all the reasons he had
    not to

speak to me last year. Nearby a covey of teenage girls keeps looking
his way, a little like newly hatched birds themselves, all legs and eyes,

despite their bare midriffs and low-rider cutoffs. Caleb just laughs.
"When I have daughters," he says, taking my arm, "they'll wear

baggy jeans and big T-shirts that say *I love my daddy*, and they'll always
love me best." They won't, of course, but for now

I can dream these girls are his girls and they have come with him
to the train station to meet me, who has traveled far into the future

just to see them, these girls who beat around us
like those moths around lamps, their wings little sparks of flame.

"Russia is big and so is China"

—overheard statement from President Bush at summit with Chinese President
Hu Jintao

Monopoly is fun and so is strip poker.
The weather is nice and so is this iced tea.
Porcupine quills are sharp and so is that pair of scissors. Be careful, ok?
The baby across the aisle from you is loud and so is some rap music.
The GED was hard and so was bungee jumping.
Pink is a color and so is salmon. Salmon is also a fish.
Bruce Willis is still hot and so is Kurt Cobain, though he's dead.
Stoplights are annoying and so are brussels sprouts.
Vitamin C is good for you and so is exercise.
I could stand to lose ten pounds and so could you.
I am lazy and you don't have anywhere else to be.
North Korea is fidgety and so is my little sister. But no Ritalin for her.
I am horny and so are most of my dumb friends.
Seven is more than three and so is eight.
The news is strange and so is my hairdresser.
Model airplanes are frustrating and so are summits.
Poisoned Halloween candy is creepy and so is Anthrax.
Used dental floss is icky and so are missiles.
Nuclear weapons are large and so is my penis.
Metaphors are always obvious and so is common sense.
Wisdom is cheap and so is bus fare.
Solar energy is easy and so is my ex-boyfriend Nick.
Armageddon is a bummer and so is Picasso.

CHRISTOPHER BURSK

Irreconcilable Differences

Khrushchev and Eisenhower, that old married couple,
were bickering again, over how often
each could blow up the other,
but I had more pressing matters to deal with:
exactly when and where I'd have a chance to
get Sally Hamilton's blouse unbuttoned.
For weeks I'd been practicing on a bra I'd stolen
from my mother's bureau drawer,
and fastened to one dining room chair
while I sat in another and let the right hand work its way down
to the clasp; it took a while: the thumb standing guard,
the index finger at work, liberating
each hook. Eisenhower and Khrushchev could have learned from me
the virtues of delayed gratification.

If I got an erection just trying it on a dining room chair,
imagine the ecstasy of doing it
with a real girl, stroking an actual nipple.
Should I devote all my attention to both breasts? Or
lavish my affections on one
at a time? Unlike the President I didn't have a cabinet of advisors.
When the U-2 went down,
and the Soviet Premier carried on like an aggrieved wife,
Eisenhower fidgeted like one more henpecked husband
caught cheating but doing his best
to make it seem as if it weren't the end of the world.

I had even more complicated negotiations
to see to: how to place one important part
of my body into an equally important part

of my girl's body. Talk about the need for diplomacy!
I had my hands full. What did my penis know
of tact, my greedy upstart, ugly American
determined once again to meddle
in someone else's internal affairs? I had a weapon
I needed to test, bombs I was tired
of stockpiling, and I intended to drop one wherever
and whenever I could—just to see how much
of an explosion it would make
and if I could survive the blast.

STEPHEN DUNN

Replicas

When it became clear aliens were working here
with their dead-giveaway, perfectly cut Armani suits,
excessive politeness, and those ray guns
disguised as cell phones tucked into their belts,
I decided we had two choices: cocktail party
to befriend them, or massive air strikes (I joked
at the Board meeting) on what might be a hospital
for children with rare diseases, but could
as easily be where these aliens spawned and lived.
Cocktail party it was, and they came
with their gorgeous women dressed like replicas
of gorgeous women, and though they sipped
their martinis as if they'd graduated
from some finishing school between their world
and ours, I must admit they were good company,
talking ball scores and GNP, even movies,
and how bright and inviting the stars seemed
from my porch. I found myself almost
having sympathy for what certain people will do
to fit in, until I remembered they might want
to take over, maybe even blow things up.
And when the dog barked from the other room,
the way she does when some creature is nearby,
about to cross an invisible line, I was sure
I couldn't afford to trust appearances ever again.
Then it was time to leave, and they left,
saying at the door what a good evening they'd had.
Each of them used the same words,

like people who've been trained in sales,
and as they moved to their Miatas and Audis
I noted the bare shoulders of their women
were the barest shoulders I'd ever seen,
as if they needed only the night as a shawl.

Upon Hearing of My Friend's Marriage Breaking Up, I Envision Attack from Outer Space

Even in September noon, the groundhog
casts his divining shadow: summer will never
end and when it does it will never come again.
I've only the shadows of doubts, shadows
of a notion. The leaves turn in tarnished
rain like milk. Hearts, rotund with longing,
explode like dead horses left in a creek,
our intentions misunderstood, misrepresented
like that day they turned the candles
upside down, thumped them out and we all
lost our jobs. Nothing personal. Handshakes around.
Of course we're not guilty
of what we've been accused of
but we're guilty of so much else, what's it matter,
I heard on the radio. I hate the radio,
how it pretends to be your friend.
You could be eating, you could be driving around
and then you're screaming, What, what did that fucker say
but by then it's someone else with the voice
of air conditioning saying, Take cover,
storm on the way. It's amazing
word hasn't gotten back to us from irritated
outer space how some creatures of spine and light
have finally had enough. Shut up, they beep back
but we're so dense, so unevolved, we think
it's just the usual interference: Bill next door
blending his Singapore Slings during *Wheel
of Fortune*. Right now they're working on something
that'll make our fillings fall out,

turn our checking accounts to dust,
something far more definitive.
There's a man starting his mower in the bedroom.
There's a woman burning photos in a sink.
I hate the phone, how it pretends to be
your friend, but I called you anyway,
got some curt, inchoate message that means
everyone's miserable, little shreds of your heart
rain down on me, twitching like slivered worms.
Upstairs, they're overflowing the tub again,
they're doing that Euripidean dance. I knew
a guy in college who stuck his head through a wall.
It seemed to decide something, to make us all
feel grateful, restored to simple things:
cars starting, cottage cheese, Larry, Curley, Moe.
It was, of course, a thin wall, a practice wall,
a wall between nowhere and nowhere's bedroom,
nothing like that 16th century woodcut
where the guy pokes through the sky into
the watchback of the cosmos. Tick, tick.
The cosmos gives me the creeps.
I like a decent chair where you can sit
and order a beer, be smiled at while you wait
for a friend who just had his sutures removed,
who rolls a quarter across his knuckles
to get them working again.

Wrong Number after Midnight

When I pick up, the voice on the other end is already off
and running: *You were right, man, you were so*
incredibly right, and now I'm more than sorry I didn't believe you
when you claimed that the only way to keep their voices out of our heads
was by using heavy-duty aluminum foil, the kind
our own mothers were crazy for when it came to preparing leftovers
for their deep-freeze oblivion. You tried to tell me:
regular foil's too thin for making any kind of proper headgear—
a ponderous buffer-zone helmet, or something less obtrusive and more
stylish, say, a wave-deflecting beret. Next time I visit,
I'll be sure to bring enough of the extra-strength for us both.

And although this sounds like something I certainly might
    have suggested—
perhaps only to my closest friends, it's true—it happens
that I didn't, and finally he stops to worry up a whisper: *This isn't*
my friend Stuart, is it? And I say *No*, and he says *Oh my God,*
man, they've gone and gotten through to you, haven't they? As if
he's the one who can't believe what he's hearing, who's never felt so
disconnected, standing in the middle of whatever room he's renting
in his suddenly less-than-accommodating life. There's no way
he can appreciate how accidentally he's reached me, how sympathetic
I really am—the one other person who might think it's worth trying,
this last-ditch defense against the aliens or the in-laws or those
frightening late-night infomercial people.
                                        It's after midnight again,
when everything that comes along is that much harder to resist,
and where I've come to live, more often than I'd like,
just a single touch-tone button away, apparently, from the madhouse.
I'm so wide awake now in the dark, it's not funny, and there's nothing

left to say along the miles of open line, nothing to do but quietly
     lay down
the receiver in its cradle, take the long walk back to sleep. And if I make it
that far again tonight, you can be absolutely sure that's when
the Venusian scout-ships will be closing in, or Patricia's mother,
and somewhere Mr. Car Wax Guru will be setting a Chevrolet on fire
to the paid-off astonishment of his TV-studio audience—one more
brilliant lesson in the virtue of sheer resilience—and he'll swear
nothing else on Earth can stand up to that kind of heat.
But three of us, more or less, in our foil-wrapped, American-as-baked-
potato wisdom, will know better. There's me, my wrong-number
     friend, and
Stuart, wherever he is right now. May his meds make him unbreakable,
and doctors never talk him fully out of his half-baked, hard-won silence.
May his friends wait until morning before ringing through to him there.

And let the plans of the space people and our relatives and anyone else
who would come to us in our woozy sleep, on this night at least,
come to naught. May they be foiled, with any luck. And with
     our blessings
or our curses, foiled again. May it turn out they've been looking,
all along, for someone else. And if they find us instead, certifiable
wrong numbers, may they have to tell us exactly how sorry they are.
And for how much.
                    Given the crush of increasingly unstable particles
in the universe, it's no small thing: how surprisingly undisturbed
we actually are, how quiet it so often is on our end of the line.
And whenever we get to thinking that's okay, there's quite enough
still ringing in our ears for one more night or for a lifetime,
here comes another one of those voices out of nowhere, saying
in so many words we haven't heard anything yet.

Unusual Summer Weather

This overstated thunderstorm is a fancy blue hat
upon the very brink of which Zeus is perched and crooning,
poking out his godly pinkie while sipping good Zinfandel

and catapulting seedless grapes down into the Nile
or into the hot and steamy redwood tubs on the weather-proofed decks
of the women of the DC start-ups. That is,

he's crashing roller coasters and hitting small children
upon their anemic heads and pulling out his loincloth pennies,
licking them for luck. He listens all day

for the plunk and holler of the children on their slides
and chain-link swings and plastic motorbikes.
That's when the Moms come running with their bras half-snapped

and their panties askance. Whereupon Zeus rubs his belly
with olive oil and powder puffs his golden hair
and bids the Orchestra pluck *Sweet Home Alabama*

and knots tiny rose blooms into the straps of his sandals
and giggles over at Venus lying on a towel
under a colossal brass lamp, sunning her glossy skin

like a lizard on a rock
while down below we bitch and moan and whine and weep
like demons, like puppies, like newborns in our beds.

Astute Chinese Aside

Lao Tsu and Confucius met once in the city. To have been a fly on the wall for that conversation! Confucius would treat the virtuous well, the bad badly; Lao Tsu treated all living souls the same. Confucius thought a poor and filial scholar is best. His host cared little for bookishness. The self-restrained, Confucius would go on, seldom would go off. To Lao Tsu the river knew where it was headed. The tea got tepid and little was said. Then the Old Sage sighed that everything, even that fly on the wall, is one ten-thousandth of the mystery. And Confucius nodded and swatted it.

. . .

Denuded, deluded, who knows what human nature is? A dull feeling that it's all near-miss—the Great Wall to the Great Mall; the inner-life to the sinner-life; *ben-xing, ren-xing*—or as it was mentioned in Mencius: *Ox Mountain was covered by trees, but it stands near a populous city. Came axes, came saws, came cattle, came sheep . . . and people who see it today think it always was treeless.* Denuded by drives, deluded by droves, who dead or alive may spell what human nature is?

. . .

Ez sez find a new Greece in China. You have your orders—Ez sez. Obstructive! Obtuse! Obstruse! Before those stony villages named for saints, before the saints, before the Athenian schemer of *The Republic*, hermits of that land would feed on ferns before taking one grain gathered under corruption. Name a Beat poet untaxable as that! I spent his century's final ticks digging for it in San Francisco, kept every pithy paper slip those dim sum diners gave me, hoping—what?—wisdom entered from the belly? *Your ability to find the silly in the serious will take you far.* So far, so good . . . but still so far, so far. Everywhere, men with crumbs and cookies with fortunes.

A Pocket Guide to Trouble

1. Genesis: Making Trouble

In those first days on the job—when God was just a beginner
in a hurry, no real résumé to speak of, when finally
it was light enough for Him to see what He was doing—
surely He must have been thinking *Don't*
let there be trouble, but He blew the line when He delivered
the official, out-loud word of God. And there was trouble.
He had all the time in the world, but no one knew yet
how long that would turn out to be. And after the backbreaking
week He'd put in already, He wasn't about to start over.

2. The Epistemology

If it looks like trouble and it sounds like trouble
and you can't stop yourself from asking everyone you see
What, exactly, seems to be the trouble?
then, okay, this time it's absolutely going to be trouble, or else
another one of those goddamn, less-than-obvious ducks.

3. The Mechanics of Trouble

From the look on your face, I'm guessing it's major car trouble—
transmission, brakes, or engine. But even a cracked block is nothing,
compared to woman trouble, heart trouble you can put a proper
    name to—
the kind that's guaranteed to really set you back: it's the labor,
not the parts. We'll get to you, one way or the other, first thing
in the morning. We'll let you know whatever we find that's not quite
beyond repair. You'll tell us what you can and can't afford.

4. Commuters in Trouble
Odysseus found himself going to an awful lot of it
just trying to get home. Jimmy Stewart, too, near the end
of *It's a Wonderful Life*.

5. The Worst-Ever Political Advice (U.S. Edition), Expressed Here as a Trouble-Filled Couplet of Epic Proportions
Let Nixon
be Nixon.

6. At the Border of Switzerland and Trouble
Even with millions of those red army knives and no standing army
to speak of, the Swiss have somehow managed to stay out of it.

7. Theatrically Speaking, We've Got Trouble
right here in River City, where the Déjà-Vu-and-Blue-Hair
Community Players never seem to run out of musicals. Or else
they do. And believe me, that's trouble too—with a capital T
which rhymes with D and that stands for *Death of a Salesman*, which
they've overhauled, lightened up, led to its song-and-dance slaughter.
In the moving words of Willy Loman's wife, *Attention must be*
paid—although
she sings them now in some unaccountably jaunty Calypso fashion.
Willy's thankfully still a salesman by day, but he's moonlighting as,
of all things, an amateur thespian. Every night he brings down the house,
desperately invoking his imagined former glory: *They loved me*
in "Oklahoma!"

8. Trouble Knows a Few Tricks
Because my novelist friend is a fan of those huge 19th-century novels,
he named his enormous, real-life dog Trouble, as in
Trouble climbed into bed with us this morning. Call for Trouble
and he comes. Sits. Lies down. But he won't roll over. Won't play dead
for anyone. Not as long as he still remembers every bone
he's ever buried with a real-life vengeance.

9. What Is the Sound of Questions Getting Harder?
A Buddhist who isn't sure about the sound of two hands clapping
is clearly a Buddhist already in trouble.

10. The Classic Overachiever
Jesus, facing the multitude with five loaves and two fishes
long before the advent of cole slaw as a side dish: predictably,
another miracle—no trouble at all.

11. Sometimes Trouble Isn't on the Menu
Like decent pizza in Nebraska—by now
you should know better than to go asking for it.

12. Like the Mountain Coming to Mohammed, Trouble
will certainly find you. It knows where you live. Sooner or later
the roof will spring its leak, the stove will go out for good,
the bedroom door will fall off its hinges, and the water in the toilet
won't stop running, no matter how religiously you jiggle the handle.
And suddenly trouble is an uncle with nothing better to do,
waiting up in the dark for as long as it takes you to come back.
If that's how it has to be. He's finished with following you.
He'll be easing into your favorite slippers, lifting a few fingers
of your highfalutin Scotch. He'll have you down cold—
even the nervous humming will be pitch-perfect. There's no way
you'll be able to say that you like what he's done with the place,
but you still can't help admiring how he's made himself this much
    at home.

13. (Always a Troubling Number)
Don't let that silver-haired Mr. Businessman's demeanor fool you:
Wallace Stevens was out there, bird-dogging for us all.
He knew thirteen sure-fire ways of looking for trouble, including
his favorite: shouting *Hey, you skinny, uninsured sons-of-bitches*
at the thin men of Haddam, Connecticut.

Elvis, Be My Psychopomp

  Sometimes I see my dead parents: at the end of the street,
   say, or just ahead of me in the ticket line. At times
they are turning into another aisle at the supermarket,
   and I want to run after them as I did when I was a little boy,
and at others, they are walking toward me, and they smile
   when they see who it is, though when I reach to embrace them,

   they vanish, like the gods in *The Iliad*.
They're my age now—or not my age, for if they are sixty,
then I am twenty again, so young and so unhappy,
   though I don't know it. When Odysseus goes
to the underworld, he sees his mother, who cannot speak until
   he sacrifices
a ram and a ewe, and she drinks their blood, though when

   she does and they talk to one another, he tries
to embrace her but can't. Aeneas, too, goes to the underworld
to seek his father, Anchises—if they can, why not I?
   I'd need a psychopomp, a Hermes or the Sibyl of Cumae,
and while I wish it could be "bright-eyed" Athena,
   who leads Telemachus here and there in search of his father,

   as I am white, male, Southern, and have lived
   most of my life in the last half of the 20th century,
I think it will be Elvis who leads me through "the darkness
   of the night with shadows all about us,"
as great Homer said, "through the empty halls and the desolate kingdom,
   as though walking in a wood by the light of the fitful moon

when Jupiter has hung the sky in shadow and black night
has robbed all things of their color." And when the Angel
of the Apocalypse taps on the Bible and says, "There shall be time
no longer," Elvis will say, "You get some kind
of decoder ring with that thing, man?" and I'll thank him:
"Thank you, Elvis!" I'll cry, and he'll say, "Look, ace, I always

played heroes in the movies, but when the director
said 'Cut!,' it was time for drugs and stupidity
and the coveting of women. The way I see it, this is my chance."
We pass signs saying "Warning: Bridge Out"
and "Hitchhikers May Be Escaping Inmates" and before I know it,
we're in the Valley of the Perversely Proud and Presumptuous

and out again, and when we cross the Nail-Studded Bridge
and I weep and say I can't walk because my feet are bleeding,
Elvis says, "Remember how, in your life, your feet were ready
to carry you to those places where you could sin?"
When we see Lord Satan devouring sinners and excreting them
out his backside, Elvis will say, "Let's slide on by—

if he catches us, not only will we be dead sons of bitches,
but so will our souls. We'll just be a bag of slop."
And we do, but not before the King of Cruelty
sees us and cries, "Elvis! What's it like in Tupelo?"
and Elvis says, "Uh, rough! But a nurse to good lads."
Then he mutters under his breath, and I think it's something

about an "undead sack of shit." So far, I figure, so good.
The trick, of course, is not getting into Hell,
it's getting out again. Bread, meat, beer, chips, ice, bait,
smokeless tobacco, beef jerky, water for washing—
everything must be refused if you wish to leave
the Kingdom of the Dead. We pass Hades,

the master of Tartarus, sometimes called Plouton
or wealthy one because of his vast holdings:
precious metals, objects buried with the dead, the wealth

of crops that spring from his soil. And Buddy Holly
and Jimi Hendrix, and Elvis says to Jimi, "Hey,
    your dad misses you, man" and Jimi says, "Give him this"

    and tries to hand Elvis a black guitar that slithers
    and undulates as fiery streaks rise to its surface like lava
and fall back again, but Elvis knows better.
    We see Janis Joplin surrounded by devilkins
stamping their crooked legs and punching each other and snickering,
    and Elvis says, "Eating out your hand like always, mama!"

    and Janis says, "Are you shitting me?
    I'd rather be a crack whore on Melrose than Lady Paramount
of these twerps." And so we pass into The Place
    of The Bad But Not Very Bad and from there
to The Place of The Good But Not Very Good
    and on to the Land of Joy, the resplendent glades, the happy

    wood, the meadow of the blessed where there
    is dancing and singing and wrestling and running,
and eventually we come to a little park, and there are my mom
    and dad at a table, watching the games and eating
and drinking what they ate and drank in life: fried chicken, martinis,
    lemon meringue pie, and I'm thinking, martinis?

    and Elvis reads my mind and says, "Beats the hell
    out of ram's blood, huh, buddy?" My father is silent,
as he always was, but my mother begins to chatter away:
    "You're Elvis Presley, aren't you? You've got
a lot to answer for, young man. What's with the hips
    and the hound dog and that stuff in your hair?"

    And Elvis says, "You think those days were something,
    lady, you ought to see what's going on up there now."
And I try to talk to her, but she can't hear me, so I tell Elvis,
    "Ask her why she died. Say 'What is death, anyway?'"

And he does, and she says, "When I was alone
　　and my new life began, it wasn't to my liking.

　　I missed my husband so much, his wit,
　　his gay merry ways, and life was sweet no longer, so I died."
Which is a pretty speech, but I don't remember my father
　　as merry or witty, and he doesn't, either,
because when I look over at him, he shrugs and smiles shyly,
　　as if to say, If she wants to remember it that way, let her.

　　The other dead draw closer, and Elvis licks his lips:
　　"We can't stay," he says, and I cry, "Goodbye, Mommy!"
but she's eating her pie again, though my dad raises his hand
　　just perceptibly and sticks out his thumb
and little finger and makes the *shaka* and wiggles it, the way
　　surfers do in Hawai'i. We pass through the Gate of Horn

　　and make our way back, and just as I can see
　　the fires of my native land, Elvis says, "See ya," and I say,
"See ya, Elvis!" and then, "Elvis, wait!"
　　Because the challenge for mythic heroes
is not slaying the enemy or freeing the oppressed, it's telling
　　the story to those who have never seen a dragon.

　　But Elvis says, "Aw, just listen to the songs, man,"
　　and I say, "But they're not in order. Also—I'm sorry—
some of them are bad!" He shrugs and says,
　　"That's the only way to tell the story" and disappears,
and I'm wondering what he means by that.
　　I wonder if I'll ever see my dead parents again,

　　and if I do—at the end of the street, say,
　　as Barbara and I take our morning walk, and I look up,
and, suddenly, there they are—if my father will look
　　at me and smile and look down, the way he did in life,
as my mother floats by, regal as always, oblivious, almost,
　　and I say, "Mommy! Remember? I just saw you

in the other world! You were drinking martinis!
    Don't be dead!" And Barbara says,
"Who are you talking to?" and they go right by,
        and just as they're about to walk away, maybe forever
this time, my mother rolls her hips, ever so gently,
        and my dad says, "All right, now, mamma—shake that thing!"

Apocalypse

If eating corndogs and watching the demo-
lition derby on TNN
Friday nights is a sign of the apocalypse,
then the end of the world is certainly being birthed
in my living room. But I shouldn't run away from it
like actors from computer simulated dinosaurs,
instead I should welcome it with open
arms and a smile, take it home and give it
a name—Pupipo or Chad. After all, it needs
love and acceptance just like anyone.
Think about it, how would you feel if everyone
feared your impending arrival? If The Iceman
tried to disguise his voice whenever you called
and everyone on the camping trip sat around
the campfire drinking hot beer trying
to get so drunk they wouldn't notice
your presence? You'd feel pretty rotten,
wouldn't you? So I'm saying, don't
abandon the apocalypse at Porko's house
in Pittsburgh and get a ticket while speeding away
in Zanesville, Ohio. I mean, Porko's
no child caregiver, he's an auto mechanic
for Christ's sake—he'll fix your VW but not
your life. Give it some time to grow, you'll
realize everything will have been worthwhile.
By junior high it'll be going steady with girls,
playing football and baseball and golf every
day, shoving the heads of unsuspecting
nerds into toilet bowls. You'll see, by
high school it'll be dating a cheerleader

named Crystal and be captain of the football
team. It'll finally get that Firebird
working. It'll graduate, go to technical
college, flunk out, get a job
at the alignment place west of town, spray
paint Crystal Hudson's name on an overpass
just before she leaves it for a guy who repairs
small engines at Rick's Small Engine
Repair. It'll spend its nights on the back porch
drinking Wild Turkey and Old Milwaukee,
pining for the good old days. Pretty
soon everything will begin to fall apart—
it'll be buying more and more shotguns
and stashing them in the closet, talking about
our right to bear arms. It'll start saying
backwoods militia groups make a lot of sense.
That's when everything will go down. You'll
be sitting around one afternoon
watching *Mama's Family* because it's on
Channel 2 and Channel 2 is the only
channel you get, and everything prophesied
will erupt. Most will die. And you'll be one
of the last remaining, driving down I-64
in a white Toronado, turning the radio
to AM 1610 for some
information—weather, tourism, fishing,
you won't care. You'll be searching for an off track
wagering facility to put 500 dollars
down on inescapable death and end up
at a British Petroleum in Burnt Prairie, Illinois,
refueling and cleaning your windshield in silence,
a Ford Aerostar on either side of you
filled with men staring at you, mumbling
to one another in Spanish.

Thanks to Andrew Berzanskis, former acquisitions editor at the University of Georgia Press, who suggested this anthology to us, and to his successor Erika Stevens as well as press director Nicole Mitchell, both of whom supported our project enthusiastically after Andrew's departure. The people who suggested poems for us to consider are too numerous to name, though Andrew Epstein and Eric Lee were of special help in bringing work to our attention.

Permission to print each poem in this book is given below.

414

INDEX OF AUTHORS